Advance Praise for

The Entrepreneur's Desk Reference:
Authoritative Information, Ideas, and Solutions
for Your Small Business

by Jane Applegate

"My wife founded a very successful small business. She doesn't read my books, but she swears by Jane Applegate. She loves Jane's new book. **What more can I say?**"

Tom Peters
Coauthor of *In Search of Excellence*
and author of *The Circle of Innovation*

"Jane Applegate's *The Entrepreneur's Desk Reference* is a lush, enlightening, and superbly written publication that **ought to be mandatory equipment for anyone who wants to succeed in business**. In my opinion, it is as crucial as a computer and a telephone for any big dreamer with a limited budget."

Jay Conrad Levinson
Author of Guerrilla Marketing series of books

"Once again Jane Applegate has written a **valuable resource that can help any entrepreneur run a more productive and efficient business**."

Jack Faris
President and CEO, National Federation of Independent Business

"**No matter how long you've been in business and whether you're a start-up or a seasoned owner, *The Entrepreneur's Desk Reference* offers concrete and practical advice, as well as comprehensive business information.** This valuable tool is great to keep next to you at your desk and ready for use on a daily basis."

Marsha Firestone, Ph.D.
President and Founder, Women Presidents' Organization

"For Jane Applegate's many fans—and I'm certainly one of them—*The Entrepreneur's Desk Reference* is a welcome addition to her many valuable resources for business owners. **It's timely, informative, and wonderfully easy to use.**"

Jill Andresky Fraser
Author of *The Business Owner's Guide to Personal Finance*

Praise for
201 Great Ideas for Your Small Business:
Revised and Updated Edition
by Jane Applegate

"I wish I had this kind of invaluable information when I launched my company 47 years ago. It took me a decade to learn these important tips for managing a successful business. From one entrepreneur to another, don't start your business before reading Jane Applegate's book!"

Lillian Vernon
Chairman and CEO, Lillian Vernon Corporation

"The most comprehensive book I've ever read for the owner of a small business. If you are in business for yourself, make sure you get your personal copy. **It could prove to be your biggest asset. "**

Wally Amos
Founder of Famous Amos Cookies and Uncle NoName Muffin Company

"Chock full of great advice, great stories, and great solutions. **It's sure to save any small business owner time, energy, and money.**"

Terri Lonier
Author of *Working Solo* and *The Frugal Entrepreneur*

"Give your business an extraordinary advantage—BUY THIS BOOK."

Harvey Mackay
Author of *Dig Your Well Before You're Thirsty*
and *Swim With the Sharks*
CEO of Mackay Envelope Corporation

"Just one of these smart ideas can help boost your business. Glean a dozen and you'll *cream* your competition."

Martha Rogers
Coauthor of *The One to One Future* and *Enterprise One to One*

The Entrepreneur's Desk Reference

The Entrepreneur's Desk Reference

Authoritative Information, Ideas, and Solutions for Your Small Business

Jane Applegate

Bloomberg Press
Princeton

First edition published 2003

1 3 5 7 9 10 8 6 4 2

Library of Congress Cataloging-in-Publication Data

Applegate, Jane.
The entrepreneur's desk reference : authoritative information, ideas, and solutions for your small business / Jane Applegate.
    p. cm.
    Includes index.
    ISBN 1-57660-086-6 (alk. paper)
1. Entrepreneurship. 2. New business enterprises--Management. I. Title

HB615 .A72 2003
658.02'2--dc21

2002015287

Acquired and edited by Jared Kieling
Book Design by Barbara Diez Goldenberg

*To my best friend, Joe Applegate, whose unwavering love,
quirky sense of humor, and support
provide a base for family harmony*

Acknowledgments

THIS COMPREHENSIVE BOOK would not exist without the tremendous writing, research, and editing skills of Joe Applegate and Cliff Ennico. Joe wrote many sections and the pithiest definitions, and copyedited the manuscript. Cliff, our dear friend and attorney, offered his expertise for most of the legal entries. John D'Aquila, SBTV Corp.'s CPA and CFO, also contributed his sage advice.

Thanks to all the experts, consultants, and entrepreneurs who shared their insights. And, also to Sarah Prior for her reporting and research on this project.

Special thanks to Jared Kieling and Tracy Tait, my terrific editors at Bloomberg Press, for their support and devotion to shaping this book. Bloomberg's John Crutcher, Lisa Goetz, and Andrew Feldman provided savvy marketing and sales support. Gail Whiteside, Bloomberg Press's insightful publicity manager, and Priscilla Treadwell, subsidiary rights director, are always pleasures to work with.

Thanks to my agent, Dominick Abel, for his support and negotiating skills.

Finally, thanks to my dearest children, Jeanne and Evan, who although they didn't like it, understood that a writer needs time alone to write and gave me the space to finish this epic.

Introduction

YOU'LL NEVER WORK HARDER than when you work for yourself. If anyone tells you something different, don't believe it. The entrepreneurial life poses never-ending challenges. On a daily basis you face obstacles on all fronts: personal, financial, and psychological. And the stress of running a business, whether it's prospering or faltering, takes its toll. You might swing from exhaustion to exhilaration during the same day. Owning your own company also requires an enormous amount of physical and mental stamina—so get in shape and surround yourself with people and resources to lighten your load.

The most successful big business and small business owners I've met have one thing in common: They set their egos aside and ask for help. They understand that they can't be experts in every single aspect of managing a business and aren't afraid to admit they don't know everything. From time to time you, too, may have to turn to experts for guidance. I wrote this comprehensive book to help hardworking entrepreneurs who can't afford to hire a team of experts—or even one expert—for every business problem.

Keep this book close at hand—you'll find detailed, practical answers to hundreds of common questions, plus real-world solutions to many daily challenges. Use it every day as an alternative to booting up, logging on, and slogging through thousands of pages of online text. Having founded three successful companies (two consulting and one multimedia website for business owners), I know that when something is troubling you, you need answers fast. You don't have time to waste on a trip to the library or surfing the Internet. This book is fluff-free—putting concise information at your fingertips.

I've organized *The Entrepreneur's Desk Reference* in a simple to use A-to-Z format with many cross-references, making it quick and easy to locate the information you need to succeed. Most sections are short and to the point. Many also include helpful tip boxes and recommended reading. There are extensive sections on common legal problems and advice on many personnel problems—from dealing with troubled employees to coping with an office romance. There's also a resources section at the end, with suggestions on where to go if you seek further information.

You'll find dozens of helpful entries about financing your business, from raising investment capital to dealing with investors to expanding to selling out when you have achieved your personal or financial goals. There are definitions of accounting terms, explanations of laws that small businesses must obey, and several entries on marketing, advertising, and public relations. The section on crisis public relations will be helpful to every entrepreneur (and to all the corporate executives who filled the newspapers and airwaves with their serious legal problems in 2002).

The Entrepreneur's Desk Reference incorporates the research I've done and the experiences I've had since I began covering the entrepreneurial market in 1988, after working several years as an investigative reporter. I applied my skills to cover "mom and pop" businesses. My colleagues thought I was crazy to go from the front page to the back page of the business section, but I was eager to chronicle the American dream rather than to glorify criminals and the dark side of the business world. I told my editors that I was happy to interview and profile hardworking people who earned their living, rather than those who stole money from others.

When my first book, *Succeeding in Small Business: The 101 Toughest Problems and How to Solve Them,* was published in 1991, I was inspired by the people I interviewed and quit my job at the *Los Angeles Times* to set up my own small business. Many people are still surprised to learn I'm one of the few journalists in the country who actually owns and manages a small business. I know what it's like to wake up in a sweat and be unable to go back to sleep because you aren't sure the payroll can be met by Friday.

Despite the ups and downs, both financial and emotional, I've never regretted my decision to devote my creative energy to helping small business owners succeed. It has allowed me to become acquainted with thousands of the most fascinating, eccentric, and dedicated people. You'll meet many of them in this book as they share their advice, inspiration, and insights. After all the interviews, meetings, conferences, seminars, phone calls, and e-mails, I am still intrigued by the entrepreneurial world.

Many of the entries in this book are based on looking for answers to the questions I had while running my own companies. I've tried to come up with the most practical answers—based on practice rather than theory. This reference book is my fourth and most ambitious project. I devoted about two years to the writing and research. I collaborated with a terrific editor, my husband, Joe Applegate, and a talented contributor, small business attorney Cliff Ennico. Our mission was to cover as many bases as possible in a readable and often entertaining fashion. I'm confident you'll find the answers you need to succeed, and you'll be pointed in the right direction if you need to find more information.

I wish you continued success in life and business!

absenteeism Employees missing in action, costing you money and lost productivity.

O FTEN SMALL COMPANIES are forced to hire young, inexperienced workers with a poor work ethic. They may think they can sleep late and miss a few hours or minutes of work, the same way they used to cut early morning classes in college. One way to reduce tardiness and absenteeism is to have a written policy that you give to new employees their first day on the job. It should state that you expect employees to show up on time every day, unless they are seriously ill or faced with a family emergency. A perfect beach day is not a family emergency.

Let employees know you will not tolerate unexcused absences and you will not pay them for missed days. Ask them to leave a message for you the night before if they are not feeling well, so you can adjust your plans or schedule accordingly. Here are some common excuses and how to handle them:

Sick child. If your employee is the primary caregiver, there isn't much you can do, except offer to pay the fee at a drop-in center for sick kids operated by a local hospital or clinic.

Broken vehicle. Weigh the cost of a taxi or car service with the cost of losing a day of productivity. It may be worth paying transportation costs for a valuable employee or sending another employee to pick them up.

Family problems. If someone is seriously ill or dying in another state, there is not much you can do to stop an employee from taking off. Ask them to brief a coworker on what can be handled by others in their absence.

accountability Being held responsible for one's actions, ethically and financially.

How often do your colleagues, clients, you, or customers actually *do* what they say they will do? A package delivered on time? A proposal completed? Unfortunately, deadlines are rarely met because people are afraid to hold themselves or each other accountable. It's easier to let something slide than to make a stern phone call, but the consequences of unmet promises are serious and expensive. Rather than creating stress, establishing clear schedules and holding people accountable actually *reduces* stress. Meeting your own obligations also forces you to focus and hunker down to do the work, rather than only to worry about it.

I have few gripes, but if someone can't meet a deadline, I hate it when they disappear. They don't return phone calls or respond to e-mail messages. They seem to vanish. Not admitting you screwed up by missing an important commitment is unprofessional and makes me think twice about doing business with you again.

If you want to make an indelible, positive impression, submit the work before it is due.

accountants The know-it-alls behind your business. (*See also* bookkeeper; economic forecasting; enrolled agent.)

Technically, accountants are men and women trained to keep track of our finances. Certified public accountants (CPAs) have passed a state-sanctioned examination. Enrolled agents (EAs), many of whom are former Internal Revenue Service agents, pass a rigorous exam given by the IRS.

In effect, the people with whom you trust your finances are the confidants of the business world. You will probably share more confidential information with your accountant than with your clergyperson. Think about it. The trail left by your money reveals your life story. If you are having an affair and use a credit card to pay for a hotel room, your accountant will know about it before your spouse does. If you order roses online, the charge will appear on your credit card and may raise the question of whether or not they were a business expense.

Your accountant should be your most trusted adviser, someone to help you sort out a variety of problems. Accountants are often among the major influences in an entrepreneur's life. We ask our accountants whether we should buy or lease a car, whether to extend a business trip into a vacation, and how much to put aside for retirement.

The best way to find a good accountant is by word of mouth. Ask business owners you respect for their advisers' names. Ask members of your trade or professional association for recommendations, especially if your business requires special tax or accounting expertise. Having an explicit, detailed job description makes a want ad more effective and helps you clarify in your own mind the duties of the position. A good CPA can often double as your business development guy and part-time chief financial officer. Our CPA helps develop cash flow projections, estimates our tax liabilities, and determines the best and quickest way to repay our commercial credit lines. He helps analyze the long- and short-term implications of the projects we take on.

If you are unhappy with your current accountant, don't be afraid to find a new one. Just don't try to interview candidates between New Year's Day and March 15 (when most corporate tax returns are due). Summer is the best time to look for a new accountant or enrolled agent. Enrolled agents work with many small business owners and have a distinct advantage in that they can represent you to the IRS, and many of them are former IRS agents. Finding a competent person to help you manage your money and file your tax returns should be one of your highest priorities.

accounts payable The money you owe people for goods and services they provide.

accounts receivable The money people owe you after you have shipped or produced products or services, sometimes referred to as *receivables*.

accounts receivable financing A popular form of financing based on the amount of money owed your business.

It is generally more expensive than bank financing, but AR lenders are willing to extend credit to smaller, less-established businesses. AR lenders are easy to find if you ask your accountant or even your banker for a referral. "By the time they find out about me, they have been turned down by traditional bank financing and don't want to give up a piece of the business to venture capitalists because they don't want to lose control," said Rebecca Karp, a former bank executive who helped finance small business owners.

The difference between bank financing and AR financing is that the lender doesn't base his decision on the creditworthiness of the client. One of Karp's clients, for instance, started a home health care agency that sends nurses into patients' homes to provide chemotherapy and other treatments. Although he had many contracts, his clients, mostly big insurance companies, rarely paid their bills sooner than sixty days after the invoice date.

"He wasn't sure he could afford to take on the new business because he had to pay nurses every other week," said Karp. "I purchased his receivables, because his clients were big, strong, stable insurance companies." With her help, his revenues increased 130 percent in one year.

Before you sell your receivables, check out the reputation and credibility of the lender. Ask for references and check with other business owners who have worked with the person.

Like many AR lenders, Karp started buying "anything that has stream of payments." She bought privately held mortgage notes and structured insurance settlements from people who preferred lump sum payout.

"I personally funded smaller, local businesses because I liked the rapport and connection with the business," said Karp.

advertising Paid commercial space on the air (radio and television), in print (newspapers, newsletters, and magazines), or on the Web. Can also include signs attached to your building, billboards, and ads painted on walls.

You totally control the message in advertising, the cost of which is usually based on the number of impressions made. Most small business owners say advertising is too expensive. I agree. But the one advantage that many kinds of advertising offer over other promotional strategies is the ease of tracking responses to it. You can add a code to coupons printed in your local newspaper and know exactly how many buy-one-get-one-free coupons were redeemed. You can track online sales and know which banner ad is drawing better than another. (Yes, banner ads still exist on many major sites.)

The most important step in effective advertising is finding the best medium for reaching your target market. This takes time and research. Ask the advertising sales reps for the magazines and radio or television stations you are interested in to send you their media kits. You want to base your ad buys on hard numbers, not emotion. Some targeting decisions are obvious: If you sell skateboards to teenage boys, check out rates in *Boy's Life* and *Maxim*. If upscale female entrepreneurs are your ideal buyer, look into *Victoria* and *More*. Upscale male readers are drawn to *Esquire* and *Fortune Small Business.*

Spend money in the places where you know your customers can be found. Unlike the venture-capital-fueled dot-coms that spent millions of dollars on Super Bowl TV spots in the late 1990s, prudent small business owners don't spend their annual advertising budget on one ad. If you're planning anything more ambitious than classifieds or small ads in a local periodical, you'll do best to rely on professionals to help you spend your ad dollars. If you can't afford a big, award-winning agency, hire a small agency whose work you like. Ask for references and speak to other clients. Set a firm budget and stick to it.

Test the rough drafts of ads on a small group of customers and clients whose sensibilities you trust to be representative and relevant for your target market. Get them into a room, show them the ads, and ask them for an honest reaction. You don't have to spend thousands on formal focus groups. Moreover, your best customers will be flattered that you appreciate their opinions.

Look for advertising bargains. Most people don't know that newspapers often slash their ad rates right before they go to press. You can also negotiate a mix of paid and remnant ads if you ask the salesperson to put your ads anywhere they have extra space. Take advantage of bargain rates after the official ad deadline passes. Small papers will be happy to take your money at the last minute if the presses haven't started rolling. You can also, in some cases, buy leftover time on cable networks if you wait until the last minute.

Work with a media buyer if you plan to buy advertising on a regular basis. They usually take a commission of 10 to 15 percent of the total ad buy, but can often negotiate much lower rates because they represent many ad buyers and have leverage with the ad sales people.

Consistency is important when it comes to wringing the most out of your ad budget. If an ad is drawing response, stick with it. You can also get a break on multiple insertions versus buying one ad at a time.

RECOMMENDED READING

Here are some good books to read if you are ready to launch an advertising campaign:

- *The Wizard of Ads* (Bard Press, 1999) by Roy Hollister Williams is based on a collection of letters and memos from Williams to his clients and friends. Williams is an ad writer and marketer whose company in tiny Buda, Texas, enjoyed revenues of $20 million in 2001.
- *Advertising Without an Agency* (Oasis Press, 1998) by Kathy J. Kobliski explains how to buy time and ad space and gives tips on writing good copy.

A/a

advertising specialties Giveaway merchandise featuring your company's logo. (*See also* premiums.)

We all have desk drawers filled with key chains, letter openers, mouse pads, and budget pens. It's hard to resist filling up a trade show bag with all the free stuff companies want you to lug back to the office.

Despite the cheesiness of most advertising specialties, businesses spend $12 billion every year on giveaways. Your challenge is to find, among the thousands of promotional items, something that reflects well on your business. If you are going to spend $1.56 on something, at least the same amount of money needs to make it back to the office.

Advertising specialties are faddish. One year, sports bottles are in. The next year, it's backpacks that turn into briefcases or colored highlighters that fit into a plastic triangle. The secret to selecting the right premium is to rely on the advice of an expert. Ask a few companies to suggest a range of premiums to fit your budget and your target market.

If you want someone to take something home, don't make it too heavy. But, if you want to be sure your best clients keep your gift on their desk, send the crystal paperweight inscribed with your company logo. There are thousands of companies that sell premiums. (One company we buy from often is **www.ipromoteu.com**.) Before you place an order ask yourself what you hope to accomplish by giving away something with your logo on it:

- Do you want customers to have your phone number and website handy?
- When they see the item do you want them to smile or to think serious thoughts?
- Do you want them to keep it forever on a shelf or use it every day?
- How much do you want to spend?
- When do you want to present the premium? Is it seasonal in nature? Is it something you'll use to draw attention to your booth at a trade show?
- Can you afford to give hundreds or thousands of these items away?

a/A

■ Do you need something so unique you are willing to have something custom made?

Make sure the premium is something your customers will like enough to keep, or you're just throwing money out the door.

advisory board An informal committee of successful, often prominent, people formed by smart business owners looking for credible, outside expertise. (*See also* board of directors.)

Most advisory board members receive little or no compensation and are not legally or financial liable for the advice they share. "An advisory board can be your tripwire," says Susan Stautberg, founder of PartnerCom, a consulting firm in New York City. "An advisory board can alert you to new companies

---

SHOULD YOU PAY YOUR ADVISERS WITH EQUITY?

When money is tight, it's tempting to offer stock in your company to your advisers, but think carefully about the ramifications. Giving advisers an equity stake in your company comes with strings attached, and those strings may turn into a noose.

On the positive side, advisers who are willing to take stock in lieu of cash, or a combination of stock and cash, usually believe wholeheartedly in you and your business. Some advisers may just be out to collect small stakes in promising companies, but don't really want to get involved beyond serving on an informal advisory board. That's OK, if their involvement lends credibility to your company.

On the negative side, if you are paying someone only with stock and you really need their help, you may find your phone calls unreturned because they are busy dealing with paying clients. Another drawback is having an adviser/investor who wants to take a hands-on approach to running your business and starts interfering with your decisions. An entrepreneurial CPA who takes a small equity stake in a few of his clients' companies told me he sees no downside to his own-

---

anywhere in the world that can wipe you out."

Stautberg forms informal advisory boards for big and small companies. One client, Gayle Martz, credits Stautberg with saving her company. Martz worked for years to solve a big problem for people who want to travel with their pets. As founder of Sherpa's Pet Trading Co., Martz designed stylish, lightweight, ventilated pet carriers, and lobbied major airlines to allow small pets to ride in the passenger cabin.

"I saw people squishing their animals into hard plastic cases and came up with a great idea," says Martz, a former flight attendant and passionate handbag collector. She designed the first carry-on bag to transport her own dog, a Lhasa Apso named Sherpa. Now the company manufactures several different pet totes for use around town or in the air.

ership role in the handful of growing companies he advises.

"Your reputation is at stake for each company you are advising," he says. "If anything, equity motivates the adviser to make certain that the information they are providing is accurate and correct, versus your motivation being fee-based."

Independently wealthy and a business owner himself, he is in the enviable position of not having to manage a full practice of accounting clients. So, he picks and chooses the companies he works with, happily accepting a combination of cash and stock.

"I view equity as a positive thing because you pause and reflect more when there is an added incentive to boost value of the company, versus just billing for your time and meeting deadlines."

A small business attorney, who also works for a reduced fee in exchange for stock in a few of his clients' companies, said he's more involved emotionally with the companies he owns. His challenge is to remain objective when they need legal advice and to wear his attorney hat rather than his investor hat.

CAREER SPRINGBOARD

Serving on an informal advisory board yourself can also be good for your career, according to PartnerCom founder Susan Stautberg. Participating on a board can

- Add to your personal network of experienced leaders
- Stimulate you to think big and innovate, virtually risk-free
- Build relationships with decision-makers at the company
- Train you to step up to a corporate board

When she needed help to improve and expand operations at her New York–based company, she turned to Stautberg, a former journalist and publisher. In recent years, Stautberg has created boards for Avon, Avis, Swissotel, and Cigna. She also formed a special advisory board for the United Nations. While the U.N. sought international business leaders, Stautberg recruited a group of pet-loving, high-profile professionals to guide Martz.

Stautberg, whose clients fondly describe her as a "walking Rolodex," first figures out what type of help business owners or executives need to build their businesses. Then, she handpicks for each one an experienced, prestigious group willing to work for a small fee and, possibly, free products.

Susan Shultz, author of *The Board Book: Making Your Corporate Board a Strategic Force in Your Company's Success* (AMA-COM, 2000), says having an advisory board is a "great first step." "An advisory board can focus on strategic issues and not get mired in the details of operation," says Shultz.

But, if you manage a rapidly growing business or are about to go public, Shultz suggests forming a formal board of directors.

affirmative action Ensuring that your business does not discriminate unlawfully against anyone at any time. (*See also* Americans with Disabilities Act.)

Every business, no matter how small, is under a legal obligation not to discriminate in its employment practices on the basis of age, race, color, religion, sex, or national origin. In a growing number of states, you cannot discriminate on the basis of sexual orientation (gay versus straight) or medical conditions, including pregnancy. If, however, you have at least one contract with any of the thousands of federal and state government agencies, you may be required to seek out minorities, the disabled, and Vietnam-era veterans, who are protected by federal and state anti-discrimination laws, and ensure that they receive an equal opportunity to compete for jobs for which they are qualified. These affirmative steps are usually spelled out in a written "affirmative action" policy.

Here is a summary of the major federal anti-discrimination laws:

The Civil Rights Act of 1964 prohibits discrimination on the basis of race, color, religion, sex, and national origin. Title VII of the act, as amended in 1991, applies to all employers with fifteen or more employees.

The Age Discrimination in Employment Act of 1967 prohibits age discrimination against individuals who are forty years of age or older. The ADEA applies to employers with twenty or more employees.

The Equal Pay Act of 1963 prohibits wage discrimination between men and women in substantially equal jobs within the same establishment. The EPA applies to most employers with one or more employees.

The Americans with Disabilities Act of 1990 prohibits employers from discriminating against persons who have a mental or physical impairment that substantially limits one or more major life activities. An employer is required to make an accommodation to the disability, if the accommodation would not impose an undue hardship on the employer's business. An employer is not required to lower quality or production standards.

The Rehabilitation Act of 1973 (Section 503). Like the ADA, it prohibits employment discrimination against persons with disabilities, but applies only to private companies engaged in federal contracts worth more than $10,000.

The Vietnam Era Veterans Readjustment Assistance Act of 1974. VEVRAA, like the Rehabilitation Act, applies only to federal contractors, and prohibits them from discriminating against three classes of veterans: those who served or were disabled in service between 1964 and 1975; those who were awarded a medal during a war or campaign; and those deemed at least 30 percent disabled by the Department of Veterans Affairs.

Generally, employers with 100 or more employees (or employers of 50 or more employees if they have federal government contracts totaling more than $50,000) are required to file an annual report to the U.S. Equal Employment Opportunity Commission on Form EEO-1, providing a breakdown of the employer's work force by race and gender. Form EEO-1 is available as a free download from the website of the U.S. Department of Labor at www.dol.gov.

State laws may impose stricter affirmative action requirements than the federal laws described above, and may impose these obligations on smaller companies. For example, a state may also prohibit companies with ten or fewer employees from discriminating on the basis of sexual orientation, pregnancy, legal immigrant status, or a number of other factors.

Your affirmative action obligation does not mean that individuals covered under these laws are given a preference in employment, or that your company must meet hiring or promotion quotas. Nor does it mean that you must hire persons who are not qualified to perform a job. It does require, however, that you take steps to seek out individuals within the protected classes to ensure that they have an equal opportunity to be considered for jobs.

Even a small company should consider having a written affirmative action policy. It could state, for instance, that in looking for new hires you will go beyond mere job postings by contacting individuals and groups who could assist in locating minority candidates. The policy could also propose that any minority candidate who turns down a job offer will be contacted to find out why. Your affirmative action policy, and the steps you take to make sure you comply with that policy, should be spelled out in your employee handbook or in a separate affirmative action policy document.

agent A person who does something for your business in the hopes of receiving a commission or other compensation based on performance. (*See also* independent contractor.)

The most common form of agent is the sales representative who generates leads for your products and services and helps you make sales and is paid a commission based on the sales volume he or she generates. An agent can, however, be anyone who acts on behalf of your business, including your lawyer, your accountant, or your Aunt Matilda who runs the store for two weeks while you are vacationing in Aruba.

One of the toughest legal questions is determining whether an agent has the right to bind your company (called the principal) to a contractual or legal obligation. Generally, sales representatives lack the power to close deals on behalf of the principal, although they may have limited authority to negotiate the sales contract or quote a suitable price subject to final approval by the principal. The contract between a company and its agent will generally specify in some detail the extent to which the agent has authority to bind the principal. When your agent's authority is limited, this must be disclosed to the customer or other people he or she is dealing with. Their business cards and letterhead should clearly state that they are your "independent agent" or "independent representative." You must clearly disclose to third parties (such as customers) any limitations on your employees' ability to act on your behalf, such as that "Vice Presidents of this company have no authority to enter into contracts greater than $10,000 without board authorization." You should review and approve (or have your attorney do so) your agents' contracts with third parties to make sure that any limitations on their authority are clearly disclosed.

Never should you allow an independent contractor to use a cor-

a/A

porate title such as "vice president" or "principal" on their business cards or stationery—this sends the signal that they have authority to bind the company, perhaps that they are even your employee.

alliances, strategic Any sort of business relationship that positively benefits one or more of the companies involved. (*See also* partnerships; due diligence.)

A strategic alliance between two companies has one mission: to increase sales in ways that benefit both companies equally. Big companies forge alliances with small ones, and small ones forge alliances with each other.

Proximity doesn't have to be an issue in crafting a strong strategic alliance. Two small companies located across the country from each other can form a strong and deep relationship. For example, Axiom Navigation Inc., based in Anaheim, California, forged a successful alliance with FleetBoss Global Positioning Solutions Inc. in Fern Park, Florida, in the late 1990s to develop

---

BEFORE YOU TEAM UP

Here are tips on creating a successful alliance:

- **Learn all you can** about the company you plan to approach via the Internet or by ordering the annual report.
- **Find the right executive** to pitch your idea to by asking the marketing department where to start.
- **Submit a concise proposal** explaining exactly how working together will benefit both alliance partners.
- **Project the financial impact** of the alliance in a spreadsheet.
- **Create a simple, clear contract** spelling out who does what, how the money flows, and what the cancellation terms will be.
- **Test the concept.** Start small and see what happens.

A/a

a new vehicle-locator product. FleetBoss, which sells monitoring equipment used by fleet operators to track delivery and service vehicles, didn't just contract with Axiom to develop a new global positioning system for fleet operators. The company president also invested in Axiom and serves on its board of directors.

Axiom, with about thirty employees and $35 million in annual revenues, was started by a group of engineers who worked for the military. The company designs tracking systems that rely on data transmitted to and from twenty-four satellites. By sending signals to three, four, or five satellites at a time, you can pinpoint the location of just about anything, according to Dave Smith, Axiom's vice president of business development.

The close relationship speeded up the development of the technology FleetBoss needed to help customers like Ted Springer, owner of Springer Equipment Company in Birmingham, Alabama. Springer, who has been repairing refrigeration units across the South for more than twenty-five years, needed to cut his expenses and clamp down on speeding by his repairmen. The system helped him cut fuel costs by about $200 a week, enabling him to quickly recoup the cost of the $10,000 FleetBoss tracking system.

alternative dispute resolution (ADR) Procedures of arbitration and mediation intended to settle disputes outside of court. (*See also* lawsuit.)

In a mediation proceeding, the parties submit their claim to a neutral third party expert who listens to both sides and makes recommendations for a settlement. Many attorneys, accountants, business brokers, and financial consultants will be able to act as mediators, provided that both parties agree to accept the mediator. Your local bar association will generally have a list of attorneys who have volunteered to serve as mediators (with pay) for certain types of commercial or employment disputes.

The problem with mediation is that there is no guarantee you will achieve a settlement—both parties must agree to the mediator's solution, and there is no mechanism for enforcing the mediated result if one party decides not to comply.

A more binding but more difficult and costly form of ADR is

a/A

the arbitration proceeding. In an arbitration proceeding both parties submit their dispute to an arbitrator (or a panel of arbitrators, for larger disputes), appointed by one of the major arbitration agencies. In the United States, the two largest agencies are the American Arbitration Association (for domestic disputes) and the U.S. International Chamber of Commerce (for international disputes). Both parties present their evidence, just as in a court proceeding, and the arbitrator renders a judgment or "award," which is binding upon the parties but may be appealed to a court of law if one of the parties refuses to be bound by the arbitration award. Generally, the parties must agree in writing to submit disputes to arbitration, and there is no assurance that a party will recover the costs of arbitration if it is successful.

Americans with Disabilities Act (ADA) A federal law requiring business owners to accommodate disabled customers and employees.

Intended to make life and work easier for the estimated 43 million Americans with some sort of disability, the ADA has sections covering public services, public transportation, telecommunications, and public accommodations. Title I applies to business owners. Its key phrase is "provide reasonable accommodations." The act, which has been challenged in court numerous times by both employees and employers, doesn't specify what is reasonable. It has been interpreted as requiring employers to restructure jobs, alter workstations, or modify equipment.

To comply, you might have to do something as simple as installing a phone with an amplifier to help a hard-of-hearing employee, or build access ramps for a worker who uses a wheelchair.

The act, which is enforced by the U.S. Department of Justice, defines disability as any one (or more) of the following circumstances:

- The employee has a physical or mental impairment that substantially limits one or more of his or her major life activities.
- He or she has a record of such an impairment.
- He or she is regarded as having such an impairment.

A disabled employee who seeks accommodation must request it orally or in writing, using plain English. The employee does not have to mention the ADA. If the disability is not obvious, you have the right to ask for reasonable documentation, but you need to come up with some solutions in a timely manner. In other words, ignoring the request is a good way to get into more trouble if the employee contacts the Equal Employment Opportunity Commission.

You don't have to give the disabled employee more time off or unpaid leave than your other employees, though, because that would create an "undue hardship" on you, the employer. According to the Justice Department's interpretation of the law, undue hardship refers not only to financial difficulty, but accommodations that are "unduly extensive or disruptive" or those that would "fundamentally alter the nature or operation of the business." If the accommodation you provide is disruptive to other employees' ability to work that may be an undue hardship.

A company with fewer than fifteen workers is exempt from most of the compliance issues, but you should still try to meet the spirit of the law around your small company. Those with more than fifteen employees can seek exemption by proving that reasonable accommodation of the disabled would create an "undue hardship" on the business. But be careful. You can't claim undue hardship because you think employees or customers will be uncomfortable being served by a disabled worker. You also have to be very careful during the application and interview process not to ask questions that violate a person's right to privacy. If someone walks with a cane, you may not ask what happened. You may ask whether or not they can do the job you are advertising. If you notice a current employee is having trouble doing his job, you may lawfully ask if he needs some sort of help.

When Congress was debating the ADA, many small business owners lodged shrill objections. Political activists claimed the ADA would push every small business in America into bankruptcy. Of course, their dire predictions never materialized. The law encourages employers to seek funding from the state or federal government to offset the cost of providing the accommodation.

a/A

There are also tax credits or deductions for certain expenses incurred by employers trying to accommodate disabled workers. For more information, see the *ADA Enforcement Guide,* available by calling 800-669-3362 or on the Web at **www.eeoc.gov**.

angels Wealthy private investors who traditionally invest in regional or local companies within their industry or area of professional expertise. (*See also* venture capital.)

Entrepreneurs dream about meeting angels, who are desirable investors for several reasons. They like to invest in companies in their industry and often provide expertise along with their cash. They prefer to invest in small companies close to home so they can keep an eye on how their money is being spent. Best of all, they're usually more patient when it comes to reaping a return on

---

PITCH TO AN ANGEL

All good investors are optimistic and skeptical. They also hate time wasters. Before you present your business idea you should be prepared:

- Assemble a top-notch, experienced management team.
- Credentials will be looked at closely.
- Create a comprehensive, well-written business plan.
- Make a list of qualified investors to target, based on personal recommendations from your accountant, attorney, and colleagues. Start with three or four people. You don't want to pitch too many angels at the same time.
- Ask your accountant and attorney to make personal introductions.
- Specify how much money you need and how you plan to spend it.

---

their investment than are venture capitalists who often say they want to make ten times their investment back in less than five years. (This happened quite a bit during the dot-com mania of the late 1990s.)

Angel investors are usually very private people. They rarely disclose how much money they invest, although a true angel will make several investments in a lifetime. Angels prefer to work on their own and in a low-key manner. They don't want to be bombarded with requests for money. In fact, if an angel gives you money, he or she will probably make you swear not to disclose the relationship. Discretion is important to angels. Many are industry leaders and they want to see if their investments pan out before letting people know what they've been up to.

Most angels invest under $500,000 in each deal, preferring to keep the amounts modest until they recoup their initial investment. Venture capitalists, on the other hand, are known to be quick to invest millions of dollars in one company because the money they put at risk is usually raised from a pool of high-risk investors and is not their own.

The best way to find an angel is to network your way into a respected trade association or professional society. Angels like to invest in their own industry and often provide hands-on help and guidance to the companies they support. Ask your attorney and accountant to recommend some high-net-worth investors who have a history of investing in your industry and region.

annual review An annual look at a company's business plan to update and adjust it for market conditions. (*See also* advisory board.)

You should be reviewing your core business operations once a week, once a month, or every quarter. But, once a year, you should spend a few days taking a hard look at where you've been and where you are going. I'm astonished at the number of business owners I meet who never stop to think about their businesses and the direction they're taking. They are too busy doing whatever they do to get through the day, not aware that operating a business by rote wastes time and money.

A full annual review should include a close examination of

- Your management team
- Your employees and their job descriptions
- Your vendors and suppliers
- Your clients and customers
- Your banking and financial relationships
- Your advisory board or lack of one
- Your personal happiness

Obviously, this review can't be done in a day. Start with the management team. Think about the people who help you manage the company. Are they all working as hard as they should be? Are they meeting unexpected challenges? Do you enjoy working with them? Is it time to reassign duties or to hire new people to fill the gaps? Is it time to part company with the slackers?

Take a close look at your employees. Do you know what they do all day? Ask them to submit short job descriptions as part of this annual review. You may be shocked at how their view of their jobs differs from what you actually hired them to do. Try shifting responsibilities and mixing things up a bit to play to people's strengths. Invest in training and development if you think a poor employee should be given a second chance. Give merit raises to hard workers. Put slouches on probation and document their problems.

This is a good time to review all your sources of critical materials and supplies. It's dangerous to be overly dependent on one source of a key ingredient or component. What happens if that supplier goes out of business? Shop around. Compare prices and set up secondary accounts with new companies. Ask your current vendors to meet the prices offered by their competitors.

Take a hard look at your customer or client list. Do you have any new names on the list? Are your marketing efforts attracting new customers? Are you saddled with deadbeats? Consider cutting off the customers who don't pay in full and on time. You don't need the aggravation and you should not be financing their purchases, unless you are a bank.

Speaking of banks—set up a face-to-face meeting with your business banker or financial adviser. Try to meet at your office to accommodate touring your facility and meeting your staff. Be honest. Explain what's going on, all about your new accounts, projected cash flow, and bad debts. Ask for detailed information about credit lines, loan consolidation, and sweep accounts. Figure out how you can save money on hidden fees and charges. Consider moving your business account from the local bank to a financial institution, such as Merrill Lynch, which pays interest on business checking accounts.

Remember: bankers hate surprises. If you have something really bad happening, tell your banker. You don't want him to call in your loan when you are least able to pay it off.

If you haven't met in person in a while, schedule a meeting with your advisory board via telephone. Savvy entrepreneurs always rely on mentors and advisers for confidential advice and counsel. (My mentors are in totally different fields, but they offer me a fresh perspective on my problems.) If you don't have an advisory board, form one.

You should review your own performance annually, too. Once a year is a good time to ask, "Why am I working so hard?" If you dread getting up in the morning, day after day, you have a problem. If you drift into the office late and start leaving earlier every day, you have to face the fact that you don't love what you are doing anymore. It may be time for a sabbatical. Many entrepreneurs find that stepping away from the business and turning it temporarily over to someone else is just what they need to feel rejuvenated and refreshed.

Consider taking a four- to six-week break if you can possibly manage it. Invest the time in yourself. Travel. Sleep. Read. Volunteer. Do anything but show up at work. Consider it an investment in sharpening your vision. Try to detach yourself as much as possible. Letting go is tough, but you can't gain any perspective if you are calling the office every day from Maui or checking e-mail twice a day. Check in once a week. See how you feel when you walk back into the office after your break. If you feel excited to be back at work, the break did the trick. If you feel queasy, it may be time to sell out and move on. True entrepreneurs have several ventures in a lifetime; you just may be ready for a new adventure.

asset sales *See* mergers and acquisitions.

attorney *See* lawyer.

audit, external A careful review of company operations, usually financial in nature, performed by an outside accounting firm. (*See also* audit, internal.)

Publicly held companies reporting to shareholders and the Securities and Exchange Commission are required to have their books audited periodically to meet securities requirements. An outside audit is more in depth and will go a lot smoother if your books and records are up-to-date and in order.

audit, internal A careful review of company operations performed by top management to make sure financial records are well organized and accurate. (*See also* audit, external.)

Digging through books and records is no fun, but better that you and your management team do it than some state or federal official on a mission. Certain things, like your business bank account statement, should be informally audited every month. If you have a pension plan, you may be required to file forms and do other administrative tasks. Look at the bank statement and each check to make sure there is nothing suspicious. No matter how busy you are, you or another top manager should personally review and sign every company check.

Every quarter, look at payroll records and your payroll tax return to make sure your payroll service is depositing the state and federal taxes in a timely manner. If not, you could be in big trouble with the taxing authorities. Never, ever skip a payroll tax payment.

Review your insurance premiums, workers' comp reports, and other routine filings. Every six months you should do a more in-depth internal audit of all bank accounts, savings accounts, pension plan operations, and other major financial issues.

Even privately held companies should hold an annual meeting. Set the date, invite your board, and use the meeting as a deadline to complete a full report on your internal operations.

audit, IRS An experience dreaded by every American taxpayer.

If you are chosen for an audit, don't panic. Run out and buy a copy of *Stand Up to the IRS,* by Frederick W. Daily (Nolo Press, 1998). It is not only comprehensive, but also extremely reassuring and starts with a chapter titled "IRS Inefficiency." An attorney, Daily offers simple explanations for everything you need to know to survive an audit. He offers tips, such as not filing an amended tax return asking for a refund, because that becomes a red flag.

The secret to avoiding an audit is not to call attention to your tax return by taking an inordinate amount in deductions. If your business expenses are approaching 50 percent of your income, you are heading for trouble. Claiming year after year of losses associated with your business is also a bad thing to do. A messy tax return or one that features round numbers instead of exact amounts can also lead to an audit.

Daily says that if you are audited, your goals are to minimize the financial damage and limit the scope of the audit. You should get your records organized, research the tax laws you based your decisions on, and keep your mouth shut. Being antagonistic or uncooperative doesn't help. Don't offer any information, respond to questions, and "in short," Daily writes, "don't go in with an anti-IRS attitude. You are not happy to be there, but make the best of it."

audit trail The documents used by an auditor to track monies coming in and going out of a business under view.

automobile expenses A company car can be purchased and depreciated or deducted in its entirety (under Section 179 of the IRS Code) if it is valued at less that $24,000 in 2001.

Check with your accountant, but there are basically two ways to handle a company car. If it is used 100 percent for business purposes, you can buy or lease it and have the company pay the bills as a business expense. If you use it for business only a portion of the time, it's best to keep a mileage log and record all expenses and be reimbursed by the company for a portion of the expenses. Auto logs aren't required by law, but they do help back up your deductions in writing. Keep all repair and maintenance receipts and write the mileage on them. An auto diary in the glove compartment is the best tool for keeping track of these details.

babies, at the office Small human beings who, after initial visits to meet parents' colleagues, should regularly stay at home or in company-sponsored day care.

D ON'T GET ME WRONG. I love babies. I've had three of my own. I like to hold them and coo at them and hand them back to their parents. I don't think they belong at work unless you, the business owner, can afford to hire a full-time nanny to look after Sweet Pea in an office down the hall or can set up a full-fledged day care center.

I do think smart business owners should consider subsidizing childcare expenses (and, to be fair, doggie day care for childless employees). If nothing else, contract with an emergency day care center that accepts kids too sick to go to school or to their regular centers. This is a compassionate and important benefit. We all know that many employees use their sick days to stay home with their sick children, not because they don't feel well.

I realize that few small companies can afford to establish day care centers, but you might consider hiring babysitters to entertain children after school if your staff expresses the need for such a service or is trying to meet a project deadline. Consider hiring sitters or tutors if enough people need help with their kids in the gap between the time school ends and the workday wraps up. You might also pay for van or bus transportation between school and after-school activities for the children of valued employees.

Providing financial support for working couples with young children is a good investment. You will earn the loyalty and devotion of your employees if you show compassion for their children. Weigh the modest costs of these child-oriented perks with the cost of keeping your most valuable employees happy, relaxed, and productive.

back order A serious problem resulting from customer demand for a product exceeding available supply.

Every mail order or Web-based retailer needs a clear policy for handling back orders, including an option for quick refunds if customers don't want to wait. The Federal Trade Commission's Mail Order Merchandise Rule requires companies to ship goods within the stated time, or, if there is no stated time, within thirty days. If there is a delay, you must notify the buyer and give him an option to cancel the order or to receive a full refund. It doesn't matter whether you are selling goods in a brick-and-mortar store or via the Internet—the same rules apply.

The electronic commerce revolution went bust when big and small companies (such as e-Toys) failed to make on-time Christmas deliveries in 1999. If you include shipping information on your website, word it carefully because after a sale it becomes a contract. If you write, "We ship the same day," you'd better do it. Better to insert the word "usually" to give yourself some wiggle room.

bailout clause A provision in a contract that allows one party or the other to terminate based on specific things happening.

Every well-written contract should have a bailout clause. No matter how well intended a business relationship may be at the beginning, there are things that can change, and you need to be able to get out of the deal if it's hurting your company or your mental health. Most big companies write contracts to their advantage and lean away from including bailout clauses. But, if the com-

B/b

pany wants to do business with you, you can be firm and craft a plan that will allow you to walk away under certain circumstances. You should always specify exactly what must happen (such as an income threshold or a material change in the market) and what happens to the money involved in the deal if you bail. Offering to return a certain percentage of what you've been paid often helps a client agree to a bailout clause. Most bailout clauses include a notice provision of thirty to ninety days, so you can't just dump the client or the project on a moment's notice. Work with your attorney to draft solid bailout clauses in all your contracts.

balance sheet A snapshot summary of operations designed to show how you allocate your company resources.

A balance sheet, statement of operations, and statement of cash flows are the three most common financial statements used by accountants, financial analysts, and business owners when scrutinizing a company. A balance sheet is intended to summarize all of a company's assets, liabilities, and equity *as of a specific date*. Of particular interest is the comparison of a balance sheet with another period of time or to a similar company. A statement of operations summarizes a company's revenues and expenses over a period of time. Depending on what method of accounting is used, accrual or cash, it might provide a measure of cash flow as well. A statement of cash flows summarizes all of the inflows and outflows of cash.

The three statements work together. If accounts receivable on the balance sheet keep growing as fast as sales on the statement of operations, yet cash seems to be in short supply, a company may be experiencing collection difficulty.

If current liabilities on the balance sheet are growing faster than current assets on the balance sheet, then the company may be living on short-term debt in excess of cash flow and heading for a cash crisis.

A balance sheet provides a snapshot of money coming in and going out. One part lists the fixed and current assets and liabilities; another shows how those assets and liabilities have been financed. An annual balance sheet should provide a complete

b/B

and accurate picture of the company's financial health at that moment in time.

Ellen Rohr, founder of Bare Bones Business, has been advising small companies on financial issues for several years. Author of *Where Did the Money Go?* (Max Rohr Publishing Inc., 1999), Rohr says she is amazed at how many entrepreneurs are running businesses without understanding the basics of financial reporting.

"Unless business owners confront the issue of understanding a balance sheet and income statement, they are putting a stake through the heart of their business," says Rohr, who wrote her book because she needed help managing the books for her husband's plumbing business.

She says business owners shouldn't rely solely on their accountants or bookkeepers to keep track of their financial health. "Very often," Rohr says, "people are held hostage by their accountants." She suggests working on your books with a partner, another business owner, or colleague who understands a bit more than you do about bookkeeping and accounting.

The key number to track is gross margin, according to Rohr. You figure your gross margin by subtracting your direct costs (labor, materials, and packaging) from your total sales. "Always watch the number of widgets sold or the number of consulting hours sold," says Rohr.

She says one number stands out as the acid test. "Your current assets [cash and accounts receivable] should match your accounts payable," says Rohr, who estimates that only one company out of a hundred keeps track of the money going out and coming in on a daily or weekly basis.

"You don't have to become a financial expert, but you have to know a few basic things," says Rohr, who in 2001, signed on as president of the new franchise division of Benjamin Franklin Plumbing. "My job is to help small plumbing companies grow as they convert to a franchise," says Rohr, who lives ten miles from Springfield, Missouri, and works in a barn on their property.

She credits a mentor, a plumbing industry leader, for teaching her everything she knows about the plumbing industry. "He took me under his wing and showed me how to read a financial statement," recalled Rohr. "I went to the bookstore to buy a book to help me and when I didn't find a book, I decided to write one."

balancing home and work The constant push and pull felt by entrepreneurs trying to maintain both a rich family life and a profitable company. (*See also* burnout; stress.)

You'll never work harder than when you work for yourself. That's why it's so tough—nearly impossible at times—to maintain a satisfying family life and a successful business. You are torn between two powerful rivals competing for your time and energy. Entrepreneurs often justify their messed up family life by saying they are providing tons of material goodies for their spouses and kids. You give them everything: the big house, the pool, the SUV, and the beach house. But, the risk is that you'll wake up one morning to an empty bed, vacant house, and a pitiful life.

In the early years, while you are building your company, you can get away with six- or seven-day workweeks and stumbling home in the wee hours to sleep. You can miss a few major holidays or send the family off to ski or to the beach without you. You can miss the preschool dance recitals, soccer games, and high school plays. But, after a few years, if your business can't survive the normal absences required by family life, you need to do some serious soul-searching.

Any business that needs its owner on duty twenty-four hours a day is a business in trouble, even if it's making good money. If you can't take a long weekend once a month and a two-week break once or twice a year, your management skills need help. Going away on a real vacation refreshes your mind and spirit and allows your employees to make decisions, solve problems, and stretch their wings.

In August 2002 we closed SBTV Corp. for a full week, giving everyone a much-deserved extra week off with pay. August was a good month to close down. Most of our clients were on vacation. Everyone appreciated the extra days off with pay and spirits were high when we returned to work.

If you are reading this thinking, I absolutely can't get away from my business, think again. Consider taking a few mornings off

b/B

SUCCESS AND SANITY

The following are some simple first steps to creating balance:

- Schedule one long weekend away every month.
- Stay home a few mornings a week to hang out with the family.
- Close your business for one week each year and give everyone an extra week off with pay.
- Force yourself to leave the office at a decent hour at least three times a week. Arrive early to make up the missed time.
- Enroll your family in your business. Make sure your spouse and kids visit the office frequently, meet your staff, and understand why you are working so hard.

---

each week to have breakfast with the kids and another morning to have breakfast in bed with your partner. Take off an extra day for one long weekend a month. Life is too short to spend it working all the time.

banker A professional money manager whose job is to assist you in deciding what banking products are right for your company's current and future needs. (*See also* corporation; sole proprietorship.)

Your business banker should act as your advocate within the financial institution entrusted with your money. I love Debra T. Jones, my business banker at HSBC's Pelham, New York, branch. Jones, the assistant vice president and branch manager, is smart, pleasant, and appears always happy to see me. The interest rates paid by HSBC are relatively low and I could make more on my money elsewhere, yet we keep our business accounts in Pelham.

And beyond the convenience? Jones thinks like I do; she anticipates my needs. When a client opted to pay their sponsorship fee in one big annual payment, Jones got the paperwork going to

B/b

park some of the funds in an interest-bearing money market account linked to our regular checking account, and the rest in a six-month certificate of deposit. She prepared all the paperwork so all we had to do was to go in and sign a few documents. No muss, no fuss.

Every small business owner should establish a strong, personal relationship with a business banker. Transfer your personal accounts to the branch and introduce yourself to the manager. Sit down and explain exactly what your business does and what kinds of banking services you need. If you have anything but a sole proprietorship, you will need a separate business banking account. If you are incorporated, you'll need your articles of incorporation, and in many cases, a business license and other records.

Apply immediately for a credit line. Ours is with Key Bank, an excellent financial institution for small business owners. Joining Costco as an executive member is worth every penny because you can apply for low Key Bank credit line rates. We applied for two credit lines before we needed the money to launch SBTV in May 2000. Having $65,000 on tap helped us through the winter of 2001 and kept our doors open until things picked up in the spring.

Apply for overdraft protection to avoid the embarrassment of a bounced check. Most commercial banks do not issue ATM cards for business accounts, but ask anyway. Decide who will have the authority to sign checks. Limit this privilege to one or two people. Decide whether two signatures are required on all checks, or just checks over a certain amount. A good business banker will ask all the right questions and suggest the right package of products and services. You shouldn't be paying any monthly fees if you have a business account with at least $2,500. Refuse to pay any fees for bank checks or traveler's checks. If you are good customer, your manager should waive these insulting fees.

Banks are not the only place to put your money. Merrill Lynch, a sponsor of SBTV, offers a Working Cash Management Account (WCMA) with interest-bearing checking and ATM privileges. You can make deposits by mail or at a bank affiliated with Merrill. You can apply for credit lines up to $100,000 (even more, depending

b/B

on the size of your business). Your money earns interest overnight and can be linked to your personal accounts. Most other major brokerages, including Charles Schwab, offer similar money market, interest-bearing accounts for business and personal use.

bankruptcy A last resort legal action taken in federal court to provide time to repay creditors, restructure troubled finances, or liquidate assets. (*See also* turnaround expert.)

Do whatever you can to avoid filing for bankruptcy. Going bankrupt should be the last resort, to be considered only after you have done everything possible to sort out your financial difficulties. In 2001 in response to a dramatic increase in personal bankruptcies through the 1990s, Congress passed a law making it tougher for individuals and small business owners to seek bankruptcy protection. During the boom, hundreds of thousands of people ran up credit card bills, bought big houses they couldn't afford, and then waltzed into court to discharge their debts.

Businesses usually file Chapter 11 bankruptcy protection, which allows a structured reorganization of your debts and a plan to repay creditors. A judge will work with a court-appointed bankruptcy trustee to carefully sort out exactly what you owe to whom and who gets paid when. If things are really dire, you might consider filing a Chapter 7 bankruptcy, which basically means that you will be forced to liquidate everything. Bankruptcy is not to be taken lightly. You'll need to retain an experienced bankruptcy attorney to work closely with your management team and advisers during the process, which can take months or years to complete. Make sure you understand all the ramifications and ask questions before you sign any documents.

Before you file the papers, make one last attempt to work out payment plans with your major creditors. While banks can be tough and push you into court, your vendors and suppliers may be more forgiving. Make a concrete proposal and explain exactly how and why you plan to turn things around. Do your homework. Base your projections on real information and don't mislead anyone. Lies and false hopes will backfire and ruin your reputation.

B/b

Avoiding bankruptcy is possible if you are willing to make personal and professional sacrifices. Always monitor cash flow carefully to avoid getting in too far over your head. Plenty of red flags start flying when you are spending money faster than you are bringing it in. If you can't pay your monthly expenses because money isn't coming in fast enough, you are experiencing a cash flow crunch. Don't fret. Take action immediately to cut your expenses.

During the dot-com bust and stock market plunge of 2000, we were unable to attract an investor and two of our sponsors went under. Rather than panic and fret, we reduced our hours, relinquished one office, stopped buying all non-essential supplies, and ceased video production. We went into a hibernation mode. We negotiated a payment plan with a major creditor and kept sending checks to show good faith and to continue to pay off the bill—slowly but steadily.

When things perked up, we doubled all our monthly credit line payments and maintained our austerity program. We landed a new sponsor, renewed a contract with another, and reduced our monthly production expenses to the minimum. We still economize when we can; for example, to keep our TV program content fresh, we produce out-of-town stories when our producers are on vacation and can hire affordable freelance video crews. We bring along the lights and videotape to save money.

If you are reading this and are in financial trouble, please don't be afraid to ask for help. Hire a turnaround expert and consult with a reputable liquidation firm. Speak with other business owners who have filed for bankruptcy. It's serious business, and you need to know all about the emotional and financial impact before you go to court.

One small jewelry wholesaler we know was totally convinced he would have to file for bankruptcy after his bookkeeper and controller "lost track" of $1 million and failed to pay the state and federal payroll taxes (both serious crimes). I spoke to him during this crisis and urged him to seek every alternative to bankruptcy. He was reluctant to ask his manufacturer for help, but the factory owner realized that if this man, his major U.S. distributor, failed,

b/B

his business would also be hurt. So, after many stressful meetings, he finally lent the troubled business owner enough money to pay the back taxes and keep the business afloat. Despite suffering two heart attacks, the distributor weathered the crisis and had a strong holiday season in 2001 and 2002.

barter A method of exchange in which buyers and sellers agree to trade in-kind products or services in lieu of cash.

Cave people were probably the first to barter, but commercial bartering has been around for at least forty years, according to industry experts. Today it's a $10 billion industry in the United States, involving more than 400,000 businesses. "Trade is the most powerful financial tool a small business can use," says Tom Austin, who founded a Dallas-based trade operation called Delta-1

OPEN FOR TRADE

Bartering works better for some types of businesses than others. It works well for professional or service business-es like dentists and graphic designers where services have a set price. It works well for hotel rooms and airline seats that are perishable commodities. It wouldn't work well for a manufacturer who needs a specific kind of machine, unless the company that makes that machine would be willing to accept something in trade.

- Find out how long the trade exchange or barter operation has been in business in its present location.
- Don't get in too deep at first. Remember, you have to find a way to pay for the products or services you are trading.
- Do not trade more than 10 percent of your gross sales. Above 10 percent, the financial benefits of trading begin to eat into your profits.
- For more information, call the National Association of Trade Exchanges (440-205-5378).

B/b

Trade Exchange and hosted a radio show about bartering. "It can make things easier when you are starting out."

The bulk of businesses-to-business barter is conducted through exchanges like Delta-1, which provide members with private currency that allows them to trade for what they want and need. "One-on-one trade is very difficult," Austin says. "If you make wheelbarrows and need dental work, it's very difficult to find a dentist who needs wheelbarrows."

In a trade exchange, the dentist would provide the service in exchange for trade currency in services or goods he needed from another member. The wheelbarrow manufacturer would have the trade currency to pay the dentist by providing the wheelbarrows to someone else in the network.

But hanging onto your cash is only one advantage of barter. Bartering allows manufacturers and retailers to move inventory that may have lost its cash market value, and enables service industries to fill empty hours. It exposes companies to a network of other business owners that may become new customers. Best of all, barter industry experts say bartering can boost annual sales by 5 percent by moving out unsold inventory or keeping professionals busy with new barter clients.

"It is the most significant marketing tool available to small business," says Susan Groenwald, president of BarterCorp, a trade network based in Oakbrook Terrace, Illinois, which represents 3,100 clients in the Chicago area. Groenwald says that 95 percent of BarterCorp's clients are small companies with two to ten employees.

Patrick Goodness, owner of The Goodness Company, a small advertising, graphic design, and public relations agency in Round Lake Beach, Illinois, has used barter dollars to purchase laptop computers, monitors, software, office furniture, peripherals, and even space in the Yellow Pages. But more valuable to Goodness, he says, are the new clients and business he has generated by exchanging his own services. "We can fill our schedule during slow times when we can't bring in cash business," Goodness explains. "It gives us a much wider variety of clients and gives us more experience so that we can increase our value in the cash market."

b/B

Don't think you can avoid paying taxes on barter transactions. Uncle Sam treats barter dollars exactly like real dollars. Barter transactions have to be reported on a Form 1099-B and must be filed along with your regular business tax returns.

benefits Perks and resources made available to employees by their employers. (*See also* employee stock ownership plan; 401(k) and SIMPLE 401(k); health insurance; pension plans; professional employer organization.)

When you are just starting out, it's tough to offer anything but the promise of a regular paycheck to your employees. But, in today's competitive climate, even the smallest business should be offering some perks. We pay the cell phone bills for one employee who is covered on his wife's insurance. Another asked us to reimburse her for train tickets, even though we aren't obligated to pay for commuting expenses.

The best approach is a customized approach. Every company

HEALTHY CHOICES

Here are the most common employee benefits programs, according to H&R Phillips Inc., Insurance and Benefits (212-812-1000):

- **HMO:** a managed care network of doctors and hospitals. Members usually pay copayments of $5 to $25 per visit and have no option to seek care outside the network.
- **Point of service (POS):** Combines an HMO with the option to go outside the network subject to a deductible and co-insurance. May require a primary care doctor's referral to see a specialist.
- **Preferred Provider Organization (PPO):** A private network assembled by a payer, such as a large corporation, which negotiates lower prices for a clearly defined group of patients.
- **Dental insurance:** New plans may require employees to wait several months before they qualify for major service such as root

B/b

and every group of employees has different needs and preferences. Some employees would like you to help with their child care expenses. Others need vision or dental coverage. It is important to be fair, and often the best measure of fairness is giving everyone an equal number of dollars to spend. Any benefits you provide are fully deductible as a business expense.

The easiest way to figure out what kind of benefits people want is simply to ask them. Look into offering group health insurance if you can afford it. Most states have special programs available for small companies with three to five employees.

At some point you may want to set up an employee stock ownership plan (ESOP), or a 401(k) plan, where you contribute some matching funds to the employee's retirement fund.

Sit down with an independent insurance broker or benefits consultant. Once you have more than twenty-five employees, you probably have to hire a human resources or personnel manager who will devote time to sorting all this out. Providing ben-

canals and dentures. Few plans cover orthodonture. Maximum annual benefits are less than $2,000.

■ **Vision care:** Coverage for eye exams and glasses; seldom includes designer frames and eyesight-correction surgery.

■ **Section 125:** This tax section allows employees to set aside pre-tax earnings for unreimbursed health care expenses, premiums, or dependent care. A Flexible Spending Account (FSA) covers unreimbursed medical, dental, and vision care. This requires careful planning and supervision.

■ **Transit checks:** Employers can cover the cost of transportation up to $65 per month using pre-tax dollars.

■ **Employee Assistance Programs (EAPs)** provide counseling for family and substance abuse problems. Most small companies are too strapped for funds to maintain a full EAP.

b/B

efits is expensive, complicated, and often exasperating, but it's a necessary part of expanding a business and keeping employees happy.

Better Business Bureau (BBB) A national organization dedicated to protecting consumers from unscrupulous business people.

The BBB has been around since 1912. The BBB has five core services: business reliability reports, dispute resolution, truth-in-advertising guidelines, consumer and business education, and charity review. There are 145 BBB offices that help about 24 million consumers each year, according to the BBB website. Most people are not aware that the BBB's dispute resolution services are free or available at a very low cost. The BBB conciliation process takes a few weeks, compared with mediation or arbitration, which can take months. The BBB also conducts mediation and arbitration services.

Before you do business with a company, it makes sense to see if complaints have been filed against it by other consumers. For more information visit the organization's website: **www.bbb.org** or write to the Council of Better Business Bureaus, 4200 Wilson Blvd., Suite 800, Arlington, VA 22203-1838.

billing *See* accounts receivable; invoice.

blue-sky laws State laws that regulate the offering and sale of securities. (*See also* corporation; limited liability company.)

Whenever you sell stock in your closely held corporation, or a membership interest in your limited liability company, to someone who will not be involved in the day-to-day operation of your business, you are selling a security and will need to comply with the federal and state securities laws.

Generally, the federal securities laws do not apply to securities sold by small businesses. Unless you are looking to raise more than $1 million in capital within a twelve-month period, you will probably not have to worry about complying with the federal securities laws. You may, however, have to comply with the state securities laws, which are known as "blue-sky" laws.

B/b

The blue-sky laws of each state vary widely in scope. They may, for example, require that your offering materials (the information you give to people to induce them to make an investment in your company) be filed with and reviewed by a state government agency. They may require that you limit your offering within the state to only so many people, or to certain kinds of people. They may prohibit entirely certain types of offerings (such as offerings by a company whose executives have been convicted of certain crimes). A few states may even require you and your partners to register as securities brokers and take the licensing exams.

To make matters more complicated, you must comply with the blue-sky laws of each state in which your investors reside. So, for example, if you plan to offer stock in your company to Cousin Joe in Arizona, your old college roommate J. Albert Gotbucks in Connecticut, and members of the Little Old Ladies Investment Club in Wisconsin, you will have to comply with the blue-sky laws in all three states.

Before offering investment opportunities of any kind in your small business, especially to people you don't know personally, be sure to hire a lawyer who specializes in corporate and securities law to help you through the maze of blue-sky legal requirements.

board of advisers *See* advisory board.

board of directors A group of experienced business people hired to provide professional advice and direction to company executives. (*See also* advisory board.)

Directors are usually paid and need to be covered by special liability insurance to protect them from legal actions by unhappy shareholders or investors. Form and work closely with an informal advisory board before creating a formal board of directors. A formal board of directors requires an investment of time, money, and energy. Because they are bound by certain legal constraints, your board members may be cautious and reactive, rather than bold and proactive. It's not that they don't want to help you; they just have to be careful not to make too many risky decisions that may hurt their reputations.

b/B

A formal board of directors is expensive. You will not only have to pay them for their services but also buy their directors' liability insurance to protect them from financial ruin if your unhappy customers or clients file lawsuits against your company and your board.

bonus A special payment given to an employee who goes beyond the call of duty to complete a project, land a new customer, or assist a colleague.

A bonus is a pleasure to give and to receive. A bonus that rewards extraordinary achievement or the attainment of a specific goal can be a powerful incentive in a small company. A year-end bonus based on merit and performance not only makes the recipient happy, but also can help offset your tax bill. Bonuses are tax deductible as a business expense; be sure to add the bonus to the recipient's payroll check so the appropriate taxes are withheld.

You should also try to give yourself a bonus at least once a year. When we signed a new contract with MasterCard, I paid myself a bonus. Although I asked the payroll service to tax my bonus at the highest rate and the final amount was shockingly small, it still felt good.

bookkeeper Master of checks and balances. A bookkeeper keeps accurate and current financial records required by the person who prepares the company tax returns.

While many business owners manage their own finances for years, once your business starts to grow, you should hire professional help. A professional bookkeeper not only tracks the money coming in and going out, but also can offer an outside perspective of your financial situation.

The best way to find a bookkeeper is by personal referral. Ask other business owners you trust to recommend people they use or have heard good things about. Interview people by phone and ask the top candidates to come in for a personal meeting. If you like someone, ask for a list of current references. Reference checking is essential, since you will have to fully trust this person with your money.

B/b

Some bookkeepers handle only the incoming and outgoing funds, writing checks and making entries in your bookkeeping software program. Others will help you draft and send invoices, as well as calling clients who are behind on their payments. Make it clear during the interview exactly what you need the bookkeeper to do for your business.

If you are hiring someone for the first time, make sure they know how to use the software program you use, or know how to convert the data to another program. Expect to pay them for the extra time it will take to bring them up to speed on your financial situation. Make sure they have a complete list of your suppliers, vendors, and customers, as well as credit card accounts, term loans, and other payables. This is a great time to clean up your files, sort out contracts, and collect missing paperwork.

Explain any special situations, such as allowing a favored customer extended terms if they are experiencing a temporary cash flow crunch. Introduce the bookkeeper, by telephone, to your business banker or bank manager and ask the manager to be available to answer any questions the bookkeeper may have.

Be sure to set up password protection on your bookkeeping software and keep track of the bookkeeper's password.

Bookkeeping Software Programs

More than 5 million small business owners use Intuit software, either QuickBooks or QuickBooks Pro. We use QuickBooks Pro because it's easy to use and our bookkeeper likes it. Microsoft Money is another popular program. Peachtree also sells a powerful small business software package. In 2001, Oracle, the giant database software company devoted to serving huge companies, invested in Net Ledger, a small company started by former Oracle programmer, Evan Goldberg, and released Net Ledger as part of the Oracle Small Business Suite. The Suite, which includes an online bookkeeping program is not only simple to use, but also serves as the basis for managing all aspects of your business, including bill paying, payroll, and managing a Web store.

Unless you are in a really unique business that requires an industry-specific software package, stick to the basics. If you oper-

b/B

ate a small business with unique needs, consider custom software. For instance, if you own a towing company, you can purchase a program designed specifically for that business for about $6,000. The program kicks in the minute you receive a call to dispatch a tow truck. It tracks the process from beginning to end, including information about the driver you send out, the car or truck you tow, and what charges are involved. There are thousands of customized software programs for small companies, ranging from beauty salons to architectural firms.

brainstorming A process in which a group of people are asked to come up with creative solutions to a problem in a limited amount of time.

Brainstorming is harder than it would seem. It's tough enough to come up with solutions to problems on your own, let alone in a group. But, if two heads are better than one, maybe six are better than two—if you set up the session correctly.

Brainstorming isn't rocket science. You just need an hour or two when you can ignore the phone, fax, and e-mail. An erasable white board or flip chart with colored markers helps. One person, not necessarily the boss, can lead the discussion. The main thing is simply not to criticize or judge the ideas as they come up. You should, however, narrow the focus to one or two topics, which increases your chances of actually hitting on a great idea.

Start by outlining the problem or challenge as clearly as you can. You'll probably realize that finding consensus on the problem is half the battle. Then let the ideas flow, the crazier the better. Prompt the facilitator to keep recording ideas down on the board or flip chart. You may want to tape the session to have a backup. A good brainstorming session isn't a competition to see who is the smartest or cleverest. It should inspire everyone to think big thoughts and share them in a limited period of time.

Sometimes the best brainstorm comes from just one person. My husband, Joe, came up with "SBTV" for the name of our company. SBTV stands for Small Business TV and is a short, memorable name for what we do. The site had been called **ApplegateWay.com**, which was too long, and people didn't under-

B/b

stand what it meant. (It was supposed to be about the Applegate "way" of doing business.) The name also created problems for IBM, which was a sponsor at the time, because they didn't want to promote Apple and Gateway products.

So, whether you need a new name for your company or a cost-effective solution to a complex problem, set aside some time to exercise those brain cells.

brand building The process that turns your company's brand into lasting value.

Building a brand takes money and time. Intel and Huggies didn't become household words overnight. David D'Alessandro, chief executive officer of John Hancock Insurance in Boston, Massachusetts, says, "You build a brand through servicing customers and making products work each and every day."

D'Alessandro started on the public relations side of his business and claims he doesn't understand how insurance policies work, but he knows about creating a strong brand. "The first thing is not to listen to the advertising agencies," he says. "They are looking to maximize their fees. Smaller companies build their brands through publicity."

He has this advice for entrepreneurs: "Build a brand by taking care of your business. You can't paper over a bad business."

When you don't have a big advertising or marketing budget, you have to rely a lot on word of mouth. "Smart business owners recognize that every encounter is an impression to be made," he says. "You can't afford to alienate too many people. Your best sales force is your customers." D'Alessandro admits he never thought he would be heading a multibillion-dollar insurance empire. When he couldn't find a job to pay for college, he and a friend opened up a window washing business with a bottle of Windex (another painstakingly built brand name) and 500 business cards. "We said we'd give customers a 10 percent discount if they called a talk radio program and mentioned how good we were," he recalls. "It was so successful, we had to hire four crews."

He is a big fan of corporate sponsorship, but he cautions you

b/B

to carefully review the deal to understand exactly what you are getting for your sponsorship dollars. "To simply put your name on something is ridiculous," he says. "But, if there are centers of influence involved (either decision makers or groups of potential customers you want to reach), it makes some sense to sponsor an event or program."

He made headlines when he threatened to pull out of the Salt Lake City Olympics after scandal erupted involving the organizing committee. He is proud of a five-year, $15 million contract Hancock has with Major League Baseball, but the company also sponsors lots of community events. "I'm a great believer in grass roots sponsorships," he says. For example, his company sponsors runners from Africa who come to the annual Boston Marathon. He sends them into schools before the Boston Marathon to meet with inner-city kids.

break even The amount of money you need to earn to cover your costs completely. Many small companies operate at the break-even point, which is a dangerous strategy if you are not socking away profits for a rainy day.

breaks Short respites from the workday required to reduce stress, maintain sanity, and promote good health.

Breaks are essential to good business health. I'm one to talk. I rarely take breaks during the workday, but I'm getting better. I also remind my staffers to take a break for lunch and at least two short breaks a day. (Our chief technical officer takes a cigarette break, which kind of defeats the purpose of a health-related break, but at least he gets some fresh air.) You should encourage your employees to take breaks because if they don't, you are violating federal, and possibly state, labor laws.

We have a water cooler, so people can get together to chat during their breaks, or to enjoy the peace and quiet alone. Drink water instead of coffee, tea, or caffeinated sodas.

A lunch break is critical, even if you don't eat lunch. Take a walk around the block, read a chapter of a good book, call a funny friend. Getting away from the office is important, especially if you

B/b

are under stress or crashing on a deadline. Sneak off to a movie if you can't think straight, or take a drive.

bribes Unethical payoffs, varying widely among cultures.

If you feel compelled to pay a bribe to make something happen, consider the advice of Laurel Delaney, an international-trade expert who works with many small firms that deal globally.

"While bribery is a legal and moral issue, one must see it in a cultural context in order to understand the different attitudes toward bribery," says Delaney. "I don't think there is any country where the people believe it is proper for those in a position of [political] power to enrich themselves through secretive agreements at the expense of another person, company, or nation. Yet, because bribery is so complex and is difficult to define on an international basis, it continues to exist."

She says there are different kinds of bribery from extortion to lubrication to subornation. For instance, two ways of disguising bribes in Japan are to purposely lose when playing golf or the Chinese table game of mah-jongg. Japanese businesspeople invite officials or others to a discreet restaurant or club that provides a salon for private mah-jongg games. Executives of the host company bring along young employees noted for their abilities to deftly lead their opponent to a successful win at a substantial loss for themselves. If guests prefer golf to mah-jongg, no problem. They can have a golf game with the company's "reverse pro," that is, a duffer who specializes in hooking and slicing his way to sure defeat.

broadband connection A "big pipe" to the Internet required by users who need to view video or audio content online or to transmit very large data files.

You've probably been hearing for years about broadband Internet connections and how zippy digital subscriber lines and cable modems will quicken the flow of information across the Web, bringing businesses and customers closer together. That hype is fading: in 2000, Forrester Research was predicting 10 million residential broadband users by 2001; in 2002, it was barely

b/B

SIGN ME UP

Here are some tips on getting a broadband connection:

- For a DSL service provider in your area, visit **www.broadbandreports.com**, a website dedicated to DSL questions and service options. Tools on the site allow you to enter your address and phone number to see what, if any, DSL services are available in your area. You can also use the site to compare plans and even place your order online.

- **Broadbandreports.com** also features editorial reviews of service providers, active forums where users can discuss different service providers, and even other broadband options, like satellite, fiber optics, and cable modems.

- Never order DSL from more than one service provider at a time. Since most local requests go through a single clearinghouse, duplicate orders will cancel each other out. Do your research ahead of time and pick a reliable DSL service provider. The typical wait for installation is still two to four weeks.

- Whichever broadband service you choose, an always-on connection makes your computer more vulnerable to hackers. Add a firewall, available as software or hardware. Hardware is easier to install: you just plug it in. A reputable hardware device is Sonicwall; some popular software brands are Norton Firewall, Check Point, and Zone Labs.

two-tenths of that. Somewhat difficult to get installed, broadband has also proved difficult to regulate, because the federal government has tried to keep the market open to many competitors. Resolving "open access" held up the AOL Time Warner merger for nearly a year. The government wanted other companies to have access to AOL's customers to avoid a pure monopoly.

B/b

But the demand for broadband remains strong because for small businesses that rely on quick information it can be a godsend. Bill Rogers owns the Hartwell Pharmacy in Hartwell, Georgia, and installed a new kind of digital subscriber line that gives his business high-speed access, telephone service, and twenty-two television channels, all over existing copper phone wires.

With the same connection he uses to get CNN and ESPN in his pharmacy, Rogers checks drug interactions online, researches side effects for medications, and tracks orders to drug companies and United Parcel Service. He can be online while attending to customers because his connection brings up Web pages in a second or two.

"We're just a small-town drugstore," says Rogers, who does about $1.8 million a year in sales. Someday soon, he says, "I'd love to get prescriptions via e-mail from doctors." (With secure transactions and passwords, this is going to be part of his future.)

According to a survey on Internet usage by the Yankee Group, a Boston-based communications research firm, 55 percent of small businesses with fewer than 100 employees have Internet access. Of the users, 65 percent have dial-up service, 10 percent have DSL and 10 percent cable modems. A DSL line costs about $60 a month and a cable modem slightly less.

Getting into the Internet at high speeds is a bit of a chicken-and-egg scenario for many small businesses, says Michael Lauricella, an analyst for the Yankee Group. "There's still a lot of confusion as to what do I do with this. And there are still not a lot of business-grade [Internet] applications that are within the right price range and that offer true productivity advantages," says Lauricella. "Small businesses won't spend money unless it's clear there's a tangible benefit."

As part of a test group for a new technology called mPhase, Rogers had no trouble getting his DSL installed. Other users aren't so lucky. DSL is available only within three miles of a local phone company's switching station, and thus can't be had in rural areas. Cable modems work through the existing cable television wiring system, so the service is concentrated in houses and apartments but not commercial buildings.

b/B

For those outside the reach of both DSL and cable modems, there is satellite, offered by companies like Starband and DirecPC, but both are now still focused on residential customers and tend to average $500 or more to install.

Lauricella calls DSL "a better business technology relative to cable. Once you get DSL installed, you're going to have a much better user experience." Lauricella also notes that with a cable modem the line is shared with other users, which makes for a slower system when they are online.

Michael Luftman, a spokesman for Time Warner Cable, says cable is virtually identical with DSL in terms of speed and ease of use. He acknowledges that cable modem service is now mostly targeted for residential use, saying, "Business is not our first priority. Cable is residential. That's where the wires go."

Opportunities lie ahead for small businesses that can take advantage of the next stage of the Internet's development, the "evernet," in which the Net is always on, like the telephone.

budget A detailed listing of expected receipts and expenses needed to run your business, including office operations, personnel, marketing, advertising, travel, and inventory, used for anticipating and controlling costs.

If you don't have a written budget, stop now and put one together. Every business needs a budget. It is your basic road map. You have to know exactly what everything costs you to rent an office, keep the phones on, buy equipment, pay salaries, travel, and so forth. You don't have to be a rocket scientist to create a budget. Keep a written list of everything that you spend money on. Use your checkbook register as a guide. You should be using a software program to keep your books, and if you do, you already have the categories.

The most important part of the budget is to know the cost of goods sold. You have to figure out exactly what you spend to make that container, pizza, or video. You need to build in a bit of a cushion in case your raw material or labor costs go up unexpectedly.

Once you know how much you need to keep the lights on every month, you'll know how much you have to bring in to cover

B/b

costs and make a profit. Breaking even is not good enough. A business isn't working if it's not making money. If the business is losing money beyond the second year, you should ask yourself why you are in business.

burnout Entrepreneuring on empty. (*See also* balancing home and work; stress.)

The first sign of burnout is a loss of confidence. The enthusiasm and buoyancy required to weather the ups and downs of the entrepreneurial life disappear when the business owner runs out of steam. If your business woes are keeping you up at night or forcing you to bury your head under the pillow in the morning, it's time to deal with the problems before stress does you in. I speak from experience, having ended up, more than once, totally debilitated and in a weeklong fog.

Right before we launched SBTV, I flew to Florence for a vacation and ended up flat on my back in my sister's rented Tuscany farmhouse. I couldn't move at all. Sipping Gatorade and taking a bite of toast twice a day wore me out. I lost my peripheral vision and my hearing tuned in and out like a weak radio signal.

If my brother-in-law, a physician, hadn't been there with me, I would have checked myself into a hospital. He debated whether or not to take me in, but when I didn't get any worse, he declared I was suffering from "nervous exhaustion" and prescribed bed rest. If you believe that only rock stars on endless concert tours suffer from that ailment, think again. Stressed-out entrepreneurs also end up in bed, unable to think or move, if they don't take care of themselves.

I learned a painful lesson in Italy and hope never to wear myself to a frazzle again. The most important thing is to admit you are freaking out and get some help. Unburdening yourself to a close friend or family member is an essential first step. Sharing your fears with someone you trust outside the office is important. It's best not to break down in front of your employees, because this will send them into a spin. (Of course, if your business is in danger of closing down, you have to decide when to discuss it with your staff.)

b/B

Make a list of the things that are upsetting you, dividing them into two categories: the things you can influence or change and the things you can't. If your biggest customer filed for bankruptcy, leaving you in dire straits, you will need time to find new customers. If you lost a chance to landscape that new hospital and have no other projects in the pipeline, you may need to offer your best employees—and possibly yourself—to another firm who may need your skills for a short time.

Checking into a spa and taking a long weekend are short-term solutions to a long-term problem. You have to be disciplined about *not* working—no one can work seven days a week for months and not suffer a mental and physical collapse. Force yourself to relax at least one and one-half days over the weekend. I work most Sunday mornings, catching up on paperwork and writing. But from Friday night until Sunday, I'm off, and I try not to think about business matters.

Be sure to book some time out for yourself during the week. Take an hour off for a manicure, massage, or lunch with a friend. Force yourself to take a walk, drive to the park or the beach. Clearing your head makes space for fresh new ideas to flow. Take care of yourself, because so many people are depending on you to take care of them.

business card Your company's miniature billboard.

If you are on a tight budget, your business card may be your only marketing tool. That's why you should invest in an attractive, eye-catching card; never settle for a cheap, print-it-yourself model. Your card should reflect your attitude and personality, so give it some thought.

If you can't afford to hire a professional graphic artist, find an art student or even a professor who moonlights. Before meeting with the designer, dig through your stack of business cards to select ones you like. This will help the designer narrow down the choices and get a sense of your particular tastes. If you don't have a company logo, now is the time to get one. You don't need something exotic or complex. Your company name in a sleek typeface will suffice.

B/b

LOOK AGAIN

Unless you own a brand new company, you probably haven't updated your logo or letterhead in the past five years. Here are some tips from Jerry Gottlieb, a partner in Manhattan-based McCaffery Ratner Gottlieb & Lane Inc., on reinventing your company's image:

■ Look at all your existing materials with a critical eye. Decide if you want to keep anything or start from scratch.

■ Visit websites operated by your competitors. Get a feeling for what works and what doesn't work on the Web.

■ Ask your employees, suppliers, and clients for feedback on the designs you like.

■ If you can't afford to hire a professional designer, hire an art student with an impressive portfolio.

Stick to traditional business card sizes and shapes. Unusually shaped cards often get tossed because they don't fit in a cardholder or scanner. If you decide on a two-sided card, put the main information on one side and leave the other for your logo or a short message.

Pick colors that suit your type of business. If you manufacture aircraft parts and deal with government inspectors, you don't want a wacky business card. If you design costumes for rock stars, go crazy.

Include your cell phone number, pager, or after-hours contacts. Triple-check the printer's proof, then ask someone else to proofread it again. Five hundred cards will last a long time, so don't order ten thousand the first time around.

b/B

business development The process of exploring new alliances, products, markets, customers, and profitable ventures for your company.

Almost no business succeeds without alliances formed through effort. A solid business development strategy combines personal contacts with cold calling and networking. Everyone in your business should be part of the business development team. The secretary who scans the mail and reads business magazines to clip interesting articles for you is on the team as much as the full-time business development director.

When we were starting SBTV, I was introduced to a young business development director for a company called mondus, founded in Oxford, England. It was one of the first online business-to-business exchanges, linking buyers and sellers of business goods and services. The company was ultimately sold for millions of dollars to an Italian telephone directory company hungry to own its database of business owners.

Together, the biz-dev guy and I cooked up ways for our companies to work together without a lot of cash changing hands. In all, it paid us about $10,000 for the business tips we wrote for its home page and the production of a streaming video commercial explaining what mondus did. They got the content and the video; we got some much-needed cash and public recognition as one of their strategic marketing partners. We were in good company with American Express and other big names.

Even the most mundane company can forge some exciting business development deals. If you own a clothing store, team up with a local dry cleaner to provide discounts to customers. If you sell software, hook up with a hardware manufacturer to package your products together. Share sales people and coordinate your sales efforts. Share space at a trade show and advertising space in the newspaper.

Big companies make great business development deals all the time. Kinko's has teamed up with Federal Express, America Online, Kodak, and other big and small partners to provide additional products and services to Kinko's customers.

If you can't afford to hire a full-time biz-dev person, make sure

B/b

your marketing director has good people skills and can present your business case to outsiders. Our chief financial officer heads up our business development efforts. (Our CFO is unusual because he can crunch numbers *and* make a lively presentation to a potential corporate client.)

For years, I did all the initial business development work. Now, I have help, but I still try to get out at least once a month to look for potential partners. A few months ago, I spent $75 to attend a marketing seminar with the hope of landing some new clients. The $75 fee generated $10,000 in income for SBTV.

Business development efforts force you to get out of your office and make some connections. So, take your suit to the cleaners, fill your pockets with business cards, and get out there networking to make some money.

business plan A document every successful business owner must suffer to develop to attract outside investors and to build internal growth.

A good business plan explains the concept of a new venture to investors, or, just as important, keeps an existing business on track. While forward-looking, its credibility derives from its grasp of present conditions. It accurately describes the market, the management team, the need today for products under development, the realities of manufacturing and delivering products, the strengths of the competition, including their ability to counter a new competitor like yourself, and reasonable projections of growth.

Many business owners speak about "the business plan" in hushed tones as if it were a sacred document like the Ten Commandments. Or they wince, remembering all the college term papers they suffered through. I'm not surprised there is so much negativity and confusion surrounding the creation of these plans because they are definitely a challenge to research and write. But, rather than dreading the planning process, why not embrace the opportunity to spend some time thinking about why you are in business and what's going right or wrong for you?

There are many excellent books and software packages out

b/B

PRE-PLAN PLANNING

Before you sit down to write either type of business plan, here are some important questions to answer:

- What is my core product or service?
- What sets my products or services apart from our competition?
- How big is the market for my product?
- What are my mechanisms for reaching that market and how much will these mechanisms cost?
- Is our market growing or shrinking?
- What are my competitors doing to capture market share?
- How can I reach more clients?
- What are my personal strengths and weaknesses as a business owner?
- What kind of people should I hire to help me achieve my goals?
- How much money do I need to keep my business going before we see any profits?
- What are my plans for expansion and growth?
- What are my sources of capital? Personal savings? Company profits? Bank loan? Credit line?
- Do I have money saved for emergencies?

Once you answer these questions, in detail, you are ready to start writing your plan. You'll need to get away from the phones and to take a couple of days off from your normal duties to get a draft completed. Don't worry about the style, just get something down on paper— or better yet, on the computer.

there to help get you into the process; some are listed below. And there is no getting around the fact that *you* have to write your own business plan, even if you hire someone to polish the final version.

B/b

THE BASICS OF THE PLAN ITSELF

Although there is no standard format, you'll need to cover these areas:

- **Executive summary.** A three- to four-page overview of your business and your primary goals and objectives.
- **Market.** A detailed and informed look at the market you serve, including a sense of whether it's growing or shrinking.
- **Competition.** What your closest competitors are doing to serve customers and clients. How can you do a better job?
- **Management team.** Who will you hire to help you run the company? Who is working with you now?
- **Financial projections.** Where is your money coming from? Are your sales going up, down, or sideways? You'll need detailed spreadsheets, which should be done by an accountant. If you are looking for outside investment, this is a critical section.
- **Board of advisers.** Who will you rely on for advice and inspiration?

You'll also want a table of contents and an appendix featuring your résumé, brochures, news clippings, and other documentation of your bona fides. Once the plan is completed, ask a trusted adviser to pass the draft along to appropriate investors or partners. Never send a business plan out on an unsolicited basis. A plan sent over the transom will most likely be tossed out or read by a very low-level staff person.

Writing a business plan will automatically set you apart from your competition because successful business owners never operate in a vacuum. You must know where you stand in your indus-

b/B

try in order to maintain your lead. My husband and I have written several plans. For the first, we used a program from Palo Alto Software. Later ones relied on the experience of our chief operating officer, Andrea Tobias, a venture capitalist who had reviewed more than 500 plans.

"Keep it succinct," Tobias advises. "The critical elements are first, to really understand your business so you can make it clear to others who may not know anything about it," she says. "You have to understand the competition and be able to explain your company's key advantages."

A good business plan has a "clear cut, three- to five-year plan, including specific goals," she says. "Don't forget to include exactly how you plan to spend the investors' money. Tell them if you are trying to raise money to hire a management team, buy or acquire technology or launch a marketing campaign. Finally, the most important thing to an investor is the management team—without good management, your plan is worth very little."

Two Types of Business Plans to Consider

You may be surprised to learn that there are actually two types of business plans: focusing plans and financing plans. The focusing plan is the one you write when your business is in its infancy or needs a new direction. Writing it forces you to do a round of homework: market research, a review of your competition, and detailed projections of the skills and resources you'll need to get started. A focusing plan also helps to revive and clarify direction for an existing business, no matter how small it may be.

A financing plan is written for outside investors. In addition to the basics, it will include comprehensive financial spreadsheets and details on how you would spend the money you raise. You also need to specify how long that money will last and how you intend to raise future funds.

"We must be convinced the CEO has his or her eggs all in one basket—the basket we're investing in," the general partner of a respected venture fund told me recently.

B/b

RECOMMENDED RESOURCES

Here are some resources to help you write your plan:

- Business Plan Pro software by Palo Alto Software is one of the most popular and easy to use programs. Check it out at **www.paloalto.com**.
- Rhonda Abrams's *The Successful Business Plan: Secrets and Strategies* (Running R Media, 2000). The classic on business planning.
- *The Complete Book of Business Plans: Simple Steps to Writing a Powerful Business Plan*, by Joseph Covello (Sourcebooks, 1994).
- *Business Plans for Dummies*, by Paul Tiffany and Steven Peterson (Hungry Minds, 1997).

buying a company The process of purchasing an existing company rather than starting one from scratch. (*See also* selling a business; valuation.)

If you don't have the stomach to start a business on your own, consider purchasing an existing enterprise. But be careful. A company is a lot more expensive than a car, and you will need to do more than take it for a quick spin around the block. You should look for a company that fits your expertise and complements your passions.

Start your research by visiting various businesses and speaking to the owners. Owners love to share war stories. If you don't have a particular kind of business in mind, attend a franchise expo—not necessarily to buy a franchise, but to get an idea of the limitless number of successful small business concepts.

Consider retaining a broker to handle your search. Go online and search the business exchanges for interesting possibilities. (U.S. Business Exchange at **www.usbx.com** is one example.) If a company piques your interest and it's in your price range, start the due diligence process. Remember it's a process, not an event. Pull together a team of advisers including your banker, accountant, and attorney. You might also look into hiring an appraiser or industry expert to evaluate the business and see how it stacks up against its competitors. You need to be sure this enterprise is right for you because it doesn't come with a money-back guarantee.

It's easy to fall in love with a business, but be wary of basing your purchase on a gut reaction or emotional response. This is the

b/B

biggest thing you'll ever buy, and if you made a mistake, you'll regret it the rest of your life. If you're also buying the building, take the time to visit the neighborhood at night and on the weekends. Check out the parking lot, lighting, and signage. Do you feel safe? Do you like the area? What other businesses are nearby?

The list below covers the important issues to review during the purchase process. The supporting documents should be copied, collated, and placed in three-ring binders. Buying a business is a full-time job, so be prepared to give it your full attention. If you already have one company and are acquiring another firm, assign your day-to-day duties to a trusted manager. You need to know:

- Is the business making or losing money?
- Are the customers loyal and happy, or disgruntled?
- Could you see yourself working with the current employees, or would you be bringing in your own team?
- Is the business current on all required payroll and other taxes?
- Are there any lawsuits or liens pending against the company?
- What kind of business structure is in place? Sole proprietorship, partnership, corporation, limited liability partnership, or Subchapter S corporation?
- If the company has private or public shareholders, will they present an obstacle to your purchase?
- What do the vendors and suppliers think of the current owner?
- Are you buying the business, the building, or both?
- Can you picture yourself working there every day?
- What is your vision for expanding the business?

Be sure to review all contracts, leases, insurance policies, legal documents, and business plans. If the deal looks serious, have you asked employees, vendors, and suppliers to express their feelings about the impending sale?

After you answer all these questions and can still sleep well at night, consider making an offer. If you are going to need financing, don't forget to involve your banker early in the process.

B/b

Be wary of seller financing. While it may seem appealing to pay the owner directly, you may regret it. Think of how you would feel if you sold a business you had built from nothing to a perfect stranger. Consider whether you want to be tied in any way to the former owner. Do you want that person to drop by to pick up the check every month just to see what you are doing wrong? Probably not.

It's much cleaner to finance the business and pay the seller outright, although many sellers nearing retirement age prefer to receive extended payments for tax or personal reasons. Rely on your financial advisers to help you make the right decision.

I recommend hiring an outside appraiser to set the valuation as you move to the acquisition stage. It's impossible for the seller to come up with a realistic price, and an independent appraisal will take some of the emotion out of the negotiation.

You'll have to decide if you will run the day-to-day operations of the business, or leave the current management team in place. Carefully weigh the pros and cons of buying an existing business with starting one of your own.

buyout An offer made to an executive by a company that wants him to leave. Also known as a *golden parachute* if the terms were agreed upon when he or she was hired. (*See also* exit strategy.)

buy-sell agreement A legal contract by which you and your business partners agree to be bought out at a specified price should certain bad things happen. (*See also* corporations; partnerships.)

Once someone legally becomes your business partner—for example, by becoming a partner in your partnership or by purchasing shares in your closely held corporation—there is only one way you legally can get rid of them. You must buy them out.

There are a number of common situations in which you may want to buy out a business partner:

■ the partner dies or becomes permanently disabled

■ the partner may divorce his or her spouse, and the court may award some of the partner's share in your business to the ex-spouse

b/B

- you and your partner may reach the point where you cannot agree on anything, and the business is suffering as a result
- the partner may file for bankruptcy, and someone you don't like may purchase his or her share of your business at the bankruptcy auction
- the partner may retire, move out of state (perhaps to trail behind his or her spouse who has been relocated by an employer), or no longer want to work in the business

In any of the above situations, you are faced with the choice either to tolerate someone owning a significant share of your business who really isn't pulling their weight and/or doesn't deserve to be enriched by the sweat of your brow, or to purchase the stake of the person you don't want to have as your partner.

The problem, of course, is that in such situations you and the unwanted partner must agree on the buyout price. If there is suspicion or hostility between the parties, it will be difficult to reach agreement on a fair price. Even reasonable and cooperative people can disagree over what a privately owned business is worth. While there are some recognized techniques for valuing a closely held business, a partner is not obligated to accept any of them. They are free to base their estimate of your business's value on wholly unrealistic expectations. That is, unless they are bound by a legal contract requiring them to accept a reasonable price.

A buy-sell agreement is a legal contract by which all (or most) of the owners of a closely held business agree that upon the occurrence of certain stated events, they (or their legal successors) may be bought out by the remaining owners for the price that is clearly stated in the agreement. The price may be a fixed amount, a formula based on the company's earnings, profits, and/or revenue for the few years immediately preceding the event, or an amount to be determined by a third party who commands the respect of all the business owners (such as the company's accountant or financial adviser). In many states, provisions in a buy-sell agreement that require a nominal or "penalty" value (such as $1) are not likely to stand up in court.

There are two types of buy-sell agreements: "redemption" and

B/b

"cross-purchase." In a redemption agreement, the company itself must purchase the stake of the departing or deceased owner. In a cross-purchase agreement, the remaining owners must purchase the stake. In most states, a corporation's ability to redeem its owners' shares is limited by law to the corporation's accumulated earnings and profits. The theory is that an unprofitable corporation should not be using its badly needed funds to bail out the owners; it should instead be saving cash to pay creditors and operating expenses. Accordingly, most closely held corporations use the "onesy twosy" or "double dip" buy-sell agreement, a hybrid of the redemption and cross-purchase agreement in which the company buys the departing or deceased owner's stake up to the legally permitted maximum amount, with any excess purchase price being paid by the remaining owners pro rata based on their percentage ownership of the company.

The death of a business owner can occur at an extremely inconvenient time for the business; there may not be sufficient cash in the business to make the payments required by the buy-sell agreement. Accordingly, many buy-sell agreements require the owners to purchase life insurance policies on each other to fund the buyout arrangement—so, for example, Partner A would take out a policy of life insurance on Partner B, naming himself (Partner A) as beneficiary, and Partner B would take out a policy of life insurance on Partner A, naming himself (Partner B) as beneficiary. If Partner A dies, the proceeds of Partner A's policy will be paid to Partner B, who then will be required by the buy-sell agreement to pay the proceeds of that policy to Partner A's estate, without having to dip into the company's operating cash flow to pay the purchase price. Increasingly, buy-sell agreements are requiring the owners to purchase disability insurance policies on each other as well.

Buy-sell agreements should be signed as soon as possible after a new business is formed. Once a business has operated successfully for a number of years, it may be difficult for the owners to contemplate situations in which they, or their estates or successors, may be bought out. Attorneys normally will charge between $500 and $1,500 for a buy-sell agreement, depending upon the num-

b/B

ber of situations that need to be covered, the complexity of the buyout arrangement for each situation, and the amount of negotiation involved.

buzzwords Jargon or slang used by businesspeople who want to appear cool.

Remember, when every other word used was "space," "monetization," "eyeballs," or "stickiness"? The fashionistas who used those terms while talking on miniature cell phones and spinning around on Aeron chairs had a ball burning billions of venture dollars. My advice about buzzwords is this: Don't use them. They can become dated and can make you appear pretentious. Industry-specific acronyms can also become uncommunicative unless you are speaking to some other propeller-head at a trade show. English is confusing enough, so please keep it simple.

B/b

capital, raising The lifeblood of every new business, required to get the business up and running. (*See also* angels; elevator pitch; starting a business; venture capital.)

Capital fuels your dreams. Without some cash, you are stuck in the daydreaming phase of entrepreneurship. With it—even a little bit—you can go somewhere. Whatever it takes to get your business started, raise enough capital just to get going. Buy one plane ticket. One laptop computer. One software suite. Work a second job. Borrow it from your mother or brother. Tap your credit cards—if you know you can pay more than the minimum balance due every month.

In the beginning, raising capital is your biggest challenge. You have to convince someone that your business idea is solid and that you are the right person to be turning that idea into reality. Your first goal is to assemble a team of trusted advisers to guide you through the process of raising money. Your attorney and your accountant are the first members of the team because not only do they know your business well, they also may have contact with potential investors. Your attorney and accountant should also be asked to review drafts of your business plan with an objective eye. You will be too emotionally involved with touting your dream business to the world, so let them pour a little cold water on your overheated prose.

Remember that the most important part of your business plan is the brief executive summary. Often that is the *only* part of the plan read by the screeners who work for venture capitalists and investment bankers. You should also hone your elevator pitch— the short, pithy summary of your business and what it can do to make the world a better place. It should be less than thirty seconds (the time it takes to ride up three floors in an elevator) and be extremely compelling. A good elevator pitch should inspire someone to ask for your business card. And if someone does, offer him two: one to keep and one to pass along to another interested party.

Most small companies start with money from personal or family savings, while many others are opened with money advanced from a credit line or credit card. The next level of financing may come from angels, usually successful entrepreneurs who have the financial wherewithal to provide cash and advice to novice entrepreneurs.

capital assets Assets, such as property, buildings, and equipment that increase or decrease in value over time, giving rise to capital gains and losses for tax purposes. (*See also* capital-gains tax.)

Historically, the United States tax system has distinguished between the taxation of capital gains and that of ordinary income. The taxation of capital gains has been given preferential treatment. Currently, the tax on long-term capital gains (for property held one year or more) is only 20 percent, as opposed to tax of up to 39.6 percent on ordinary income, depending on the taxpayer's bracket. The creation of this preference reflects a fundamental decision by Congress that not all income from dealings in property has the same characteristics. In order to receive this preferential treatment, a taxpayer must sell or exchange a capital asset.

The value of property often changes over time, and the increase or decrease in value is taken into account or realized in the year the property is sold or exchanged for other property. If the property is a capital asset, special rules apply. When the property is not a capital asset and is sold at a gain, the gain will generally be taxed at the same rate as ordinary income, no matter how long the property was held.

There are two principal requirements in order for the capital gain and loss provisions to be applicable:

- There must be a capital asset.
- There must be a sale or exchange of that capital asset.

Section 1221 of the U.S. Internal Revenue Code defines a capital asset by listing the types of property excluded from capital asset treatment. In other words, capital assets include all classes of property not specifically excluded by Section 1221. Thus, the following are *not* capital assets:

- **Inventory stock in trade and property** held primarily for sale to customers in the ordinary course of a trade or business
- **Depreciable business property and real estate** used in a trade or business
- **A copyright; a literary, music, or artistic composition;** or similar property held by a taxpayer whose efforts created such property or in whose hands the property has the same basis as it had in the hands of the person whose personal efforts created it
- **Accounts or notes receivable** acquired in the ordinary course of trade or business for services rendered or from the sale of inventory assets or property held for sale in the ordinary course of business
- **Short-term non-interest-bearing government obligations** (state or Federal) issued on or after March 1, 1941 and acquired before June 24, 1981, on a discount basis
- **U.S. Government publications** (including the *Congressional Record*) which are received by: (1) a taxpayer from the government without charge or below the price at which they are sold to the general public or (2) a second taxpayer who receives the publications from the first taxpayer described in (1) and who determines his basis in the publication by reference, in whole or in part, to the basis of the publication in the hands of the first taxpayer

For example, you acquire shares of stock in XYZ Corporation on January 1, 2001, for $100 a share. You hold the stock for eighteen months, selling it on June 30, 2002, for $150 a share. Because stock in a corporation is not among the excluded assets in Section 1221, the stock is a capital asset. During the time you own the stock, you do not have to pay taxes on the increase in the stock's value. When you sell the stock, though, you will have to pay taxes at the capital-gains rate. Because you owned the stock more than one year, your sale of the stock will qualify for the 20 percent long-term capital gains rate.

capital-gains tax Tax paid on the profits earned by selling appreciated property, stocks, or other valuable merchandise.

A capital gain is the difference between the cost of a capital asset and the price you get when you sell it. The tax code defines a long-term capital gain as one that results from the sale of any investment held for more than a year. A capital loss can be deducted against ordinary income, but only up to $3,000 a year, according to *Tax Savvy for Small Business* (Nolo Press, 2001) by tax lawyer Frederick W. Daily.

cash-basis accounting A method of accounting based on cash coming in and flowing out of the business.

cash flow The essential flow of dollars into a business to meet overhead, payroll, and other monthly expenses. (*See also* invoice.)

Without steady cash flow your business will sputter and die. But unless you are selling ice cream cones on a busy beach boardwalk in July, you will have a tough time predicting cash flow. Even the ice cream guy will have a bad Sunday if a thunderstorm hits.

The best you can do is put away something from every check to tide you over the gaps. If you establish a small emergency fund, you won't be making payroll from your personal account every few weeks. Apply for a small credit line (most banks will consider $10,000 a good starting amount). Savvy business owners also encourage their clients to pay in a timely fashion.

Send out clear invoices to the right person and follow up with a phone call to ensure its arrival. Paper invoices are generally preferred over e-mail.

Ask to be paid when your bill is due and keep careful notes of the conversation. Track your accounts receivable on a simple spreadsheet and mark due dates and arrival dates on a calendar.

Providing something that people want to buy is only the first step. Once they buy it, it is then your job to keep the cash flowing, the lights on, and your bills paid.

cash flow crunch A lack of cash that can kill an otherwise healthy business by preventing it from paying its bills or meeting payroll.

One quick solution for a cash flow crunch is to apply for a commercial credit line to get you through the dry spells. Key Bank Corp. is a leader in offering excellent rates for these lines through Costco. Joining at the executive membership level costs about $180 a year (versus $35 for regular membership) and allows you to access the bank's affordable, flexible line of credit. (You can also get into the stores to shop earlier than the general public, which is a great perk and time-saver.) There are plenty of other financial institutions offering small business credit lines, such as American Express.

The best way to avoid a crunch is to keep careful track of when invoices go out and follow up quickly if you aren't paid on time. Cash flow and collections experts tell me you have a much better chance of collecting an overdue bill at thirty days than at ninety days. Make sure invoices actually go out the door. If necessary, e-mail, fax, and mail them to the right person. Then, have someone follow up to make sure they got to the right person in the accounts payable department. Get to know the people who cut the checks. Send them flowers and birthday cards. If they like you, they are more apt to pay you first.

C corporation A traditional corporation that pays a corporate tax on its earnings. Stockholders must also pay income tax on the dividends they receive. (*See also* corporation.)

ation A process in which minority-owned businesses attest to hat the majority owners are women or members of an ethnic minority. (*See also* woman-owned business.)

Uncle Sam and big corporations like to prove that they are giving a piece of the action to small companies owned by women and minorities. The only way they can really prove this is to deal with officially certified companies. The certification is a pain in the neck, but it may be worth it. You'll have to fill out a huge application and provide copies of tax returns, corporate filings, and management biographies to prove that the company is truly owned and controlled by a woman or minority. The process has become so strict because too many companies hire a woman or minority to front them, but are still owned and operated by white men.

You'll need your accountant, bookkeeper, and attorney to work on this project. You'll be interviewed and be subjected to a site visit to make sure you aren't acting as a front for anyone.

If you are up for this, you can work with numerous certifying organizations around the country. The two biggest are the Washington, D.C.-based Women's Business Enterprise National Council (**www.WBENC.org**) and the Women's Business Development Center in Chicago (**www.WBDC.org**). They'll be happy to send you information on certification. Minority men and women can apply for certification by the National Minority Supplier Diversity Council (**www.NMSDC.org**) in New York City.

client A person who does business with a company by signing a contract or agreeing to work on a limited, long-term, or short-term basis.

If you sell any sort of professional service, you are dealing with clients. Clients are the demanding people you have to please in order to be paid for your work. You can find new clients through personal referrals or by advertising your services. One of the best ways to get clients to come to you is by establishing yourself as an expert in your field. This can be accomplished if you are quoted by the press or write articles for industry trade magazines. Such media exposure will increase not only your

C/c

name recognition, but also your value in the public's opinion.

My best advice when pitching your services to new clients is to go to the highest level person you can find. If they like what they hear, they'll kick your proposal downstairs with their implicit stamp of approval. You may even be able to approach one of these higher-ups outside of the office. At cocktail parties or industry functions, I have openly "stalked" executives I needed to meet. I just introduced myself and whizzed through my ten-second sales pitch. Top executives are polite and most will give you at least twenty seconds of their time before turning away. The very next morning, I called their assistant and said, "I was speaking to Mr. or Mrs. So-and-so last night at the Heart Fund Ball and I'm following up." Making it known that initial contact has been established could make it easier to get a real meeting. You're not lying to the assistant; you *did* speak with the boss at the party/ballgame/ banquet, and they probably said something polite, like "nice to meet you."

Keep in mind that the best new business proposals are short and sweet with a clear deadline for response. Offer a list of references with your proposal so a prospect can save time if she wants to check up on your reputation. Be aware of what other consultants in your field are charging and place yourself at the high end. You can always negotiate down, but you can't negotiate up.

COBRA Acronym of the federal law that protects your health insurance benefits if you change jobs. (*See also* health insurance.)

Insurance you obtain under COBRA is expensive because you have to pay the full cost of continuing the coverage, plus a 2 percent administrative fee to the company that handles the paperwork. But, for the entrepreneur itching to quit his regular job, COBRA is better than nothing.

Under the Consolidated Omnibus Budget Reconciliation Act (COBRA) of 1985, you can continue receiving coverage for eighteen to thirty-six months. That said, you should still think twice before quitting your job. If your employer was paying 50 percent of your health benefits, you will be paying all of the costs under COBRA. If you are about to be fired, try to negotiate extended health insurance benefits as part of the severance package.

If you are firing employees, consider paying their benefits for a few months to soften the blow. Be sure to explain their rights to continued coverage under COBRA and stand back when they start screaming about how expensive it will be.

And finally if, like many entrepreneurs, you are covered by your spouse's health insurance plan and your spouse should die, the employer has to offer you continued coverage, but is not obligated to pay a dime for your policy.

A related law, the Health Insurance Portability and Accountability Act of 1996, is set up to allow workers to change jobs without losing group insurance. It also requires health insurance companies that serve small groups of employees (five to twenty) to provide coverage. The act also increased the deductibility of medical insurance premiums paid by the self-employed (heading up to 100 percent) and requires health insurance plans to pay for inpatient coverage for mothers and newborns for at least forty-eight hours after a normal delivery and ninety-six hours after a C-section. (This last provision was in response to hospitals' releasing mothers a few hours after they gave birth.)

collections The constant challenge of collecting money that customers and clients owe you.

"The check is in the mail" has become a big joke for many business owners waiting patiently to be paid by clients and customers. Whenever the economy begins to slow, the cash flow crunch squeezing small companies worsens.

"Most of my bookkeeper's time is spent trying to get us paid," says the owner of a small Florida-based market research firm, whose largest high-tech client owed him $500,000. "I add 2 percent interest if an invoice isn't paid in thirty days, but it's a joke," he said. "My client just says, 'Make it due in forty-five days'."

The real question: Why should a business with eight people be paying the expenses for a multibillion-dollar computer maker? Rather than getting upset, credit and collections expert Eric Shaw suggests taking strong action against deadbeat clients, no matter how big they are. "Have the manager of your bank call your creditors and their bankers to find out what's going on," suggests Shaw, president of New York Credit, based in Marina del Rey, California. Or send the collection letters via an overnight delivery service or certified mail, requiring a signature and return postcard from the Postal Service. You need to document all your collection efforts in case you end up in court, Shaw says.

Rather than suing big clients, he suggests speaking with your attorney about filing a "writ of attachment." "Suing a client can take years," said Shaw. "Instead, for about $2,000, you may be able to get a writ of attachment within sixty days. It will bring the company back to the bargaining table." The rules vary from state to state so check with your lawyer. If you do want to look into filing a writ, it's easy to find a company's bank account and branch by looking at the front of a check they've sent you. You can also order a Dun & Bradstreet credit report, (**www.dnb.com**) which usually includes a company's bank information. Other credit bureaus are Equifax, Experian, and TransUnion.

If attaching your client's bank account seems extreme, try some preventive medicine by buying credit insurance. The biggest issuer is Baltimore-based American Credit Indemnity Co., but there are others. The insurance premium costs about one quarter of 1 percent of the sales you want to insure, according to Shaw.

Shaw has another great tip: make your bank the beneficiary of the credit insurance policy. Then, ask your banker for a lower interest rate on your commercial credit line or loan. "The one [interest] point you save pays for the credit insurance policy," says Shaw.

commercial liability insurance Coverage for the unforeseen costs of doing business and engaging in lawsuits.

There are several standard types of liability coverage in the United States, and you should consult with an insurance agent to find out which is best for your company. Most businesses should be insured for at least $100,000 per event and $300,000 overall, but many businesses will require at least $1,000,000 per event and $3,000,000 overall, depending on the statistical likelihood of risk. For example, a publishing company that specializes in science fiction novels, with a low likelihood of lawsuits, will not need as much liability coverage as a publishing company that specializes in instruction manuals for heavy machinery, where one mistake in the text of a manual can lead to industrial accidents and possible loss of life.

commission A fee paid to a salesperson based on the total amount of the sale.

If you are selling anything to the public, you might rely on commissioned salespeople at some point. Most industries pay salespeople a commission against a draw—the draw being a modest salary to help pay their living expenses. The amount of the commission paid depends on your industry. My literary agent receives 10 percent of the deals he negotiates. My business development person receives between 10 and 15 percent, depending on the size of the deal and how much time he spends putting it together.

Julie Jackson, co-owner and manager of Gallerie Michael, a fine arts gallery in Beverly Hills, California, came up with an innovative pooled commission plan to keep her sales team happy. A few years ago, she was making most of the big sales because her contacts in the entertainment industry were very strong (she was once married to actor Alan Ladd's son). She said her salespeople resented that she was making much more money than the rest of them because she had more clients. The other salespeople were also reluctant to provide good service to her clients if they happened to drop in when Jackson wasn't working in the gallery.

To reduce ill will and resentment, Jackson established a system where everyone working on a particular shift pooled all of their sales into one pot and split the combined commission at the end of the month. So, for example, if a four-person team sells $700,000 worth of French art, they split the 10 percent commission of $70,000 four ways.

Jackson also set up a system of hiring rookie salespeople who are only paid a salary for the first three to six months. If they prove themselves valuable, they are added to the "A team" and can share the pooled commission. Jackson told me that her novel approach to paying commissions has boosted morale and sales at the same time.

complaints The way customers let you know you have failed to meet their expectations.

A good complaint can be extremely helpful. It is a wake-up call to let you know you are about to lose a customer or client. Every business needs a process to handle complaints, and you have to tell customers how to report problems. If you have a very small retail operation, you can instruct your staff on how to accept and handle complaints. You should keep some sort of written record on a short form or even an index card. Teach your staff how to ask good questions and collect all the details about the complaint. It's tough to resolve a vague complaint about poor service.

Offering a no-questions-asked, money-back guarantee is a powerful way to reduce complaints and build customer loyalty. Rather than engaging in a long discussion, debate, or process, just hand the unhappy customer a replacement item, full credit, or cash. You will generate an enormous amount of goodwill and probably keep those customers rather than losing them.

Set up a process to gather feedback from your customers before they complain. A short survey handed out at the sales counter can be filled out while a transaction is being processed. Plan an in-store raffle and add a few customer service questions to the entry blank people fill out. Or, send a simple postage-paid postcard to your mailing list, asking for honest opinions about your business. The feedback can be invaluable for improving your customer service.

computer security Being vigilant about protecting your company's business documents, e-mail, and communications.

Don't think because you are small that you aren't vulnerable to a crippling security breach or nasty virus attacking your computer system. "The hackers are getting more malicious and more clever," says Andy Faris, president of the American divisions of Message Labs Inc. in Minneapolis, Minnesota (**www.messagelabs.com**). "Traditional security measures aren't working anymore, so you have to step up your vigilance and improve security."

Experts say your confidential information is most vulnerable when you send it over the Internet in the form of e-mail. In 2001, 10 million e-mail messages were sent around the world every day,

LOCK THAT BOX

Here are simple first steps for computer security:

- **Change passwords often.** Defy hackers by adding one uppercase letter to your password.
- **Install firewalls and antivirus software** that updates its virus definitions frequently via the Internet.
- **Limit use of free e-mail account**s (Hotmail and Yahoo!) by employees at work.
- **Don't download any attachment or open any e-mail** unless you know what it is and who sent it.
- **Encrypt sensitive data.** Don't send financial information online unless you are sure it is secure.
- **Think about using an anonymizer to hide your identity** while visiting websites (**www.anonymizer.com**).
- **Read privacy policies** and don't give sites the option to share your data with third parties or for marketing purposes.
- **Be aware of widespread viruses** and take the time to download patches offered by software makers.

and the number is expected to grow to 35 million messages a day by 2005, according to Accenture, a high-tech consulting firm.

The 2001 scourge, Sir Cam, assaulted e-mail systems for weeks. United Kingdom–based Message Labs, which provides e-mail filtering services worldwide, intercepted 10,000 Sir Cam messages a *day* being sent to its 500,000 subscribers, according to Faris. The Sir Cam virus could delete files and forward confidential company information to unwitting recipients, Faris says.

In 2000, the Valentine's Day Love Letter virus caused an estimated $2.6 billion in losses in seventy-two hours, according to industry analysts. In 1999, the Love Bug virus infected networks, causing an estimated $10 billion in damage, while the Melissa virus cost an estimated $393 million in 2001.

C/c

"I would suggest that all companies, big and small, do a thorough review of their security," says Faris, whose company offers the e-mail filtering services for about $2.50 per user per month with a one-year contract. If a mysterious hacker isn't trying to shut down your website, a disgruntled former employee could be. Doing things as simple as changing system passwords frequently can prevent a major security breach.

"If a business owner doesn't take proactive steps to make sure their information is secured, it's the equivalent of putting their secrets out on the front doorstep when they go home at night," says Robert Lonadier, director of security strategies for the Hurwitz Group in Framingham, Massachusetts. "The typical hacker is a bored teenager with a modem and access to news groups," says Lonadier. "Data in transit (e-mail) and data at rest (company files), financial information, and customer files need to be protected in some manner, otherwise the safe bet is that it will find its way into the wrong hands."

Lonadier says lax password security results from sharing passwords or scribbling them on sticky notes and sticking them on computers or inside desk drawers. "It's amazing how common-sense gets ignored when it comes to security issues," says Lonadier.

He recommends that every business owner spend fifteen minutes making a detailed list of critical information assets. Figure out who really needs access to specific information and then limit access to everyone else. Keep close tabs on who has access to financial and other confidential information. Think twice about e-mailing confidential documents and contracts unless you use a secure method like one offered by VeriSign, which has a service for small companies interested in paying for secure document transmission. The service costs about 20 percent of what it costs to overnight a document, according to the company.

Faxing, if the recipient has a secure fax machine or gets faxes at his or her personal computer, or mailing to clients or customers is usually safer then sending proprietary data via e-mail. "People get lulled into the convenience of the electronic medium without thinking through the implication of having [sensitive] documents travel through cyberspace," says Lonadier.

To immediately increase password security, he recommends including one uppercase letter in your password, which extraordinarily increases the difficulty of guessing it. This is a very simple and effective tool against hackers. "If you have the computer equivalent of locks on your doors and The Club on your car, the casual hacker may be turned away," he says.

Another problem is the push to open your computer systems and website to your customers. The concern is this: If you want to give legitimate customers a password to log on to your site and check order status twenty-four hours a day, you are also giving a hacker an open door to dig deeper into your computer system. You'll have to balance the pros and cons of open access with the risks of being hacked. "With large numbers of computer systems being interconnected front end to back end, there is an opportunity for errors and vulnerability," says Lonadier.

Security experts warn against posting too much personal information about your executives on your website. If you tell the world your chief information officer has three kids, loves to jog, and lives in San Jose, he or she is vulnerable to being threatened by a computer criminal.

confidentiality agreement *See* noncompete agreement; non-disclosure agreement.

consultant A person who gets paid for his or her expertise.

contract A legally binding piece of paper or e-mail exchange, which can get you into legal trouble if not drafted properly.

To most people, "contract" means a formal document prepared by a lawyer with lots of numbered sections and "whereas" clauses. Because of this, you may be tempted to think that a less formal document or an exchange of letters or e-mails cannot create binding legal obligations.

A binding contract does not have to look like an intimidating legal document. Any piece or pieces of paper or any e-mail exchange by which you promise to do something (for example, deliver goods) in exchange for someone else's promise to do

C/c

something (for example, pay for the goods), is a binding contract no matter who drafts it and no matter how sloppy it is. Especially in these days of e-mail and Internet message boards where people can post notes for each other in real time, the risk of creating a contract by accident has never been greater.

Every state has a law called the Statute of Frauds, by which certain contracts are required to be in writing and signed by both parties to be enforceable. These will include such matters as the sale of real estate, the sale of personal property having more than a certain value, and any contract expected to take more than one year to perform. Any type of agreement not listed in your state's Statute of Frauds may be enforceable even if it is only oral. So be aware of the following:

■ Your invoices, purchase orders, and other standard buying and selling documents create legal contracts once the other side accepts them, so be sure your terms and conditions of sale are printed on the back of each of these forms. For example, it is illegal in most states to charge interest on overdue accounts unless you warn the customer first in writing—your invoice form is an excellent place to do this.

■ If you are making an offer or quote for new business by way of an informal letter and want to leave room for further negotiation, be sure to include a statement that "this letter does not create a legally binding obligation of our company, which can only be accomplished by a written agreement satisfactory to our legal counsel" or language to that effect.

■ Never make promises in an e-mail you do not intend to keep and be sure to put a tag line at the bottom of each e-mail saying, "Contracts with our company may not be entered into electronically, but only in a written instrument signed by our president," or words to that effect.

■ If you use e-mail as a regular means of doing business with your suppliers and customers, be sure to agree on a protocol by which either party can verify that the other side's transmission was duly authorized.

■ When drafting a contract for your business, whether doing it yourself or using a template, always have your final draft

BE A HERO TO YOUR LAWYER

Here is a "magic paragraph" that should be included in every contract you use in your business. It may look like legalese, but it will prevent a lot of misunderstandings, and make you a hero to your lawyer:

This agreement contains the entire understanding of the parties and supersedes any and all previous verbal and written agreements or understandings. There are no other agreements, representations or warranties not set forth in this agreement. This agreement will bind, and inure to the benefit of, the parties and their respective successors and assigns. Any modification, amendment or waiver of any provision of this agreement may be made only in writing signed by both parties. The failure by any party to exercise any rights granted herein upon the occurrence of any event set forth in this agreement shall not constitute a waiver of any such rights upon the occurrence of any such event. In the event any provision of this agreement is held to be in violation of any law, statute, regulation, ordinance or court order, this agreement shall be deemed modified accordingly and to the extent necessary to comply therewith and shall otherwise continue in full force and effect. This agreement shall be governed by, and construed in accordance with, the laws of the State of _____, and any action, claim or proceeding under this agreement shall be commenced exclusively in the federal or state courts located in the State of _____. This agreement may be executed in several counterparts, each of which shall be an original and all of which together shall constitute one and the same instrument. Section or paragraph headings in this agreement are for convenience of reference only."

C/c

reviewed by your attorney before sending it to anyone. Most attorneys will charge only one or two hours of their time for this service unless extensive revision is necessary.

■ If the other side wants to use its form of contract, always have it reviewed by an attorney, even if the contract is clear and easily understandable. There may be important provisions missing from the contract that should be added to protect your interests, and unless you are an expert in contract drafting you will not know what these are.

contractor *See* independent contractor.

copyright A legal monopoly designed to protect the creators of original works of authorship such as literary, dramatic, musical, artistic, and other intellectual works. (*See also* independent contractor; work made for hire.)

Copyright is a form of legal protection, or legal monopoly, provided by U.S. law. Generally, the owner of a copyright has the exclusive right (and the right to license others) to:

■ Reproduce the work in copies or phonograph records

■ Prepare derivative works based upon the work (for example, a novel based on an original movie screenplay)

■ Distribute copies or phonorecords of the work to the public by sale or lease

■ Perform the work publicly

■ Display the copyrighted work publicly

■ Perform the work publicly by means of a digital audio transmission, in the case of sound recordings

Some public uses of copyrighted material are permitted. A book reviewer who quotes a paragraph from your latest book or a student who quotes that paragraph in a book report (making sure to attribute it correctly to you) is entitled to do so under the fair use doctrine and does not have to pay you royalties for doing so.

Only the author or those deriving their rights through the author can rightfully claim copyright. Where an employee or, under specified terms, an independent contractor originates a work, the employer and not the employee is considered to be the author.

To claim copyright on a work, all you need to do is include the standard copyright notice (the letter "C" in a circle followed by your name and the publication date, as in "© 2001 by John J. Doe") on the title page.

It pays, however, to register your copyright with the Copyright Office of the Library of Congress in Washington, D.C. Registration establishes a public record of your copyright claim, and generally you cannot sue someone for infringing your copyright if you haven't first registered the copyright. Registration may be made at any time within the life of the copyright. To register a work, you must send a properly completed application form (free from the Copyright Office's website at **www.loc.gov/copyright/forms**), together with a nonrefundable filing fee of $30 for each application, and two complete copies of the work. Different rules and fees apply for sound recordings, CD-ROMs, and other copyrightable works.

A work created on or after January 1, 1978, is ordinarily given protection for a term enduring for the author's life and an additional 70 years after the author's death. In the case of a jointly authored work prepared by two or more authors who did not work for hire, the term lasts for 70 years after the last surviving author's death. For anonymous and pseudonymous works (unless the author's identity is revealed in Copyright Office records), and for works made for hire, the duration of copyright will be 95 years from publication or 120 years from creation, whichever is shorter.

There is no such thing as an international copyright that will automatically protect an author's writings throughout the entire world. Protection against unauthorized use in a particular country depends, basically, on the national laws of that country. However, most countries do offer protection to foreign works under certain conditions, and these conditions have been greatly simplified by international copyright treaties such as the Berne Convention, to which the United States is a signatory.

Some authors are concerned about registering copyright for their works, on the grounds that publicizing their work will make it easier for others to rip them off. Since it is not possible to sue someone for infringing your copyright unless you have registered,

C/c

and registration is convincing proof of the approximate date of your work's creation, there are few arguments against prompt registration of all of your important works, such as marketing brochures, advertising copy, and website content.

corporation A legal entity that limits your personal liability for business debts and obligations, but at a significant cost. (*See also* limited liability company; partnerships and limited partnerships; sole proprietorship; Subchapter S corporation.)

When you do business in unincorporated form (as a sole proprietor, for example, or as one of several partners in a partnership), you have no protection from the business's debts, obligations, and legal liabilities. This means that if your business is sued, all of your personal as well as business assets are at risk. There is no legal separation between you and your business.

One way to limit this liability is to form a corporation. Unlike a sole proprietorship or partnership, a corporation is a legal entity; it is separate and apart from the people who own it and run its business. By forming a corporation, you and your business partners (if any) have had a "child," and the child now runs the business. You and your partners are merely the "puppeteers" who pull the strings and make the child do its thing.

By forming a corporation for your business, you and your partners will be largely protected from the business's debts, obligations, and liabilities. This means that if the business is sued, only the assets owned by the corporation will be at risk. Your personal assets (meaning anything you do not specifically contribute to the corporation) will be safe. There are two exceptions, however:

1. Once you form a corporation, the business must be run in the corporation's name. You must open a separate checking account for the corporation, and all monies must flow through that account (*never* your personal account). You must use the corporation's name on all of your letterhead, stationery, business cards, invoices, purchase orders, and other correspondence. Whenever you sign any document or letter on behalf of the corporation, you must always sign as the "president" or

PROS AND CONS OF CORPORATIONS

Pros:

■ You have limited liability for your business activities. If the corporation is sued, only the assets you and your partners have contributed to the corporation are at risk.

■ A corporation (especially one formed in Delaware) may give the impression that you intend to be a "big business" someday and give you more credibility with venture capital sources.

■ While corporations are taxable entities, they usually pay taxes at rates lower than those of their individual owners.

Cons:

■ Corporations are expensive to form. Expect to pay between $1,000 and $3,000 in legal and filing fees in most states.

■ Corporations are expensive to keep alive. You will have to file reports with government agencies and keep detailed written records (called resolutions) of your corporation's activities.

■ Corporations require discipline. If you don't use the corporation and treat it with respect, you lose the limited liability that a corporation provides and your personal assets will be at risk.

■ If a corporation distributes all or a portion of its income to its owners (called a dividend or distribution), the income is effectively taxed twice, once at the corporate level and again at the individual level. You and your accountant may have to develop complex strategies to avoid double taxation.

C/c

other authorized representative of the corporation. Failure to follow this discipline will lead people to think that they are doing business with you personally, and if something bad happens they may try to "pierce the corporate veil" and reach your personal assets.

2. If, by your own negligence or willful misconduct, you injure someone else (for example, by hitting them with your car) while on the corporation's business, you will still be personally liable for your own behavior. Your business partners, however, will have limited liability for your behavior as long as they did not actively contribute to the injury (for example, by allowing you to get into your car and drive away when you are obviously under the influence of drugs or alcohol). Forming a corporation is no substitute for a good personal-liability insurance policy.

In exchange for limited liability, you must be willing to accept a certain amount of complexity in your life once you form a corporation. Corporations are expensive to form and operate, and you must be willing to do a lot of legal paperwork to keep the corporation alive and kicking. In most states, you will have to file an annual report with the Secretary of State's office, and you will have to document every meeting of your business partners and every business decision that is outside of the course of ordinary business in formal resolutions. The paperwork can be a pain, but if you don't do it regularly, you risk losing the limited liability shield that your corporation provides.

Because the corporation is a legal entity, it is considered a taxpayer and must pay its own federal and state income taxes. The tax rates for corporations are generally lower, however, than the corresponding rates for individuals. For example, the federal tax rate for the first $100,000 of a corporation's net income is only 15 percent, compared to more than 30 percent for the first $100,000 of an individual's taxable income. If a corporation distributes any of its net income to its owners (called shareholders) in the form of a dividend or other legally permitted distribution, the owners will have to report the dividend as income on their personal income-tax returns and pay taxes accordingly at their personal tax rate. For this reason, corporate income that is distributed to its shareholders is said to be taxed twice. To avoid this problem, many corporations elect to be treated as a Subchapter S corporation for tax purposes.

Generally, you should form a corporation in the state where your principal office is located. While many large companies are incorporated in Delaware for legal and tax reasons, the advantages of a Delaware corporation are not as attractive for a smaller business. For example, if you form a Delaware corporation that has its principal office in Michigan, you will have to pay Michigan's corporation income and other taxes as well as Delaware's. By forming the corporation in Michigan you would have to pay only Michigan's state taxes. If, however, you are a fast growing, high-technology company that will be seeking outside capital in the near future, forming a Delaware corporation may be advantageous because it will make your business more attractive to the venture capital community. Some small businesses incorporate in Nevada because of that state's peculiarly generous tax and secrecy laws, but there is a risk that by forming a Nevada corporation you may be perceived as a fly-by-night business with something to hide (unless, of course, you are actually based in Nevada).

Forming a corporation essentially involves a tradeoff: In order to get the limitation of liability that a corporation provides, you must be willing to tolerate the paperwork, complexity, and possible tax burdens that go with owning a corporation. If you feel you do not have the discipline to run a corporation, you may want to consider the Limited Liability Company as an alternative.

cost controls The checks and balances a company has in place to avoid spending too much on products or services.

crisis PR A strategy for handling public relations during an emergency by following a rehearsed plan of action.

When the Air France Concorde crashed in July 2000, killing all 113 aboard, airline officials were immediately on the phone, radio, and television, explaining, consoling, and commenting on the tragedy. They were prepared for the worst and executed a detailed crisis management strategy, including dealing with hysterical relatives and the world press.

But, a few years ago, when a massive shelving unit fell on a shopper, crushing her to death, executives at a West Coast home-improvement store lost control of the situation. "It was a nightmare," recalls Christen Brown, a veteran media coach and president of On Camera, based in West Los Angeles. "They didn't handle it well because they never anticipated anything like that would happen in their store."

No matter what kind of business you own or manage, and no matter how well things are going, you aren't immune to a crisis: your stock price can plummet, a terminated employee may return

---

PR DISASTER TRAINING

Consultants like Brown and Cohn charge $2,500 to $5,000 a day. A media training program for a large company can cost up to $80,000. If you don't have a budget to cover these costs, there are still things you can do on your own:

■ Spend some time outlining worst-case scenarios for your business.

■ Make a list of questions the press and public may ask after a disaster.

■ Designate an articulate company spokesperson. It doesn't have to be the owner or CEO.

■ Practice answering all the tough questions.

■ Make a list of local and national press contacts who cover your industry.

■ Send background information and an introductory letter to several reporters so they know something about your company.

■ Try to set up a meeting with a few reporters who may be interested in covering your company.

to the office with a gun, your bookkeeper might embezzle, or your product could make someone ill.

Brown and other PR and media consultants recommend that every business—big and small—have a written crisis-management plan, including designating a company spokesperson, making a list of media contacts, and composing a detailed strategy for handling employee, media, and community reaction.

"Make a list of all the possible scenarios and all the questions people would ask," advises Brown, a former TV reporter. "Once you know the questions, use role-playing to rehearse the answers to those questions with the company spokesperson."

Robin Cohn, author of *The PR Crisis Bible* (St. Martin's Press, 2000), managed the media after the crash of Air Florida Flight 90 in the 1980s. Cohn says most business owners and executives believe it couldn't happen to them. "If I had a dollar for every time an executive said that to me," she says, "I'd be a rich woman." Cohn says she once helped a small restaurant deal with the press during a well-publicized case of alleged food poisoning. "The restaurant managers invited the media in to see the kitchen and paid all the medical bills for the ill person," she recalled. "They showed compassion and concern for the person with the problem. When it turned out the food hadn't made the person sick, they wound up looking even better."

She warns business owners to be on the lookout for low employee morale. "Disgruntled employees are more likely to go to the media or go on the Internet to complain," she says. "And, if something has gone wrong, tell employees about it. Don't let them find out by watching TV."

Cohn and other media consultants often play the hostile news reporter when working with executives in their training sessions. "I ask very, very hard questions," she says. "They have to learn that the press will ask the worst possible questions and they have to come up with an answer—without losing their temper."

culture The look, feel, and texture of life around your company. Culture is comprised of attitudes, policies, vision, and outlook.

customer service The number one priority for any business that intends to grow and prosper.

If you don't serve your customers well, you won't be in business very long. But customers are loath to complain unless they have had a really horrific experience with your products or a staff member. So, it's up to you to find out what you are doing right or wrong. The most direct and effective approach is to ask customers if there is anything else you can do for them. For example, a bookstore clerk caught me by surprise when she asked me if I had found everything I was looking for in the store. It was a great question. If I hadn't found a book or magazine I wanted,

---

TRAINING FOR GOOD SERVICE

Here are some tips from Friedman to get your employees thinking about customer service:

■ Create some sort of customer service training program. Start with a brown-bag lunch discussion or one-hour session during a catered breakfast.

■ Discuss the kind of problems that came in over the phone that week and how they can be handled better next time.

■ Establish an "on the spot recovery" strategy, which consists of three steps: apologize, acknowledge, and rectify. Ask the consumer, "What is it you would like me to do to make you happy?"

■ Rehearse how you want people to answer the phone at your company. "The first four to six seconds of any conversation sets the tone," says Friedman. "If the welcome is done properly, even if I'm upset, I'll feel there's an intelligent person who can help me."

■ When speaking to a customer, take full responsibility for making the customer happy even if it's not your fault.

---

she was ready to find it for me and add it to my tab.

Asking a handful of long-time customers to share their opinions and experiences is another good way to improve customer service. Take a small group of loyal customers out for breakfast and ask them what you are doing right and wrong. Ask for specific examples and suggestions to improve your day-to-day operations.

Set up a short survey on your website and offer a discount or other incentive to people who complete it. A five-star hotel in Dallas gained instant feedback from guests by handing out a brief survey to fill out while the desk clerk was printing out the final bill.

Empowerment was a big buzzword in the 1980s. Everyone from the janitor to the CEO was empowered to do whatever it took to please a customer. A lot of this was wrapped into the "total quality management" craze, but the part about encouraging every employee to keep customers happy is still a solid concept. The old saw is that you get 80 percent of your business from 20 percent of your customers, so you want to make sure that 20 percent are happy campers.

Nancy Friedman, founder of the Telephone Doctor training company (www.telephonedoctor.com) says it's especially important to brush up your employees' telephone skills when consumer confidence goes down and "you really need to put on your customer service hat."

C/c

D&B (formerly Dun & Bradstreet) A business-to-business information service that collects and cross-references data about companies worldwide. (*See also* due diligence.)

THE SERVICE HELPS COMPANIES check on one another's creditworthiness, sales figures, holdings, market share, and other key indicators. To "Dun & Bradstreet" a company is usually part of the due diligence process of examining a prospective partner or debtor. The process is similar to the one used when you apply for a car loan: the seller will check with a credit bureau—the U.S. big three are Equifax, Experian, and TransUnion—and assess your personal credit history.

A report on your company by D&B would be more thorough: It would list the name of your accountant, your gross sales, the names of your key suppliers, customers and products, and perhaps biographical information about you and other principals. Listing your company with D&B is free. To create or correct an entry about your company, call 800-234-3867 or visit their website at www.dnb.com.

DBA (doing business as) An official legal filing, also known as a *fictitious name statement,* that publicly records information about the owner of a business and the name under which the business is operating. (*See also* trade name.)

debt restructuring A plan to reorganize the repayment of debts to make it less onerous to and more manageable for the business owner or manager. (*See also* turnaround expert.)

deductions Expenses you can legally deduct from your income to reduce your tax burden. (*See also* expenses.)

There are hundreds of legitimate business deductions you can take advantage of. The small business network section of the American Express website, **www.americanexpress.com**, lists a few common deductions to get you started, including bank service charges, health insurance, parking, postage, and rent.

For further information, spring for a copy of *422 Tax Deductions for Your Small Business,* by Bernard Kamoroff, CPA (Bell Springs, 2001). It's a great book filled with all sorts of quirky, but legal, deductions. For the straight facts, order IRS publication 535 for business expenses and IRS publication 463 for travel, entertainment, car, and gift expenses (you can download this publication for free at **www.irs.gov**).

defamation Saying or writing negative things that aren't true about other people or companies with the intent of hurting them. (*See also* invasion of privacy.)

Free speech is your right to say whatever you want about whomever you want, within limits. Similarly, you have the right to protect your reputation against malicious attacks. The law of defamation seeks to balance these two opposing interests.

Defamation is usually divided into two branches: libel and slander. Libel is written defamation; slander is oral. The primary difference between the two is that in libel, you do not have to demonstrate that you were actually harmed by the false statement—anything that appears in print is presumed by the court to have damaged your reputation, whereas the plaintiff in a slander

D/d

action must prove actual harm to his or her reputation resulting from a false statement made orally.

If you are being sued for making a defamatory statement about someone, your opponent must prove that:

- you made a statement of fact about that person (opinions cannot be defamatory);
- the statement was defamatory (reasonably likely to injure the person's reputation);
- the statement was made with actual malice (if the person is a celebrity, a politician, or another public person) or with reckless disregard for the truth (if the person is anyone else); and
- you published the statement, that is, made it known to a third party.

So, for example, a statement that "lawyer X isn't the brightest light on the Christmas tree" will probably not get you sued, whereas the statement that "lawyer X has been sued ten times in the past year for malpractice" will (if false) potentially lead to a lawsuit.

Note that in a defamation action your opponent does not have to prove that your statement was false or misleading. Quite the contrary, you have the burden of proving that the statement is true, or was uttered in a privileged context (say, in a court of law, or on the floor of the U.S. House of Representatives).

The best way to avoid legal action for defamation is not to make defamatory statements without checking your facts first. E-mail and the Internet have made it easy to say things in a fit of anger about competitors, employees, suppliers, customers, and others that you will live to regret later. There are cases in which Party A made a defamatory statement via e-mail about Party B that was intended only for Party C's private consumption, but Party A accidentally hit the Reply to All button and the defamatory e-mail message was transmitted to thousands of people around the world. When doing business via e-mail or the Internet, remember that if you act in haste, you may well repent at leisure.

d/D

depreciation The decline in value of an asset over time as it wears out or becomes obsolete. Depreciation is a tax-deductible business expense. (*See also* deductions; expenses.)

The key word here is *obsolete*. Much of the high-tech equipment that an entrepreneur uses to start a business becomes obsolete practically overnight. The IRS allows faster rates of depreciation for computers and other classes of business assets. Moreover, following the September 2001 terrorist attacks, the Bush administration included a provision in the tax-stimulus package that allows accelerated depreciation for high-tech equipment—a provision that expires in 2004. The rules are complex, and you'll need the careful attention of an accountant in weighing the pros and cons of fast depreciation. A greater tax deduction will help your new business retain more cash, but it also decreases the value of your fixed assets, and thus shrinks net profit.

direct public offering (DPO) The act of selling stock in your company to customers, clients, and associates.

DPOs, pioneered by San Francisco securities lawyer Drew Field, in the late 1980s, never really caught on as he hoped they would. They are still an option if you have a loyal group of customers or clients who want to buy stock in your company. You have to meet state and federal regulations and offer shares only to qualified investors.

Direct public offerings are considerably less expensive than traditional offerings because they are subject to less severe review by state and federal regulators. The key to a successful DPO is to have a natural affinity group—a set of customers who are both knowledgeable and enthusiastic about your business and who, of course, have money to risk.

Also recommended: Show a history of profit and at least two years' fully audited books. It is also a good idea to assign an employee to work full-time on the DPO for at least six months. For more information, check out Drew Field's website at www .dfdpo.com.

D/d

disability insurance Benefits paid when you are unable to work if you were prudent enough to purchase it.

You are three times more likely to be disabled than to die on the job, according to insurance industry experts. So, smart entrepreneurs purchase disability insurance for themselves and, often, key employees. It is not cheap, but if you are willing to wait sixty to ninety days before collecting benefits, you can reduce your premium. (I've paid $3,500 per year for minimal benefits of approximately $1,200 a month.) It's tough to get disability insurance if you work at home because insurance companies contend you can fake accidents if no one is watching you. It took me a year and a diligent broker to convince his company to write me a policy a few years ago. Certain professions have a tougher time getting coverage, including used car salesmen, real estate brokers, and people who perform stunts. (Performing stunts I know is dangerous, but is selling cars and houses that risky?)

Disability insurance is a very customized form of insurance, so speak to an independent broker and find out the best coverage for you and your family. Be sure to pay the premiums with a personal check and not a company check so the benefits will be paid to you and not the company.

disaster plan The cheapest and best form of self-insurance. Also called *Disaster Recovery Plan.* (*See also* crisis PR.)

You may not want to think about a disaster befalling your business, but with a solid disaster recovery plan in place, your business should be able to survive any crisis.

When creating such a plan, you should first spend some time figuring out how to protect your business records and computer data. No matter what kind of business you operate, arrange for a set of your key business records—customer database, payroll records, bank records, and tax information—to be kept by your attorney or accountant. If they don't have the space, keep one set of records at home or in a secure, waterproof storage facility.

Before the end of each workday, require everyone on your staff to back up their work. While it seems like a hassle, getting in the habit of backing up data on a daily basis is critical in case of emergency. You can lose dozens of files if your hard drive crashes.

Collect home phone numbers and assign a team of employees to keep in touch with everyone else should an emergency arise. You might also want to add remote call forwarding to your list of telephone services. With it you can forward calls from your office line to anywhere without actually going into the office.

Recruit a few key employees to serve on your disaster recovery committee. Rely on them to do the research and to draft a comprehensive disaster recovery plan for your approval.

Here are a few key questions to start your planning process:

- Where would we work if the office lost all power or was damaged by fire or flood?
- Can we arrange to share space temporarily with another business?
- Do we have copies of all our essential business records in case our computer systems are damaged?
- How would we keep in touch with our customers, clients, and suppliers if we can't get into the office?
- How would we keep in touch with each other?

RECOMMENDED RESOURCES

- *Business Continuity Planning: A Step-By-Step Guide*, by Kenneth L. Fulmer (Rothstein, 2000)
- *Manager's Guide to Contingency Planning for Disasters*, by Kenneth N. Myers (John Wiley & Sons, 1999)

distribution A system needed to get what you make into the hands of the people who want to buy it.

If you make any sort of product, before you go too far you need to figure out a way to get it out the door and into the hands of customers. A distribution system requires careful planning and integration of all your operations: production, packaging, inventory control, shipping, customer service, and returns. When you are small and make one product, like cheesecake brownies, your distribution system can be as simple as this: You bake as many brownies as the local café owner orders, put them in a box, drive them over to the café, collect a check, and go home. If your brownies take off

D/d

THE DISTRIBUTION AGREEMENT

Here are some of the important provisions to be negotiated:

■ **Territory.** Most distributors will want an exclusive territory, but you may not be willing to grant this until the distributor proves worthy and competent. A useful compromise is to grant exclusivity with the condition that the territory will become nonexclusive if sales targets aren't met or the distributor breaches the agreement.

■ **Minimum sales targets.** Especially when you are dealing with an overseas distributor, it is important to set clear and reasonable sales targets or minimum purchase requirements.

■ **Suggested retail prices.** While you are legally prohibited from setting the prices that the distributor will charge the ultimate buyer, there is nothing wrong with suggesting a retail price range.

■ **Customer lists.** Make sure you are allowed to see the distributor's customer lists. You should know who the ultimate buyers of your goods and services are, even though you have no direct relationship with them. This is important for market research purposes and statistical profiling of customers. Besides, you may have other stuff you want to sell them without involving the distributor.

■ **Audit.** You have the right periodically to audit the distributor's books and visit the distributor's facilities to make sure they are not hiding information from you. You should also make sure that your products and services are being appropriately stored, that the distributor is using appropriate packaging or advertising materials, and that the distributor is in compliance with the agreement.

d/D

and you begin selling them to ten cafés, twenty schools, and Costco, you'll need a much more complex distribution system.

Most manufacturing companies rely on custom software to manage and track their operations. These proprietary software packages include modules to track products from creation to sale and return.

distributor A person who buys your product and resells it, hoping to make a profit on the markup. (*See also* agent.)

When you are selling goods or services in the marketplace, there are two types of representatives that can help you: the sales agent and the distributor. A sales agent (such as an independent sales representative) scouts out and identifies prospective buyers, makes the sales pitch, negotiates the sales agreements (if any), and arranges the terms and conditions of sale, subject to your final approval. But, the sale actually takes place between you and the buyer. The agent receives merely a commission, or other agreed-upon compensation, on the sale. A distributor, on the other hand, buys your goods and services, takes delivery, pays for them (or takes them on consignment), and then turns around and resells them in the marketplace, hoping to make a profit on the markup. Virtually all wholesale and retail vendors and "jobbers" are distributors.

When dealing with third parties to help sell your goods or services overseas, it is very important to specify in writing whether the relationship is one of agency or distributorship. Third-party intermediaries in European and Asian countries generally perform both functions and aren't always clear about the nature of the relationship, thereby exposing you to unintended legal liability in the host country. For example, if you do business in a European country through an agent, you will be deemed to be doing business in that country and will be subject to that country's taxes, import/export restrictions, foreign exchange rules, and other regulations governing international commerce. If, on the other hand, you are selling to a distributor in that country, the distributor takes on most of these responsibilities.

Finding reliable people to sell your products can be challenging. Most entrepreneurs start by working with someone who represents similar products to many outlets. If you sell a food product, find a

D/d

food broker who will add your product to his or her line. If you make cosmetics or bath gels, you'll need to find a distributor with a solid relationship with major drug chains and grocery stores. Be sure to read the fine print in any distribution agreement and keep the initial agreement as short and simple as possible so if things don't work out, you are free to work with someone else.

double-net lease A lease in which the tenant pays rent to the landlord, as well as all taxes and insurance expenses that arise from the use of the property, but the landlord pays maintenance expenses. (*See also* lease.)

dress code The most important set of guidelines for projecting a company's image. Whatever the written policy, the dress code is established by the leader of the company.

Forget casual Friday. Forget casual any day. The laid back—no, *sloppy*—business dress popular in the late 1990s and early 2000s is long gone—and thank goodness it is. I would never have entrusted my money to a bunch of young guys wearing psychedelic rock band T-shirts over ripped Levis, but apparently many venture capitalists did. (Unfortunately, their casual attitude toward clothing extended to the spending of other people's money.)

In early 2000 the business world came to its senses. Country Road, an Australian retailer known for its low-key, monochromatic work clothes, launched a clever campaign called, "Business is NOT Casual," and encouraged people to once again dress for success. Unfortunately, the chain didn't survive.

While it's OK to dress casually around the office on a day when you don't have any important meetings, you should never show up in the same clothes you would wear to wash the car. Clean blue jeans are fine for the company picnic, but every other day, if you are a guy, you should be wearing khakis or creased slacks with a collared shirt, at a minimum.

Pants are fine for women business owners, but buy nice, high-quality ones and some tailored jackets or blazers. Wear a bit of lipstick, a scarf, and some jewelry. Make sure your hair is neatly combed. Set a good example for your staff, because no matter

HOW CASUAL GOT THAT WAY

"When my firm went casual on Friday, you couldn't find a staff person around after 1 P.M.," says Vincent Rua, an accountant and entrepreneur who owns three Christopher's men's clothing stores in New York state.

Although it feels like casual Friday has been around forever, it began when Levi Strauss created a campaign to promote sales of casual clothing in 1992. Levi sent its *Guide to Casual Business Wear* to 30,000 human resources managers. Since then, the company that makes Dockers casual clothes has aggressively promoted casual dress at work, through videos, fashion shows, brochures, and media campaigns. "Now, 80 percent of all companies offer some form of business casual dress policy," says Amy Gemellaro, spokesperson for Levi's Dockers and Slates clothing lines. "People want options; they want to dress how they feel. Nobody wants a mandate."

The casual dress campaign dramatically changed the way Americans dressed for work, according to fashion industry experts. "Levi Strauss never intended to promote sloppy casual dress with people wearing blue jeans with holes and sandals to work," says Rua.

"The way we dress affects the way we think, feel, and act and the way others respond to us," says Judith Rasband, founder of the Conselle Institute of Image Management in Provo, Utah. "No matter whether they work at a large, small, or home-based business, people do not work as hard when they are wearing relaxed clothes."

what you say in a company dress code, your employees will follow your example.

If you have a problem with a great employee who dresses like a slob, tread carefully. If you single out one employee and criticize his mode of dress, you could be at risk for an employee discrimi-

D/d

LOOK LIKE A MILLION BUCKS

"There's a lot of confusion about casual dress codes, with people showing up for work in outfits they should walk their dogs in," says Sherry Maysonave, author of *Casual Power: How to Power Up Your Nonverbal Communication and Dress Down for Success* (Bright Books Inc., 1999).

If you have been waiting for a reason to establish a new dress code for your sloppily dressed employees, here are some practical tips:

- Decide exactly what kind of clothes you want your staff to wear from now on.
- Set a good example. If you dress like a slob, why should they dress up?
- Be aware of what is customary dress for your industry. If you are in the fashion business, you probably know what's in style this season. If you spend your day selling paper goods to the truck stop operators, you probably don't have to wear a suit.
- Be conscious of regional differences in workplace dress codes. People tend to dress more conservatively in Chicago and trendier in Los Angeles.
- If you are uncomfortable establishing a new dress code on your own, hire a local boutique owner or fashion consultant to present a workshop to your staff.
- Make sure you enforce the new dress code fairly and uniformly. Don't allow a few favored employees to get away with wearing whatever they want.
- Be sure your dress code includes a requirement that employees show up for work with clean hair, clean faces, clean hands, and clean nails.

nation suit. One idea is to bring in a professional fashion consultant and have everyone attend a "dress for success" workshop.

d/D

Author and fashion consultant Sherry Maysonave says it's important to find a good look for your employees—a look that reflects the culture and goals of your business. You can set different dress codes for different departments, but you must be consistent.

Maysonave reminds employers to be very clear with new hires about how you expect them to dress. Hand them a copy of the dress code and ask them to acknowledge in writing that they understand the rules. Then, you have a leg to stand on when somebody shows up in a bathrobe and fuzzy slippers.

due diligence An audit of a company's business and legal affairs, usually in advance of a sale or partnership venture. (*See also* confidentiality agreement.)

Due diligence ensures that the representations you have made about your business are "true, accurate, and correct in all material respects," as the lawyers say. A team of investigators, which may include accountants and lawyers if the transaction is big enough,

CHECKLIST FOR DUE DILIGENCE

Before you go into business with anyone, it pays to find out as much as you can about its practices and reputation. Mergers and acquisitions specialists rely on a checklist of things to explore before considering a purchase. Among the things to research during the due diligence process:

- How solid is the company financially? Does it pay its bills on time and in full? Check with Dun & Bradstreet for a credit rating.
- Has anyone sued the company? Check federal, state, and local court filings to determine if any lawsuits are outstanding or if any legal action is pending against the company or its principals.
- What kind of reputation does the company have? Are the principals honest and trustworthy? Check with vendors, suppliers, and competitors.
- Does the company make quality products or offer quality services? Check with customers and clients.

D/d

will descend upon your company headquarters and tear through your files, examine (and perhaps make copies of) relevant documents, and interview your employees and staff. You will have to explain any issues or discrepancies the investigating team finds. The scope of the inquiry will depend on the nature of the transaction, the amount of money involved, the length of time you have been in business, and other factors, and may be negotiable in advance.

Before agreeing to any type of due diligence inquiry, it is important to have a nondisclosure or confidentiality agreement with the person conducting the due diligence inquiry and the agents who are performing the inquiry on the person's behalf. Otherwise, there is a risk that your sensitive information and trade secrets will be leaked to the public generally or, worse, used by the party conducting due diligence to compete unfairly with you. Regrettably, some companies use due diligence inquiries as fishing expeditions to get the dirt on their competition so that they can compete more effectively with them.

■ Does the company respond promptly to customer complaints? Check with the Better Business Bureau to see what, if any, complaints are on file or whether any disputes have been resolved.
■ Is the company's technology solid? If it's in the medical or biotech arena, do the products, drugs, or equipment do what they are supposed to do?
■ Is the company profitable? Dig deep into its books and records to review all contracts, agreements, and accounts receivable.
■ Speak with former executives and employees to collect first-hand insights about the company.

If you feel good about the company, its products, and management based on answers to the above questions, you are probably going to have a positive working relationship.

d/D

economic forecasting Projecting how the bigger economic picture will affect your day-to-day operations.

WHEN THE FOLKS AT MERRILL LYNCH want to know which way the economic winds are blowing, they ask Stan Shipley, their senior economist. But when John D'Aquila, founder and CEO of SelectWinesLLC.com, wants to know what lies ahead for his luxury wine business, he speaks to everyone from the guy selling him Chinese-made baskets, to his paper box supplier, to the UPS deliveryman.

"We, like many small companies, could never afford the luxury of hiring an economist to work for us," says D'Aquila, part owner of the seven-employee business based in Harrison, New York. "It's unrealistic for small companies to have this kind of help."

But even if you can't hire a professional economist, you can set up a do-it-yourself economic forecasting model without spending a dime. The secret is to figure out the barometers that affect your particular industry and watch carefully for signals.

There's no excuse for being blindsided by shifts in the economy. In fact, there is so much free information out there that the challenge is sorting through it to find what applies to your particular business. D'Aquila reads trade magazines, but also the mass-

BASIC ECONOMICS

Here are some tips for spotting economic trends:

■ Get personally acquainted with all your suppliers and vendors. Order by telephone rather than online. Ask specific questions. If the sales rep is not willing to disclose information, or doesn't know enough, ask to speak with the sales manager.

■ Get to know your delivery people. They know who is moving in and out of your neighborhood, who's hiring and who's laying off.

■ Speak to merchants who sell cosmetics and over-the-counter drugs. Sales of these products traditionally increase during tough economic times.

■ Visit your competitor's websites at least once a week. Check out their special offers and new products. Order their catalogs and samples.

■ Get to know the executive directors of trade groups. They are in touch with members across the country and often are the first to spot trends.

■ Subscribe to a monthly industry trade journal and a weekly newsletter.

■ Register to attend the next regional or national trade show. If you can't afford to rent exhibit space, visit the expo floor and check out your competition.

market business publications, with an eye to trends affecting the sales of fine imported wine.

"Because I'm in a luxury business, I look at the size of bonuses paid to people working on Wall Street," he explains. "I also track hiring trends and see which companies are laying off workers and which may be hiring."

He asks his box manufacturer whether the company is selling more or fewer boxes than it did last year at this time. And, he asks what kinds of companies are buying more boxes. If you think

e/E

about it, box makers are in the position to know the financial health of any industry that uses their products. So, if you buy boxes or packing materials, get to know someone at the company who knows what's going on with the sales.

"I also ask the UPS and FedEx guys how busy they are day to day," says D'Aquila. "I want to know how late they are finishing their deliveries and whether they are delivering a lot of computers and expensive items." Why grill your delivery person? If people are buying things, you know consumer confidence is still strong. If the delivery workers are driving around with half-empty trucks, things are looking bad.

D'Aquila, who operates a small wine store as well as a busy website, says he watched much bigger online wine players go out of business in the early months of the post-2000 recession. With many e-commerce businesses gone, he was able to afford more wine-oriented keywords on search engines. This low-cost marketing strategy is driving more traffic to **www.SelectWinesLLC.com**.

With bigger players out of the way, he was also able to stock more unusual and limited-edition vintages, including wines he had not previously been able to obtain from his suppliers. "If my wine suppliers are offering me deep discounts on wines they never offered me before, I'm suspicious," he says. Tuning into these economic signals tells him that his big and small competitors are flagging, and that's good news for his own company.

"If you befriend everyone you work with, you'll be surprised at how much information you'll get," he advises.

elevator pitch A short presentation about your business you can give to someone trapped in an elevator with you for less than three minutes.

Legend has it that some lucky entrepreneur, somewhere, was riding in an elevator with a venture capitalist. In the time it took for the elevator to descend to the lobby, he described his business model, obtained a business card, and miraculously got a funding commitment. That legend has inspired entrepreneurs across the planet to perfect a short, pithy pitch highlighting the great products or services their company offers and why some-

E/e

one with big bucks should invest in their companies.

A good pitch is honed with hours of practice—I'm serious. Draft a few points and practice your pitch in front of a mirror. Try it out on colleagues, and then use it at your next business meeting or networking event. You should know it cold.

A powerful pitch works if it results in someone's asking for your business card. That's a sure sign your pitch was effective and intriguing. Be sure to ask for a business card in return. I'd recommend waiting a few days and then, if there's an e-mail address, send a note about your encounter. If you don't get a reply, wait a day and place a phone call.

e-mail Efficient but entangling, the form of business communication most in need of control.

Most people have a love-hate relationship with e-mail. It is an efficient tool to transmit important information, but it also sucks away all your time and can become an obsession. E-mail is great for short bursts of important information such as meeting times, travel arrangements, or a brief exchange of ideas. It should not replace detailed memos or formal proposals.

Anyone who sends sensitive financial information through cyberspace is making a big mistake. Even if the text of your e-mail is encrypted or sent in code, the information at the top of the e-mail, called the message header, alone contains enough information—both visible and behind-the-scenes—to enable a competent hacker to learn the name of your Internet service provider, the Internet address of your personal computer, or both. With that information a hacker can easily probe the defenses of your machine or network. And copies of all your e-mails, whether you've deleted them or not, will continue to exist either on your PC or somewhere in a networked system. That's why we still prefer to mail or fax important proposals to clients.

E-mail is insidious and creates enormous pressure on people to respond immediately. In the not-so-distant past if you wrote a proposal, printed it out, and mailed it, it would take about five days to land on my desk. The proposal would sit in my in-box for a few days. Once I opened it and read your proposal, I would have

e/E

another two or three days to craft a reply. Ten days could easily pass before I responded to your proposal.

With e-mail, people hope—and sometimes expect—that you will respond in ten seconds, not ten minutes or ten days. But you don't have to feel pressured by technology. Discipline yourself to check your e-mail only once or twice a day—not every ten minutes all day long. You can't get any work done if you are reading and responding to e-mail. You might also consider directing an assistant to screen and respond to all but the most critical e-mail messages. Free yourself from e-mail and recapture the time you used to spend thinking and working.

employee A person who works for you whose activities you direct and control. (*See also* independent contractor; work made for hire; wrongful termination.)

Generally, anyone who works for your small business will be either an employee or an independent contractor. The distinction is critical because when you have employees you have lots of legal obligations. Your obligations to part-time and full-time employees are basically the same, although you can offer part-timers fewer benefits than full-timers. Unlike independent contractors, employees have certain costs attached to their wages, and enjoy certain extra legal protections. If you have employees, you may have to

- pay overtime wages and obtain workers' compensation insurance;
- withhold Social Security and Medicare taxes;
- make contributions to federal and state unemployment and workers' compensation schemes;
- pay unemployment compensation benefits if you dismiss or lay off employees who are entitled to them;
- pay state income, sales, use, and other taxes in that state if an employee works out of a home office in another state;
- provide paid sick leave, vacations, health insurance, and retirement benefits, and include them in your bonus and employee benefit programs;
- comply with federal and state laws designed to protect employees against unfair or discriminatory treatment.

E/e

WHO'S AN EMPLOYEE?

Here are some key signs. If most of the following apply to you, chances are you have employees and not independent contractors.

- You provide them with detailed training, and require them to do things your way.
- You require them to work on your premises and use your equipment.
- They work only for you or are otherwise economically dependent on you for their income, even if only for part of a year, and even if you allow them to work for other companies.
- You reimburse all or most of their out-of-pocket expenses.
- You guarantee a regular wage amount for an hourly, weekly, or other period of time, regardless of their performance.
- You prohibit the worker from advertising her services to others, or maintaining a viable business location outside of your premises.
- You provide the worker with employee-type benefits, such as insurance, a pension plan, vacation, or sick pay.
- You hire a worker for an indefinite period, rather than for a specific project or period of time.
- You hire a worker to provide services that are key aspects of your regular business activity (for example, if you are a law firm and you hire an attorney whose work you will present as your own).

On the other hand, an independent contractor receives none of these benefits. You pay him for his services and that's it.

Whether a worker is termed an employee or an independent contractor may be one of the most difficult determinations an

e/E

employer has to make. While the rules are complex and fact-specific, "it's basically common sense," says Roseann Padula, a labor and employment lawyer with the firm of Sullivan, Schoen, Campane & Connon LLC in Hartford, Connecticut. "When it looks, smells, and feels like an employee-employer relationship, then it probably is. Basically, if someone is working for you as an independent contractor, and you are getting too good a deal, be sure to check the situation twice," says attorney Padula, with tongue only partly in cheek.

While having a written agreement with a worker stating clearly that he or she is an "independent contractor" is helpful, the IRS and state regulators are free to look beyond the contract to the actual relationship between you and the worker. "A big mistake employers make," says Padula, "is to hire independent contractors to do the same job that some of their current employees are already doing, and subjecting the 'independents' to the same working conditions and other requirements as the 'employees.' Even if the independent contractors are working for other clients, they are likely to be considered your employees under these circumstances."

If you are not sure whether a worker is an independent contractor or an employee, you can file IRS Form SS-8, Determination of Employee Work Status for Purposes of Federal Employment Taxes and Income Tax Withholding, with your regional IRS office. Few employers do this for fear of alerting the IRS to their often informal relationships with workers. If you are concerned that some of your independent contractors may actually be employees, you should speak to an attorney who specializes in labor and employment law as soon possible.

"You don't want to take chances here," says attorney Padula. "The IRS claims it loses about $20 billion a year in taxes from employers who misclassify their employees as independent contractors. The IRS is ruthlessly going after employers who play games in this area." For a detailed description of the criteria the IRS uses to distinguish employees from independent contractors, see IRS Publication 15-A, Employer's Supplemental Tax Guide.

Generally, unless you have a written employment agreement with

E/e

your employee, an employee is considered to be an "employee at will" and may be terminated for any reason (and may quit for any reason) with or without notice. If you do not handle the termination properly, however, you may expose your business to a wrongful termination lawsuit from the terminated employee.

When you hire a new employee you should have an IRS Form W-4, Employee's Withholding Allowance Certificate, on file for each employee no later than the first day of work, to know how much federal income tax to withhold from an employee's wages. You must also verify that the new employee is legally eligible to work in the United States, by requiring the employee to complete Immigration and Naturalization Service (INS) Form I-9, Employment Eligibility Verification (available as a free download from the INS website at **www.ins.usdoj.gov**). In addition, if your employees receive tips from customers as part of their compensation, they must complete and give to you IRS Form 4070, Employee's Report of Tips to Employer, no later than the tenth day of each month, reporting tips received during the immediately preceding calendar month. No later than January 31 of each year, you must furnish a copy of IRS Form W-2, Wage and Tax Statement, for each employee to whom you paid wages during the immediately preceding calendar year.

All IRS forms and publications, with instructions, are available as free downloads from the IRS website at **www.irs.gov**.

employee-assistance programs The means of insuring your investment in employees by helping them with common problems such as depression and substance abuse. (*See also* health insurance.)

Most small companies can't afford formal employee-assistance programs, but you can show good faith when employees are in trouble by lending an ear in a private setting. You may be asked to refer them to a counselor or community clinic for help available on a sliding scale.

You can also do the right thing by offering employees access to an affordable health insurance plan that includes some coverage for mental health problems. Most health plans will let a primary care physician diagnose and treat drug or alcohol abuse as a med-

e/E

ical problem. But if your employee is seriously addicted to alcohol or cocaine, you may be faced with having to decide whether to personally pay for their stint in a private rehab hospital or letting them tough it out on their own. Some employers will allow an employee to file for short-term disability benefits if they swear to get some help in overcoming their addictions.

Once you are on financially stable ground and turning a profit, beef up your insurance package to offer more comprehensive benefits for mental health and substance abuse.

employee fraud *See* fraud.

employee stock ownership plan (ESOP) A program that sets aside company stock for purchase by qualified employees, usually at a discount. (*See also* benefits; pension plan.)

Most small companies are too small to set up an ESOP. Only a C corporation can set up one and you'll need a team of savvy advisers to execute the plan. Most ESOPs are established by a successful small business owner who is nearing retirement and wants to reward long-term employees with stock. In simple terms, the company sets up a trust and makes annual contributions of stock or cash to the trust. The trust is set up to meet tax rules for a profit-sharing plan. Over several years, the owner slowly transfers ownership to the beneficiaries of the trust—the loyal employees. Employees usually have ownership established in proportion to their salaries, according to tax attorney Fred Daily.

One drawback is that an ESOP cannot keep out long-term employees who aren't members of the owner's family. The tax-code rules under section 404 are very complex, and you'll need a team of professionals to guide you.

Daily said unless your business is worth $1 million or more, you shouldn't get involved in establishing an ESOP. If you want to explore this option, hire an experienced tax or estate attorney and a securities expert who has established ESOPs for similar companies.

E/e

employer identification number (EIN) A number provided by the IRS to businesses for tracking of payroll taxes and other information. (*See also* employment taxes.)

An EIN is your company's nine-digit Social Security number. Every business needs one and you can get one assigned pretty easily through a local or regional IRS office. You'll need an EIN to open a business bank account and to work with a payroll service. The first two digits represent the state where your company is based; the other digits are assigned randomly. To apply for an EIN, you'll need to fill out IRS form SS-4, which you can download from the IRS website **www.irs.gov**. If you apply for a number by mail, it can take several weeks. You can speed up the process by calling the Tele-EIN number listed for your area and speak to an IRS rep over the phone. There isn't any charge for an EIN. Remember: You need a separate EIN for every business you operate.

employment taxes Social Security and Medicare contributions, which an employer must withhold from employees' paychecks and deposit with the U.S. government on a regular basis. (*See also* unemployment taxes.)

The Federal Insurance Contributions Act (FICA) provides for a federal system of old age, survivors', disability, and hospital insurance. The old age, survivors', and disability insurance is financed by the Social Security tax. The hospital insurance is financed by the Medicare tax. Each of these taxes is reported separately.

Social Security and Medicare taxes are levied on both the employer and the employee. As an employer, you must withhold and deposit the employee's part of the taxes and you must pay a matching amount. Social Security and Medicare taxes have different rates and only Social Security tax has a "wage base limit"—the maximum wage that is subject to the tax for the year (currently $72,600 but adjusted for inflation each year).

The employee tax rate for Social Security is 6.2 percent. This is the amount withheld. Your tax rate is also 6.2 percent. This is the amount you pay. Thus, the total Social Security tax rate currently is 12.4 percent.

e/E

The employee tax rate for Medicare is 1.45 percent. This is the amount withheld. Your tax rate is also 1.45 percent. This is the amount you pay. Thus, the total Medicare tax rate currently is 2.9 percent. There is no wage base limit for Medicare tax, meaning that all covered wages are subject to the tax.

If you are an employer, you must deposit the income tax you withhold on behalf of your employees using IRS Form 8109, Federal Tax Deposit Coupons. If you are a new employer, the IRS will send you a federal tax deposit coupon book about six weeks after you receive your employer identification number (EIN). There are two deposit schedules: monthly and every two weeks. Before the beginning of each calendar year, you must determine which of the two deposit schedules you will use. The rules are quite complicated, but generally if you plan to report $50,000 or less of taxes during the fiscal year, you are a monthly schedule depositor. If you plan to report more than $50,000, you are a biweekly schedule depositor. If you fail to make a timely deposit of federal tax, you will incur a penalty ranging from 2 to 15 percent, depending on the lateness of the deposit.

Each quarter, all employers who pay wages subject to Social Security and Medicare tax must file IRS Form 941, Employer's Quarterly Federal Tax Return.

The best source of information about Social Security and Medicare taxes is IRS Publication 15, Circular E—Employer's Tax Guide, which is available as a free download at **www.irs.gov**. Because the IRS gets extremely difficult when Social Security and Medicare taxes are not paid on time, most small businesses use a payroll service that automatically makes the withholding deductions and deposits on a regular basis. Two well-known payroll services are Automatic Data Processing (ADP) (**www.adp.com**) and PayChex (**www.paychex.com**), but a fast-growing competitor on the Web is PayMaxx in Franklin, Tennessee (**www.paymaxx.com**).

enrolled agent An income tax specialist licensed by the IRS to prepare returns and filings. (*See also* accountants; taxes.)

Enrolled agents are the unsung heroes of the tax-preparation world. They have been around since the 1800s and really know

E/e

their stuff, because they have to pass an intense licensing examination given by the IRS. Because the examination is so tough, most EAs are former IRS auditors or examiners. If they have five years' experience working for the IRS, they don't have to take the grueling exam. There are about 24,000 enrolled agents in the United States.

For some reason, they don't have the cachet of a tax attorney or CPA and generally charge a much lower hourly fee. A tax attorney bills at $125 to $400 an hour; CPAs may charge in the $200 range; an EA charges $50 to $150 an hour, depending on where you live, according to Fred Daily, author of *Tax Savvy for Small Business* (Nolo Press, 2001). "They offer good value and are reliable for tax return preparing and routine tax matters," writes Daily. "Many EAs offer bookkeeping and accounting assistance."

CPAs are licensed and regulated by the state. Some states issue licenses to public accountants, but they aren't as highly regarded as CPAs. A tax attorney is a lawyer with a special degree in tax law. If you have a big problem with the IRS or a complicated tax situation, spring for a tax attorney.

entertainment expenses Uncle Sam's share of your fun.

Before you pick up that tab, remember you can only deduct 50 percent of your entertainment expenses if they are directly related to doing business (a catered business dinner during a big negotiation), or they are associated with the business (an evening out or tickets to a ball game after a long business meeting).

One perk: Transportation to and from the event is fully deductible. If you fly off to woo a special client, most business-related travel expenses, including airline tickets, taxi, bus, and limousine fares, and hotel rooms are also fully deductible.

Uncle Sam wants you to have an employee party or picnic and lets you deduct 100 percent of the cost. Be sure to invite everyone to the party, but don't overdo it. You can use the party as a morale-booster and you don't have to discuss business. In all cases, keep good records, including a written guest list and the nature of any business discussed.

Before you order lavish gifts for your best clients, remember

e/E

you can deduct the cost if the gifts don't exceed $25 per person per year. You can also deduct the cost of engraving, wrapping, and shipping the gifts.

entrepreneur From the French, to undertake. A businessperson who perceives and fulfills a need in the market for profit; vitality is created by the entrepreneur's dual role. (*See also* Kirton Adaptation Innovation Inventory.)

Entrepreneur is a grand word that few people can spell. But you wouldn't be reading this book if you weren't one. Most entrepreneurs are born, not made, and many are serial entrepreneurs—people who start more than three ventures in their lifetime. Entrepreneurs take calculated risks, not stupid ones. Entrepreneurs are usually bad employees. I know I was.

I was always getting in trouble for insubordination. Once I couldn't control myself and called my boss a jerk. He reported me to his boss and I was ordered to attend private counseling sessions to get over my anger. The psychiatrist told me that the newspaper was, metaphorically speaking, a military-industrial complex, and that I had violated protocol by insulting my commanding officer. I remember laughing so hard I almost fell of the chair. I realized at that moment that it was time to start my own company.

Most entrepreneurs experience a similar flash of realization and leave the corporate nest to take a flying leap into the unknown. I'm sure glad I did, and if you are on the fence and teetering, go for it. You'll be glad you did.

Equal Employment Opportunity Commission (EEOC) The commission responsible for enforcing certain federal laws prohibiting employment discrimination.

The federal Equal Employment Opportunity Commission, or EEOC, was established by Title VII of the Civil Rights Act of 1964 and began operating on July 2, 1965. The EEOC enforces the following federal statutes:

■ **Title VII of the Civil Rights Act of 1964,** as amended, prohibiting employment discrimination on the basis of race, color, religion, sex, or national origin

E/e

- **The Age Discrimination in Employment Act (ADEA) of 1967,** as amended, prohibiting employment discrimination against individuals 40 years of age and older
- **The Equal Pay Act (EPA) of 1963** prohibiting discrimination on the basis of gender in compensation for substantially similar work under similar conditions
- **Title I and Title V of the Americans with Disabilities Act (ADA) of 1990,** prohibiting employment discrimination on the basis of disability in the private sector and in state and local governments
- **Section 501 and 505 of the Rehabilitation Act of 1973,** as amended, prohibiting employment discrimination against federal employees with disabilities
- **The Civil Rights Act of 1991** providing monetary damages in cases of intentional discrimination.

With its headquarters in Washington, D.C., and through the operations of fifty field offices nationwide, the EEOC coordinates all federal equal employment opportunity regulations, practices, and policies. The commission interprets employment discrimination laws, monitors the federal sector employment discrimination program, provides funding and support to state and local Fair Employment Practices Agencies (FEPAs), and sponsors outreach and technical assistance programs.

Any individual who believes he or she has been discriminated against in employment may file an administrative charge with the EEOC. After investigating the charge, the EEOC determines if there is reasonable cause to believe discrimination has occurred. If reasonable cause is found, the EEOC attempts to conciliate the charge by reaching a voluntary resolution between the charging party and the respondent. If conciliation is not successful, the commission may bring suit in federal court. As part of the administrative process, the EEOC may also issue a right-to-sue notice to the charging party, allowing the charging party to file an individual action in court without the EEOC's involvement.

The EEOC receives approximately 80,000 private sector charges annually. These are relegated to one of three categories:

e/E

Category A charges are given priority investigative and settlement efforts due to the early recognition that discrimination has likely occurred; Category B charges require further investigation to determine if a violation has occurred; and Category C charges include nonjurisdictional and unsupported charges that are closed immediately. Settlements are encouraged at all stages of the process.

equipment The minimum set of goods required for excellent work.

One key skill of entrepreneurship is to balance your equipment needs with the tasks needed to get the job done. My best advice for equipment is always to rent it, lease it, or buy it used. It doesn't pay to buy anything new, except some kinds of precision tools for scientific purposes—and even those you can probably find secondhand. Shop around for the best deals, and whatever you buy, be sure to adequately insure it.

equity Ownership of an asset, usually expressed in shares of a company. (*See also* shares.)

It seems like magic: People are willing to give your company hard cash in exchange for paper. Of course they're buying ownership, or equity, which derives its value from what buyers perceive to be the future profitability of the company. Equity is a great early source of money for a company that can make a persuasive case that its product or service will sell big. But with it you give up control to investors who will demand incessant growth and profitability.

equity, taking Accepting all or part of payment in company stock instead of cash. (*See also* venture capital.)

If someone really believes in your business model, they may be willing to work for a piece of the action—equity rather than cash, but it takes a special kind of investor. My sister, Andrea, left a lucrative position as a venture capitalist in France to work as a part-time COO when SBTV Corp. was in its infancy. She was compensated in shares and hopes someday to receive her deferred compensation. During the dot-com mania, landlords, gardeners,

E/e

TAKING STOCK

Robert Klug suggests answering the following questions before you decide to take equity in a client's firm:

- Have you taken a good look at the market to understand the potential earnings?
- Are there big players who can get together and cremate you?
- Does the company have the right product, placement, price, and distribution?
- Do you trust and believe in the founder?
- Can you afford to lose your investment?

and software programmers were anxious to take a reduced salary if they received stock options. Then, in 2000, the stock market tanked and thousands of people were left with worthless stock certificates and no jobs.

At the height of the Internet boom, Robert Klug and Christine Soderbergh were so impressed with their client, Doug Lopez, the founder of windows and skylights company 1stWindows.com, they decided to take equity in his new online venture, rather than be paid their regular fees.

"I loved the idea of reinventing an industry," says Klug, founder of Microscape Web Solutions, a Web designer in Newport Beach, California. Klug designed the 1stWindows.com website in exchange for a share of the business, and takes an active role in its management. "It's an all equity deal—I did all the Web work for the equity, because it was a great idea at the right time." Soderbergh, president of Keefer/Soderbergh Public Relations in Pacific Palisades, California, opted to take equity in lieu of a full monthly retainer because the company "met all the criteria venture capitalists look for in e-commerce start-ups ... Doug Lopez was passionate; he was eating and breathing windows and he really wanted to attack the marketplace."

Lopez was so committed to creating the best online site for

windows, he sold his rental properties and moved into a small apartment to raise the cash he needed. "The best thing for me about this business is that orders are paid in full, up front," says Lopez. "We put the money from the orders in a money market fund and earn interest, which helps to pay the rent."

Klug says he is happy he took a risk and invested his time and efforts in Lopez's business. "I'm an entrepreneur, and I love other entrepreneurs," says Klug. "It was the right time, right place, right product, and he was the right person to run the company."

equity capital financing The process of raising money by selling stock. (*See also* initial public offering; venture capital.)

estate planning Making sure your business doesn't die when you do. (*See also* family business; family limited partnership; gift tax; limited partnership; succession planning.)

Few people like to think about their own death. Yet one common reason for starting any business is to create something that will outlive you, a legacy for future generations. Making sure this happens, and that the business doesn't die when you do, by having a comprehensive estate plan is one of your primary responsibilities as an entrepreneur.

Every business owner needs to have an estate plan and a will—it's as simple as that. "Your ownership of any kind of business is an asset," according to Joseph Sweeney, an attorney in Fairfield, Connecticut, whose practice is limited to estate planning. The purpose of having an estate plan is so that "when you die, the asset doesn't just disappear. It gets transferred to your heirs. If you don't have a will, the intestacy laws—the laws that govern the distribution of a person's property if she dies without leaving a will—of your state will determine who receives your business, and it may not be who you want to be."

Some examples cited by Sweeney include:

■ **You own a business 50/50 with your spouse, and you work together in the business.** You have two siblings, but you are not close to them and do not want them to have any part in your business. If you die without a will, the intestacy laws of

E/e

your state may divide your assets one-third to your spouse, and one-third to each of your siblings. Thus, your siblings may end up owning two-thirds of your business, effectively becoming the bosses of your surviving spouse.

■ **You own a very successful business that is worth more than $1 million and die without a will.** The estate is clobbered by federal estate and gift taxes and state death taxes. Your heirs have to sell the business to a stranger in order to raise enough cash to pay the tax liability.

"Every business needs a succession plan," says Sweeney. "You need to think carefully about who should run the business after you die and plan accordingly. If there are key employees without whom the business will fall apart, you should by all means include them in your estate plan, or give them an ownership stake in the business while you are still alive. If you are not sure that a particular child or heir will be ready to take over the business when you die, you can set up a trust in your will by which your trustee —your business partner, for example, or that key employee—can run the business until such time as they feel your child or heir is ready."

"You should also review and update your estate plan every few years or so," Sweeney adds, "because things change." For example, if your will leaves everything to your surviving spouse, and you later divorce, your ex will be legally entitled to your entire estate, including your business, until you revise your will so as to exclude her.

RECOMMENDED READING

■ *The Family Business Succession Handbook*, edited by Mark Fischetti (Family Business, 1997)
■ *Keeping the Family Business Healthy*, by John L. Ward (Business Owner Resources, 1987)

estate tax *See* estate planning; gift tax.

e/E

exit interview An opportunity for a business owner to learn from her soon-to-be former employees' experience.

No matter how upset you are when you have to terminate employees, don't let them get away without an exit interview. It's really important to find out what went wrong so you can avoid making the same mistake in the future. Prepare a few simple questions and try not to get too emotional. You want a departing employee to make constructive suggestions, not go on a rant about what a terrible boss you were. Ask for a few suggestions about what you could have done to make the employee's experience at your company more productive or pleasant and leave it at that. Make notes and put the final report in the employee's file.

exit strategy A game plan for reaping the reward for all of your hard work. (*See also* buyout; buy-sell agreement; estate planning; franchise; harvesting; initial public offering; mergers and acquisitions; selling a business; succession planning.)

Just as trees do not grow to the sky, businesses do not last forever. Even if your business grows into a giant, sooner or later you and your partners will want to spend the rest of your lives doing something else. You will need a plan to convert your ownership of the business into hard, accessible cash—in short, an exit strategy.

It will be difficult to attract outside capital for your business without a solid exit strategy. Investors are, of course, interested in the growth of your business, but ultimately their commitment of capital hinges upon their ability to recoup their initial investment and make a healthy profit. On average, venture capitalists and other professional investors will want to see a return on their investment within three to five years. They do not work in the business and cannot take out compensation the way that management can, so the only practical way for them to "cash out" of their investment is for you to sell the business or to make a public offering within that three- to five-year period. You will need to state your exit strategy clearly in your business plan and other investor documents, along with convincing evidence that the

E/e

strategy can be executed within your investors' time frame.

Even if you are not looking for outside capital and you only wish to build a legacy so that future generations of your family will not have to worry about earning a living, you still will need an exit strategy; only in this situation, it is called a succession plan. Who will take over your business when you die or retire? Where will your retirement income come from? Will you continue to take a salary or a consulting fee for reporting to the office one or two days a week during retirement? Or, will you require the next generation of business owners to buy out your stake in the company? Painful though it is to realize that you will not live forever, planning for your eventual departure from the business is one of the most important things you can do to ensure that the business will have a future after you're gone.

Among the most common exit strategies adopted by business owners:

- **Initial public offering (IPO).** In an IPO, the company sells its shares to the public to be traded on a stock exchange or over-the-counter. The investors can convert their ownership stake into cash, the majority owners usually can maintain control, and the potential return is extremely high.

- **Selling the business.** The owners of the business may determine to sell it to another, perhaps much larger, company. By selling the business, you can receive either cash or stock in the acquiring company (which, if the acquiring company is publicly traded, may be immediately sold for cash). You may also negotiate employment, management or consulting agreements by which you and your partners can continue to run the company for a number of years.

- **Mergers.** In a merger, two or more companies combine into a single entity. The resources of the two companies are combined, and current management may be allowed to stay on to help run the new, combined company. Mergers may, however, entail new partners or bosses and less control by the former managers. To avoid becoming taxable to the business owners, mergers must be structured as stock-for-stock exchanges with very little cash changing hands. If the other company is a privately held company like yours, this stock will not be freely tradable, and you may have to wait years after the merger before you can cash out your investment.

■ **Buyout.** In a buyout, one (or more) of the stockholders buys out the others. The seller usually receives cash, while the other owners remain in control of the company, ensuring at least some continuity of management. Because the buyers are individuals like you, however, they may not have sufficient cash to pay the buyout price all at once. You may have to accept payments in installments over several years. If the new owners are less than competent managers, there is a risk they may "run the business into the ground" and default on their obligations, leaving you with a worthless company and no retirement income.

■ **Franchising.** If your business uses a business plan that can be easily copied in multiple locations, you may want to consider selling the business plan to others. In a franchise transaction, the seller receives up-front cash, plus a percentage of revenue during the life of the franchise. Current management remains in control of the company granting the franchise (called the "franchisor"), with few if any of the risks of running the franchised operation, and the same business plan may be sold over and over again. The potential for large-scale growth through franchising is great. Franchising a business is an expensive proposition, however: You will be required to prepare an offering circular (similar to a prospectus in a stock offering), have it approved by the Federal Trade Commission, and then have it re-approved by regulators in each state before you establish a franchised operation in that state. If your business concept has not been successfully proven in at least several different locations before you launch the franchise, there is a significant risk that no one will want to buy your franchise.

■ **Succession plan.** Regardless of how you ultimately plan to cash out of your business, you will need to plan for someone to take over the management of the business should you become ill, die, or otherwise be forced to retire. Without a clear suc-

E/e

cessor, whether a family member or a key employee, your heirs may be required to sell the business at a distressed price in order to generate the cash necessary to pay your medical bills or estate taxes.

expenses Costs deductible from income. Unlike investments, expenses do not result in greater assets. (*See also* deductions; taxes.)

Expenses can be headaches or blessings. Just about everything you need to buy for the legitimate operation of your business is tax deductible. You don't need a receipt for every small thing; in fact, business expenses less than $75 do not require individual receipts.

Apart from rent, utilities, telephone bills, Internet access, and car payments, there are all sorts of business expenses that business owners often overlook. Here are a few categories to remember:

- Postage and shipping
- Petty cash
- Taxi and airline expenses
- Consulting fees
- Business gifts (up to $25 per person per year)
- Education to polish business skills
- Service charges (bank)
- Seminars and courses related to work
- Videotapes and business books
- Beverages and coffee for the office
- Association dues

Check with your accountant for help in setting up a chart of accounts that will enable you to keep close track of legitimate business expenses.

exporting Selling your products or services to customers abroad. (*See also* freight forwarder; global trade.)

Federal officials involved in promoting international trade are urging small business owners to enter the global game, especially since the U.S. economy began slowing down in 2000.

e/E

TIPS FOR TAKING ON THE WORLD

Ferris Corp., which makes medical products, won the Illinois Governor's Export Award two years in a row. Marketing chief Jeff Dzuria offers the following tips, which worked for his company:

- **Get company-wide commitment.** Every employee at Ferris is a vital member of the international team, from customer service through engineering, purchasing, production, and shipping.
- **Research and map out** your export journey. Do your homework.
- **Know where you want to go** and go there. Know your destination.
- **Take that decisive step** and follow it up with sensible judgment. Jump in with both feet first, but keep them firmly planted on the ground.
- **Keep your ego in check.** Don't let the prospect of 'going global' inflate your ego and cause misjudgments.
- **If it smells, looks, or feels bad, don't try to rationalize otherwise.** Trust your instincts.
- **Make personal contact** with attentiveness, courtesy, professionalism, and consistency. In-person visits are vital to building a relationship with rapport.
- **Factor in a three-year lead time** for world market penetration. It takes time and patience.
- In a global marketplace, **welcome the unknown.** Don't let the prospect of the unknown frighten you. Rather, learn to welcome it, take it apart piece by piece, and then slowly digest it all. The rewards can be great.

"We've been telling small business owners now is the time to get involved in exporting," says Jean Smith, assistant administrator for trade at the U.S. Small Business Administration. "Take

E/e

EXPORT COUNSELING ON THE WEB

The SBA offers free seven-week export training classes at Export Assistance Centers around the United States. Visit **www.sba.gov** or check out these other good sites:

- www.Tradecompass.com
- www.Worldskip.com
- www.Stat-usa.gov
- www.Tamtam.com

---

those profits and put them into expanding into overseas markets."

Smith says there are about 200,000 small companies engaged in international trade, a fraction of the 24 million businesses in America. However, she points out that only about 12 million firms have products or services that are exportable.

Having a product or service that works at home and abroad is the first step toward export success. Medical items such as Poly-Mem, a drug-free and irritant-free wound therapy treatment made by Ferris Corp., are among the U.S. goods finding eager customers overseas. In 1988, Robert W. Sessions patented the formula for PolyMem that stimulates healing and reduces painful wound dressing changes. Now, it's known worldwide as "The Pink Dressing."

Going global wasn't always part of Sessions's vision. His company began its sales efforts, as most small businesses do, with a strictly domestic focus. But marketing chief Jeff Dzuira said he visualized the world as a single market. He researched and contacted every government office that he could. Working with the resources of state and federal agencies helped his company win the Illinois Governor's Export Award two years in a row.

"I learned of a subsidy available to us through the federal and state governments that would help fund our participation in Medica 96, the world's largest annual medical device exhibition held in Dusseldorf, Germany," says Dzuira. "That venue launched our international sales campaign. The first Medica show yielded us

e/E

over 140 qualified leads worldwide and secured us our first large block of distributors."

He acknowledges that going global requires a serious investment of time and money. Companies without financial resources cannot make international deals. "Our packaging needed to be redesigned with multilingual text and accompanying instructions for use," he says, adding that he often relied on suggestions from his local distributors.

It takes effort to build a small business into a world-class operation. Regulations have to be followed and payment methods have to be put in place. It took Ferris three months to secure an international distributor, and sales didn't materialize instantly. Due to the complexities involved in marketing medical products abroad, the company had to seek approval from the U.S. Food and Drug Administration.

Despite the delays, the effort was worth it. "It's truly rewarding knowing that at the end of the day, not only have international sales been spectacular, but people worldwide have benefited from a very remarkable medical product," says Dziura. "The lessons I learned have not come from seminars, textbooks, or advice; rather, they have come from practice in the global playing field, which hones the skills necessary for succeeding in the marketplace."

Export-Import Bank

Known as the "Ex-Im Bank," this institution offers a range of affordable loan programs for small companies interested in going global. One of the bank's most popular programs for small businesses is special short-term credit insurance, by which Ex-Im guarantees payment from foreign customers, which, in turn, enables U.S. businesses to offer credit at rates charged by U.S. banks, typically far below the rates in many foreign countries.

As of late 2001, about 1,100 U.S. small businesses were participating in the short-term insurance program, under which the Ex-Im Bank would pay 95 percent of the money owed to a U.S. business if the buyer could not pay for commercial reasons, such as bankruptcy, and 100 percent if for political reasons, such as the

E/e

outbreak of war. The cost to the U.S. business is about $940 on a $100,000 transaction. To be eligible for Ex-Im Bank financing, goods and services must be shipped from the United States to a foreign buyer. Other programs include medium-term credit insurance and a guarantee for a line of credit. For details visit the Ex-Im website at **www.exim.gov**.

e/E

factoring A form of accounts receivable financing popular with businesses coping with a predictable, but seasonal, sales cycle.

FACTORING HELPS COMPANIES in the clothing and furniture business cope with an extended sales cycle. A factor buys a company's receivables, and provides the company with a percentage of the cash value up front so the company can pay for supplies and meet payroll. Then, the factor goes after the customer to pay the balance.

Factors take a hefty percentage of the amount due, often 15 to 20 percent, but they do take responsibility for collecting the balance. Many companies prefer to apply for a commercial credit line, which charges less interest than a factor. The upside is that you are your own banker, weathering the dry spells with borrowed money and paying it back when the checks come in. The downside is that you are the one going after slow payers, in addition to running the business.

Fair Credit Billing Act A federal law that enables consumers to resolve disputes with credit card companies and other creditors.

Have you ever been billed for merchandise you returned or never received? Has your credit card company ever charged you twice for the same item, or failed to credit a payment to your account? The federal Fair Credit Billing Act establishes procedures for resolving disputes such as these quickly, painlessly, and without the involvement of lawyers.

The law applies to open-end credit accounts, such as credit cards, revolving charge accounts (such as department store accounts), and overdraft checking accounts. It does not cover installment contracts, such as car, appliance, or furniture loans.

The Fair Credit Billing Act applies only to disputes about billing errors such as

- unauthorized charges (under federal law your liability for unauthorized charges is limited to $50)
- charges that list the wrong date or amount
- charges for goods and services that you didn't accept or that weren't delivered as agreed
- mathematical errors
- failure to post payments and other credits
- failure to send bills to your current address, provided you notified your credit card company of a change of address at least twenty days before the billing period ended

Disputes about the quality of goods and services are not billing errors for purposes of the Fair Credit Billing Act, so the dispute procedure does not apply. If, however, you buy unsatisfactory goods or services with a credit or charge card, you can take the same legal actions against the card issuer as you can take under state law against the seller.

Fair Credit Reporting Act A federal law to protect consumers against unfair use of information supplied to credit reporting agencies. (*See also* D&B.)

Most credit bureaus gather and sell information about you— such as if you pay your bills on time or have filed bankruptcy—to creditors, employers, landlords, and other businesses. Under the Fair Credit Reporting Act, you must be told if information in your file has been used against you. Anyone who uses information from a credit bureau to take action against you—such as denying an application for credit, insurance, or employment—must tell you,

f/F

and give you the name, address, and phone number of the credit bureau that provided the consumer report.

At your request, a credit bureau must give you the information in your file, and a list of everyone who has requested it recently. A credit bureau may provide information about you only to people with a need recognized by the law, such as a creditor, insurer, employer, or landlord. If you tell a credit bureau that your file contains inaccurate information, the credit bureau must investigate the terms, usually within thirty days, by presenting to its information source all relevant evidence you submit, unless your dispute is frivolous.

You can dispute inaccurate items with the source of the information. If you tell anyone, such as a creditor who reports to a credit bureau, that you dispute an item, they may not then report the information to a credit bureau without including a notice of your dispute. In addition, once you've notified the source of the error in writing, it may not continue to report the information if it is, in fact, an error.

Fair Debt Collection Practices Act A federal law that tells you what you can and cannot do to collect your outstanding debts.

The federal Fair Debt Collection Practices Act requires that certain debt collectors not use unfair, coercive, or abusive practices when seeking to collect personal, family, and household debts from consumers.

Only personal, family, and household debts are covered under the act, including money owed for the purchase of an automobile, for medical care, or for charge accounts. Moreover, the act restricts only the actions of a debt collector, such as a collection agency or repo person, who is not actually the creditor. Thus, a small business or creditor seeking to collect its own debt that does not fall into the personal, family, or household category may not be subject to the restrictions of the act. Of course, state criminal laws usually will prevent you from engaging in extreme tactics to recover your outstanding debts, so consult with an attorney familiar with these laws before you decide to take action against a recalcitrant debtor.

F/f

Fair Labor Standards Act A federal law that requires overtime pay for certain employees working more than a forty-hour week, among other things. (*See also* employment taxes.)

The federal Fair Labor Standards Act establishes minimum wage, overtime pay, record keeping, and child labor standards affecting full-time and part-time workers in the private sector and in federal, state, and local governments. The act is enforced for the private sector by the Wage and Hour Division of the U.S. Labor Department.

The act requires overtime compensation (at time and one-half) for all hours worked over a prescribed threshold (typically forty hours per week) for nonexempt employees, as well as a minimum wage of not less than $5.15 per hour. Generally, executive, administrative, and professional employees, outside sales employees, and employees in certain computer-related occupations (as defined in Department of Labor regulations) are exempt from these requirements.

Usually, an employer is subject to the act's minimum wage provisions only if it is engaged in interstate commerce and its annual gross volume of sales made or business done is not less than $500,000 exclusive of certain taxes. There are many exceptions to this requirement, however. For example, an employee of a firm that does not meet these requirements is subject to the act's minimum wage requirement if he or she engages in interstate commerce activities (such as using the telephone to contact out-of-state customers or crossing state lines on company business). You should not assume that you are exempt from the act's provisions without first consulting a qualified labor attorney; even if you are exempt from the act's requirements, state law may impose similar requirements on firms like yours, and must be taken into account. In certain states, for example, a company engaged in construction or other similar activities must pay its workers no less than the prevailing wage for similar work in the region in which the work is performed.

What about employees who receive tips? Under the act, those who customarily and regularly receive more than $30 a month in tips may consider tips as part of wages, but the employer must pay

f/F

at least $2.13 an hour in wages to a tipped employee. If an employee's tips combined with the employer's direct wages of at least $2.13 an hour do not equal the minimum hourly wage, the employer must make up the difference.

family business Entrepreneurship with the risk/reward of lifetime employment. (*See also* estate planning; family limited partnership; succession planning.)

The fate of your family-owned business hinges on whether you have a clear succession plan. Despite all the books, publicity, and admonitions, most family business owners still don't have a clear succession strategy. In fact, 25 percent of senior generation family-business owners have written a will but not completed a succession plan, according to a national survey released by the Family Firm Institute in Boston, Massachusetts.

Although 81 percent of those polled said they want their business to stay in the family, 20 percent aren't sure the next generation is committed to keeping the business under family ownership. Experts advise owners to make succession plans that meet the best interest of the business rather than family expectations.

"It's harder for people to make good business decisions when there's family involved because the family issues seem to thicken the plot," says Andrew Sherman, a Washington, D.C., attorney and author, who counsels families. The family drama unfolds when children do what they think they're supposed to do and agree to work for the business under duress. These reluctant heirs often feel pressured by a parent who is obsessed with keeping the business in the family.

Sherman says family business owners should remember they have many options. "You don't have to turn over management decisions to your children, even if you feel it's right to give them the stock," says Sherman. "You could sell the business, transform the business, do a joint venture, or sell it to an employee or outsider."

No matter what course you take, Sherman emphasizes the need to put it in writing. He also suggests being very honest with a child who may want to take over the business, but who you feel

F/f

SUCCESSFUL SUCCESSION

Alfred Scheid, owner of Scheid Vineyards in Monterey County, California, offers these tips for keeping peace in your family business:

- Make sure your kids go out into the world and get five years' experience in an unrelated business.
- Don't be the employer of last resort for your kids.
- If you hire your children, compensate them fairly.
- Don't set higher standards for family members. Treat all employees the same.
- Keep family affairs and business dealings separate. If a personal issue requires immediate attention, discuss it over lunch or while taking a walk.
- Accept that there may be rocky times in a complex family business relationship. Have the courage to be honest, open, and communicative.

---

doesn't have the skills or personality to run it. "Of course, you are going to offend somebody," says Sherman. "But if your life's work is going to be run into the ground, who benefits from that?"

Not every family business falters. Some actually make a smooth transition from one generation to the next. Many wineries, for instance, are traditionally family run. (The Gallos come to mind when one thinks of famous family-owned wineries.) Alfred Scheid, owner of Scheid Vineyards in Monterey County, California, devised a recipe for passing his business to the next generation. "In our office, the fact that you are family is out the window," says Scheid. "When the kids came in, we had to make some strict rules. We don't discuss family issues at work. But very frequently we ask, 'Are you free for lunch today?'"

Scheid says he didn't assume that his children would take an interest in the business. His oldest son, Scott, was in his early forties and working on Wall Street as a trader for E.F. Hutton before he transferred to a Costa Mesa, California, branch office. One day

f/F

his father called to ask if he would be interested in working in the family business. "I saw the offer as an opportunity to put together a business and a chance to learn from someone who is a real mentor to me," says Scott Scheid.

Scott Scheid, who served as chief operating officer, was destined to eventually take over the reins from his father. His younger sister Heidi was working for Ernst and Young in Los Angeles before she joined the company. She is now the chief financial officer. "My daughter had completed her master's degree, got married, had a baby, and was on maternity leave when she came to the office for a visit," recalls the senior Scheid. "We had a problem with our computer that day, and she fixed it; I gave her a job offer, matched her Ernst and Young salary, and she never went back to her other job."

Although Scheid likes having two of his four children working for the business, he says he would not have offered his kids a position unless they had some "real world experience" to bring back to the company.

"What traditionally happens is kids work at the family business during the summer, they go off to finish college, and then they come back and need a job," says Scheid. "But, what do they bring to the party?"

Having also been an investment banker for E.F. Hutton prior to starting the winery, Alfred Scheid says he saw a lot of unhappy family business successions. "I've seen so many failures when sons or daughters feel obligated to step into their parents' shoes," says Scheid. He recommends that kids have at least five or six years of outside work experience before they return to the business. He suggests that the time be spent doing things totally unrelated to the family's industry sector. "The more foreign the business is to your kids, the better," says Scheid.

Scheid's second rule is don't hire your kid just because they need a job. His youngest son wanted to work for the winery right after college. Scheid put him to work six days a week as an intern, pounding stakes, riding a tractor, and living in a trailer by himself. "We'll see if he comes back," says Scheid.

Scheid may have strict standards, but he knows how to keep

F/f

his employees happy. "Everyone is well compensated, but not overly compensated," claims Scheid. "My kids' salaries are in the 80th or 90th percentile for the industry." While the kids who work for the company have equity, so do the siblings who don't work for the company. In fact, all of the children hold equal amounts of stock.

A couple of times a year, Scheid hosts a Sunday night family dinner. "Unless it's a dire emergency, business just doesn't come up," Scheid says. "It's fair game to say, 'Call me Monday.'"

RECOMMENDED READING

■ John L. Ward, Ph.D. and Craig E. Aronoff, Ph.D., two leading family business experts, have published *Family Business Ownership* (Family Enterprise Publishers, 2001) as part of their Family Business Leadership Series. They have eleven other titles covering every aspect of family business. *Family Business Ownership* is packed with advice, anecdotes, and graphics.

family limited partnership (FLP) A common method for a business owner to transfer a business to the next generation with a minimum of federal estate and gift tax liability. (*See also* estate planning; family business; limited liability company; limited liability partnership; Subchapter S corporation; succession planning.)

An FLP is fairly straightforward and can be illustrated with one example. The parents of a family own of a closely held corporation or limited liability company engaged in a trade or business. They have three children, one of whom, the daughter, is interested in working for the business. The parents form the FLP as a limited partnership under state law. The parents then contribute their interest in the company to the FLP in exchange for general partnership interests (totaling 10 percent of partnership capital and profits) and limited partnership interests (the remaining 90 percent interest). For protection from liability, the parents may also transfer their general partnership interests to a limited liability company or S corporation.

Now the parents give half of their limited partnership interests to the children, dividing up the interests as they think best. Their daughter may or may not become an employee of the FLP. Each

f/F

year the limited partners will be allocated their proportionate share of the company's profits and losses. If the company is an LLC, S corporation, or other "pass through" entity such as a general partnership or business trust, the limited partners will also benefit from the future appreciation of the company's assets and properties.

For gift tax purposes, the gifts of limited partnership interests can be planned so that the discounted value of the gift falls within the $11,000 annual gift tax exclusion. Therefore, the gifts will be free of federal gift taxes. For estate tax purposes, gifts of limited partnership interests remove value from the client's taxable estate, thereby reducing the amount of estate tax due upon death.

Adoption of a FLP also has some non-tax benefits:

■   The owner(s) can give interests over time in a FLP that owns assets such as real estate with less difficulty than giving undivided fractional interests in the real estate itself over time.

■   The owner can ensure that assets stay within the family. For example, the FLP partnership agreement could contain language that requires all partners to first offer their partnership interests for sale to the other partners before selling or otherwise transferring the interests to non-family members.

■   An FLP provides a level of protection from creditors of the partners. Generally, even if a partner is forced to transfer his FLP interest to a creditor, the creditor will have none of the rights of a partner. Therefore, the creditor will be entitled to receive only his pro rata portion of partnership distributions, which are usually at the discretion of the general partner.

■   An FLP provides protection in divorce situations because partnership interests are generally considered separate property, and the courts generally do not award partnership interests to spouses.

■   An FLP encourages other family members who own an interest in the partnership to be interested in the management of family assets and to learn the family's wealth management philosophies.

F/f

The tax rules governing FLPs are highly complex, and the Internal Revenue Service has for some time viewed FLPs as being overly generous to the taxpayer when transferring wealth between generations. Accordingly, the drafting of the FLP partnership agreement and the preparation of any supporting valuation should be undertaken only by experienced professionals.

Federal Insurance Contributions Act (FICA) The federal law that authorizes the withholding of taxes for Social Security and Medicaid. (*See also* employment taxes.)

Because the taxes are not applied to wages greater than about $40,000 for a single taxpayer (the figure changes yearly with inflation), FICA sometimes causes headaches for entrepreneurs with employees who also work at other jobs. An employee may believe he's overpaying his FICA taxes if he's already earning more than $40,000 elsewhere. Do not give him a refund. Every employer is required to withhold FICA taxes regardless of what an employee claims to pay out of another paycheck. A refund is available to the employee from the IRS.

FIFO (First In, First Out) A means of accounting for inventory, in which earlier acquisitions of inventory are deemed to be sold before later acquisitions. (*See also* LIFO.)

There are a number of ways to account for purchases and sales of inventory. The two most commonly used by entrepreneurs are LIFO, or "Last In, First Out," and FIFO, or "First In, First Out."

If you purchase inventory in lots and wait until all of the items in that lot have been sold before purchasing the next lot, it does not matter whether you use LIFO or FIFO to account for that inventory; the results will be the same. Few, if any, businesses, however, operate in this fashion. If you purchase inventory at different times and at different prices, your resulting profits may vary significantly, depending upon whether you use LIFO or FIFO accounting.

FIFO accounting assumes that when sales out of inventory are made the items sold were the ones first purchased or acquired by you. LIFO accounting assumes that when sales out of inventory

f/F

are made the items sold were the ones last purchased or acquired by you.

The best way to illustrate FIFO is to demonstrate how it contrasts with LIFO. Let's say you start a retail bookstore at the beginning of Year 1. During the year, you buy 1,000 copies of *Entrepreneur's Desk Reference* at $10 each and sell 900 of these books for $15 each. At the end of the year, you count the number of copies of *Entrepreneur's Desk Reference* on hand. If there has been no pilferage or other loss, you will have 100 copies on hand. To summarize, your opening inventory (at the beginning of the year) is zero; your purchases are 1,000 copies at $10 each for a total of $10,000; and your closing inventory is 100 copies at $10 each, or $1,000; so your cost of goods sold is $9,000.

At the beginning of Year 2, your opening inventory of *Entrepreneur's Desk Reference* is 100 copies at $10 each, or $1,000. Suppose that during Year 2 you buy 1,000 more copies of *Entrepreneur's Desk Reference* at $11 each and sell 1,000 copies at $16 each. At the end of Year 2, you count the copies on hand. Again, assuming no losses or pilferage, there will be 100 copies on hand.

If you cannot identify which copies of *Entrepreneur's Desk Reference* were bought when, you may use either LIFO or FIFO to figure out the value of the inventory on hand. The results are set in the box at right.

Notice your profits under FIFO would be higher because FIFO assumes that the higher-priced copies of *Entrepreneur's Desk Reference* bought in Year 2 remain on hand, whereas LIFO assumes that the lower-priced copies bought in Year 1 remain on hand.

In determining whether LIFO or FIFO accounting is more suitable for your business, you will have to compare the results across all product lines. It generally will not be possible for you to select LIFO accounting for one product and FIFO accounting for another, unless they constitute clearly distinct and separate product lines. Even then there may be restrictions on your use of FIFO versus LIFO accounting. Certain regulated businesses, for example, are required by law to use either LIFO or FIFO accounting. Similarly, if you adopt LIFO or FIFO accounting, it may be difficult to switch

F/f

YEAR 2:
SALES OF *ENTREPRENEUR'S DESK REFERENCE**

	LIFO	FIFO
(1) Beginning number of copies	100	100
(2) Cost per unit	$10	$10
(3) Total cost, opening	$1,000	$1,000
(4) Copies bought (no. of units)	1,000	1,000
(5) Cost per unit	$11	$11
(6) Total cost of purchases (line 4 x line 5)	$11,000	$11,000
(7) Total cost, beginning and purchased (line 3 + line 6)	$12,000	$12,000
(8) Ending number of copies	100	100
(9) Ending cost per unit	$10	$11
(10) Ending total value	$1,000	$1,100
(11) Cost of goods sold (line 7 – line 10)	$11,000	$10,900
(12) Sales	$16,000	$16,000
(13) Profits	$5,000	$5,100

*In this example, it does not matter in Year 1 whether you use LIFO or FIFO because there was only one purchase— that is, the last purchase and the first purchase are the same.

to the other system in subsequent years. Your accountant should help you make the decision to choose FIFO or LIFO accounting, preferably before you have set up your bookkeeping system and have commenced operations.

f/F

financial statement The record of financial data required to plan your company's future. (*See also* balance sheet; gross profit; income statement; profit and loss statement.)

"Future" is the key word in this definition. The purpose of creating a résumé of your company's past—and financial statements deal only with the past—is to make adjustments for future performance. Some entrepreneurs disdain financial statements, trusting their experience and instincts. It's like driving a car: you don't need to look at the dashboard to go down the highway. But over the long haul you need to know how much gas is in the tank. Financial statements are the dials and lights on the dashboard.

A new business or one in flux (growing or shrinking) should have financial statements prepared and analyzed monthly. The balance sheet and the income statement (also called the profit and loss statement) are the two basic reports. The balance sheet shows what the company is worth by listing assets (such as cash, inventory, and equipment) and subtracting liabilities (including wages, taxes, and debts). The income statement compares revenues and expenses to show how profitably—or unprofitably—the business is performing.

firing employees Never to be taken lightly, terminating any employee should involve legal counsel. (*See* employee; hiring.)

When an employee repeatedly violates a company policy, you should document in writing the time, date, and nature of the offense. You should also document your counseling sessions and any action taken. Documenting everything is essential should you have to create clear grounds for a legal termination.

Dr. Mark Goulston, an author and psychiatrist who specializes in workplace issues, recommends giving a problem employee thirty days to shape up. "It takes thirty days for a change in behavior to become a habit and six months for a habit to become the automatic way a person does things," he say. "If they haven't changed in thirty days, it's not going to happen."

Personnel experts also advise employers to be clear about at-will employment. Although it varies state to state, most states allow either the employer or employee to terminate the working

F/f

PROBLEM STOPPER

Most employers and employees dread performance reviews, but done correctly, they can prevent small problems from becoming big ones. Here are some tips:

■ Consider conducting quarterly, rather than annual, reviews of your employees.

■ Begin by asking the employee to evaluate himself. Most people will own up to their shortcomings when questioned with respect.

■ Heap on the praise before you present your written evaluation. If the employee is hardworking, rarely absent, and never late, mention those qualities up front.

■ Be as specific as possible about areas needing improvement. Don't just say, "I don't like your attitude," or, "you didn't bring in that big new customer." Point out calmly that not landing that huge new account means that there will be smaller pay increases and a smaller contribution to the profit sharing plan.

■ Give employees time to explain exactly the circumstances of situations you bring to their attention, and explore what could have been done differently. Get the facts rather than launching into criticism. Avoid a tirade, at all costs.

■ End the conversation by making a list of very specific changes that need to be made. Set deadlines for improvement, and make it clear you plan to hold the personal accountable.

relationship at any time, for any reason. Be very careful not to turn a job offer letter into a binding contract. Always have an experienced labor lawyer review every document before you present it to a potential employee.

George Scharm, a former police officer, is founder and presi-

f/F

dent of TSS Consulting Group, based in Gurnee, Illinois. The group conducts employee background checks. He reminds business owners not to treat employees like family. "You don't want an employee to think the business is his family," warns Scharm, because "when they are fired, they feel like they've been thrown out of the family. This can lead to workplace violence."

If you have tried counseling and warnings, have documented the problems, and have decided that firing is inevitable, be very careful when it's time to do it. Be sure to be courteous, polite, and have your termination discussion in private. Scharm suggests conducting a short exit interview and being generous with severance pay, even if the person doesn't really deserve it. It helps to do everything you can to end on a civil note.

Human resources expert Dolores Ennico says that many business owners believe that Friday is the best day to fire someone, but she disagrees. She says an unstable or lonely person fired on a Friday will have a very tough weekend and may return to work on Monday with violent intentions. She recommends firing people on Tuesday or Wednesday.

fixed expenses Costs that remain stable from one accounting period to the next.

Rent, interest, utilities, salaries—those expenses that occur regularly (including quarterly, such as insurance premiums), are also the easiest to account for. Variable expenses such as raw materials, extra labor, travel, and shipping are harder to track, but the effort is worthwhile because they are also easier to cut.

401(k) Employer-sponsored retirement plan that encourages employees to contribute part of their income on a tax-deferred basis. (*See also* pension plan.)

franchise Borrowing on another entrepreneur's success and paying for the experience. (*See also* exit strategy.)

A franchise is not, as many think, a separate type of small business entity. It's a contractual relationship between two businesses, known as the franchiser and the franchisee. Typically the fran-

F/f

SHOPPING LIST

Here are some tips for choosing a franchise from Jim Amos, CEO of Mail Boxes Etc. and chair of the International Franchise Association:

- Give yourself plenty of time to do careful research; most franchise agreements are for ten years or more.
- Talk to as many franchise owners as possible, and learn from their experience.
- Compare different franchises within a given industry, and aim to identify the competitive advantage of each.
- Call some of your potential customers, and make sure there is a market for the prospective business.
- Consult professionals. At the least, you should talk in detail to your own lawyer and accountant before making any commitment.
- Don't get financially strapped: plan for more expenses than you think you'll have, for longer than you think it'll take.
- Make sure you are ready for the commitment. Owning a business is always hard work.

---

chiser owns trademarks, service marks, and a ready-made business plan for selling a particular product or service, The franchiser sells or licenses the business plan as a turnkey package to franchisees. Franchisees are people who want to get into the field but who do not have the experience or capital to launch the venture themselves. The franchisee runs the operation in a particular location or designated territory, but is required to adhere closely to the master plan established by the franchiser and pay royalty fees (generally a percentage of gross sales) to the franchiser each month or quarter.

So many franchises have been offered fraudulently over the years that the Federal Trade Commission (FTC) and state depart-

f/F

THE FRANCHISE AGREEMENT

A buyer's key questions:

- What are the fees to be paid to the franchiser, and when are they payable? The agreement should list every penny you will have to pay to run the franchise business, with no costs that surprise you later.
- Is your territory exclusive—in other words, can the franchiser set up another franchisee in your territory without your consent?
- Can the franchiser sell its products and services directly (for example, via the Internet) to people in your territory and bypass your franchised business?
- What if the franchiser merges with another franchise that has a store or outlet in your territory? Will yours be protected?
- Can you set up your own website for the franchise business, or must you participate in the franchiser's website?
- How much training and support will the franchiser provide for you and your staff? Will they be available by telephone if you have questions?
- Is there an association of franchisees of this franchise? If so, who are the members in your geographic area?
- If you die or become disabled, or if the franchise business just doesn't work out for whatever reason, will the franchiser help you find a buyer for your business or pay you fair market value to personally take over your business?

ments of consumer protection have stepped in to regulate them. If you decide to buy a franchise, the FTC requires the franchiser to give you a Uniform Franchise Offering Circular (UFOC) at least ten business days before the closing of a franchise sale. The

F/f

UFOC is a disclosure document, similar to the prospectus for an offering of securities (and often as complicated), which describes the franchise and the operating results achieved by other franchisees, both locally and nationwide. You will also be required to sign a detailed franchise agreement describing training and support, if any, that the franchiser will provide you, and fees you will owe the franchiser. Franchisers are usually inflexible in negotiating the agreement because they want all of their franchisees to operate under the same set of rules.

Franchise consultants can help you select and evaluate a franchise opportunity, review and understand the offering circular, and help you negotiate the agreement, although it's best to have an attorney also review the agreement on your behalf. Generally, franchise consultants are paid by the franchiser as a percentage of the up-front franchise fee.

Keld Alstrup, a franchise consultant based in Tuxedo Park, New York, who works with dozens of franchises as part of the nationwide Franchise Network (**www.frannet.com**), advises: "When buying a franchise, especially one that hasn't been around for a long time, the best thing to do is to talk to the franchise's other franchisees, even if you have to travel around the country to do it. Ask lots of questions, such as: Are you happy? Does the franchise company give you support? Are your gross and net revenues what you expected they would be? Franchise owners believe in supporting each other, and you will get extremely candid and honest responses."

Why buy a franchise when you can go it alone and not have to pay all the franchise fees? Alstrup replies, "When you buy a franchise, you are buying a proven concept that has worked for other people. While, of course, there's never any guarantee of success, franchises fail at a much lower rate than their independent competitors. Besides, there are franchises nowadays for just about every type of business. Do you really want to start your own business only to have a national franchise, whose owners receive lots of advertising and technical support, open a competing store down the street from you? It may be better for you to grab the franchise territory you want before someone else beats you to it."

f/F

fraud When truth is stretched until it hurts. (*See also* values.)

In business sometimes you have to stretch the truth a bit. If you stretch too far, though, it's considered fraud. You can be sued and possibly (depending on the type of fraud) sent to jail.

When you commit fraud, you make a false or misleading statement about a material fact. False or misleading statements come in two varieties: An untrue statement such as "our sales went up 100 percent last quarter," when in fact they went down 100 percent; and a material omission or half-truth such as "our leading sponsor, XYZ Corp., renewed their commitment for another year," when in fact XYZ Corp.'s renewal was for half the amount of money as the previous year.

An untrue statement is material if it would cause listeners to change their behavior if they knew the truth. So, for example, the statement "our sales increased by $1 million" when in fact they increased by $999,990, is probably not fraud; but the statement "our sales increased by $1 million" when in fact they increased by $750,000, is misleading and probably fraud.

The misrepresented fact must be one that a reasonable person would find material. So, the statement "[a leading expert in your industry] is on our board of advisers" when in fact he or she has not committed to serving on your advisory board, is probably fraud; but the statement "everyone knows only people born under the astrological sign of Aries make good chief executives, and our CEO is an Aries," when in fact he or she is a Gemini, is probably not fraud, despite being demonstrably false.

Statements of opinion or predictions about the future are generally not considered fraud but harmless puffery. The following statements are probably not in themselves fraudulent:

- "Our company is the best in its industry."
- "We predict that our sales will double next year."
- "We think a 10 percent stake in our company is worth $100,000."

Employee Fraud

The statistics are chilling: Employee fraud and abuse cost American businesses about $400 billion a year. Trade-secret theft con-

F/f

LOCKS AND KEYS

Here are more tips for protecting your business from theft and fraud:

- Limit access to valuable equipment, inventory, and checks. Lock up everything you can.
- Segregate responsibilities within the accounting department so that no one person controls all the financial functions.
- Make sure employees use their allotted vacation time. Most embezzlement plots are uncovered during the employee's absence because these schemes require the perpetrator to cover their tracks at all times.
- Carefully check the references of new employees. In many instances, criminals have a history of fraudulent behavior. Bring in outside help to review your security procedures if you suspect trouble.

tributes to about $250 billion in annual losses to businesses. Lack of security and controls make smaller companies with fewer than 100 employees more vulnerable to theft and fraud than larger ones, according to a two-and-a-half-year study by the Association of Certified Fraud Examiners.

"Many small business owners operate with few, if any, controls in place," says Tom Rafferty, a CPA, forensic accountant, and partner in the accounting firm of Mintz Rosenfeld & Co., based in Fairfield, New Jersey. Rafferty compares the lax supervision and record keeping, unsecured inventory, and poor delegation of responsibilities in small businesses to an open bank vault for dishonest workers. "Small businesses very often have a comptroller or bookkeeper who controls every facet of the organization's finances: accounts receivable, accounts payable, purchasing, and payroll," he says. "You have to hope that individual is honest." Some separation of authorities and some checks and balances are a good idea, to avoid giving any one person free rein.

f/F

Most employee fraud and embezzlement falls into off-book or on-book schemes. Off-book schemes occur primarily in cash businesses where employees ring up part of a sale into the cash register and pocket the rest. These scams include skimming, where money from a sale is pocketed before it is rung into the register; voids, where sales are voided under the guise that a customer returned goods; and under rings. "If you're running a neighborhood deli, it can be tough to figure out what's going on," says Rafferty.

On-book schemes are more complicated and are perpetrated by falsifying and manipulating accounts receivable, accounts payable, inventory, purchasing, and payroll records. In lapping, one of the more sophisticated schemes, an employee removes cash from a customer's account for personal use by falsifying documents or stealing a check. Money from a second customer's account is credited to the first customer's account, a third customer's funds credited to the second, and so on until the final account in the chain is adjusted with a false charge.

Inventory frauds usually involve an employee ordering excess inventory and converting it to personal use. Rafferty says these frauds can be easy to pull off because a full inventory is often taken only annually. In other on-book scams, payments on slow-paying accounts are diverted or phony purchasing orders and vendors are created.

So, how does a small company without the resources to hire a big accounting or security firm protect itself? Here are Rafferty's three rules for preventing fraud:

Rule 1: Have your bank statements sent to your home and review them before anyone else. Carefully review the statement and checks. Do you recognize the names of your vendors? Do the amounts of the payments make sense? Does your signature look legitimate?

Rule 2: Pay only original invoices, never photocopies or statements. Stamp the original document "paid" once you sign the check.

Rule 3: Be on the lookout for confusing accounting records, out-of-balance accounts, unexplained adjustments to any ac-

counts, and cash shortages. When confronting employees, be alert for unreasonable and convoluted explanations.

Rafferty also recommends being attuned to changes in your employees' behavior or lifestyle. "If the opportunity is there, under certain circumstances, the very dear family friend who has been the bookkeeper for years may decide to take out a loan with every intention of repaying it," he says.

If you do suspect employee fraud or scam, don't overreact. Collect evidence quietly. Then, call your attorney and local law enforcement officials for advice. You don't want to wrongly accuse anyone of a crime in today's litigious society.

freelancers *See* independent contractor.

freight forwarder A key member of your export team. The forwarder ships goods abroad and can be instrumental in collecting payment. (*See also* exporting; and exporting subhead, export-import bank.)

Vickie Reilly, president and founder of A.V. Reilly International, Inc. in Wooddale, Illinois, helps big and small companies move their goods out of the country safely. Her firm, with forty employees, is a member of the High Tech Forwarder Network, whose members ship about $1 billion worth of products overseas every year. The group, with sixty-seven member companies, was founded in 1992.

"Our client base is comprised of companies with sales ranging from $20 million to $250 million," said Reilly. "We ship a lot of high-tech products with a high value. We look for things that aren't just run-of-the-mill, not just a box or crate that has to go from here to there."

In recent years, more small firms have become more comfortable with exporting. "There's a whole big world out there," said Reilly. "If your domestic marketplace slows down, you look to emerging countries for business."

She said smart business owners call a freight forwarder from the start to develop an export plan. "It's best to call one before you get the order," she advises. "Terms of sale are widely confusing and very different domestically versus internationally."

f/F

Her firm ships goods to seventy countries. "We ship the most to and from Asia," she said. They also ship copper-mining equipment to several African nations, including Ghana and Zambia, and "high-tech components from Scotland," she said.

She recommends shopping around for a competent freight forwarder long before you solicit an overseas order. Advice from her firm is free, and they can save you time and money.

F/f

gift tax Tax placed on gifts given to any person while you are still living. (*See also* estate planning.)

GIFT TAXES BASICALLY are taxes that supplement the federal estate tax. You may give up to $11,000 a year in cash or assets to an unlimited number of people each year without incurring gift tax liability, so long as there are no strings attached. Married couples can give, as a couple, up to $22,000 as a gift per year to as many people as they want. If an individual gives more than the $11,000 annually, the excess is applied toward his lifetime gift-tax exclusion. The exclusion was $1,000,000 in 2002. If at any point the gifts you gave during your life or left in your estate exceed that exclusion, you pay gift tax on the excess amounts over $1,000,000. Any gift transferred between spouses (where both are U.S. citizens) of any size is 100 percent gift tax free.

giveaways *See* advertising specialties.

global trade Selling your products or services overseas with patience, contacts, and diplomacy. (*See also* exporting.)

Despite the economic chaos affecting many Asian countries and the volatile stock market, American entrepreneurs still yearn to go global. But, it takes more than a plane ticket and a hotel room to sell internationally.

Collecting facts and figures is a start, but international business experts say small business owners are often surprised at the level of formality still found abroad. America's fast-paced, informal culture, geared toward getting the deal done quickly, is often at odds with European and Asian business culture.

"In Europe, you will need formal introductions," says Tracey Wilen, author of *Europe for Women in Business* (Wilen Publishing, 1998) and coauthor of *Asia for Women on Business* (Stone Bridge Press, 1995).

Overseas companies are also much more rigidly structured and hierarchical than American ones—executives rise through the ranks after years of hard work. Wilen says women and young people riding the entrepreneurial wave in the United States won't find many of their contemporaries sitting across the table from them during negotiations in Europe and Asia.

American women should also be prepared to face a variety of obstacles, including gender bias, cultural prejudice, and sexual harassment. Wilen, an executive with Cisco Systems in San Jose, California, is a veteran business traveler and adjunct professor of International Business at Golden Gate University in San Francisco. She says American business people still don't realize the importance of establishing a relationship before trying to do business.

To boost the credibility of your company, she suggests arriving fully equipped with company statistics, referrals, letterhead, and business cards translated into your host's language. Hire an interpreter before you make the trip and meet with the interpreter before your first business meeting. If you can afford it, bring along an associate to important meetings. If you are a woman business owner, bringing a male colleague may increase your credibility and stature in the eyes of your foreign colleagues.

"They are thinking, you are only one person, how can you know everything?" says Wilen. "While we are thinking, why do they need all these people at the meeting?"

She says American businesswomen should be prepared to field

sexually offensive comments in Japan and accept the post-workday dinner ritual that usually involves a long night of heavy drinking in a bar. Cultural factors will also color your success. For example, your German hosts will politely listen to your entire presentation and follow the agenda, but your Italian colleagues are likely to disregard the agenda and prefer having a conversation. While Germans are punctual, Italians may be thirty minutes to an hour late. Wilen says that the French can be aggressive inquisitors and will debate you on every point. You may think the deal is sinking, but this is just the way they do business. The French will also want to negotiate in French, even if they speak English.

In Asia, elaborate rituals are followed, from a ceremonial exchange of business cards down to complex table seating arrange-

SAVOIR FAIRE

Here are some of Tracy Wilen's do's and don'ts that apply in almost every European and Asian country:

■ Do dress in conservative, formal business attire. Women are advised to be particularly conservative in Asia. Always wear a suit jacket and pantyhose. Avoid red suits and flashy jewelry.

■ Do arrange formal appointments and confirm them by fax, e-mail, or telephone well in advance.

■ Do display respect for and interest in the culture, history, and heritage of your host country.

■ Don't use first names until invited to do so. Observe courtesy titles unless you are specifically given permission to use a first name. In many European and Asian languages, there is no proper translation for "Miss" or "Ms." so women should be prepared to be called "Mrs."

■ Don't categorize Western Europe or Southeast Asia as one homogenous region.

g/G

ments that hark back to the days of the Samurai warriors. Follow every protocol to establish yourself as person to respect, Wilen advises. While she believes, "technology and the Internet are also very helpful in making small companies seem much bigger than they are," you'll still have to spend time in the country in order to make a deal.

Wilen recommends contacting the U.S. Department of Commerce for help. The department offers a variety of services to assist small business owners, including preparing a list of potential business partners and setting up appointments. Fees range from several hundred to thousands of dollars.

The Commerce Department's Matchmaker program has helped thousands of business owners go abroad. Molly Costa, project manager of the matchmaking program, says fees can range from $2,500 to $4,000, depending on how many countries you want to visit, plus travel costs.

Call 800-USA-TRADE to be referred to the appropriate government agency or program. Also, check out this helpful book: *Start and Run a Profitable Exporting Business,* by Laurel Delaney (Self-Counsel Press, 1998). Her book is filled with practical advice, contacts, resources, and forms. It also explains how to use the Internet to find international business opportunities.

goodwill In accounting, the value of a company above the sum of its assets. In practice, the quality of your business relationships.

grassroots politics Wielding political clout through the efforts of business or community alliances.

If you don't like how the current administration is handling the issues affecting your family or your company, stop complaining and get involved in the political process.

"If you don't blow your own horn, someone will use it as a spittoon," quips Ted Fowler, chief executive officer of the Golden Corral Corp., a restaurant chain based in Raleigh, North Carolina, with 460 steak restaurants in thirty-eight states. Fowler, who also serves as vice-chairman of the 230,000-member National Restaurant Association, says small business owners can make a big

G/g

difference when they make their opinions known to lawmakers. For example, he says grassroots lobbying efforts by restaurant owners lessened the financial impact of the Clinton administration's minimum wage increase. Although the NRA didn't prevent Congress from increasing the federal minimum wage, efforts by restaurant owners pushed lawmakers to include tax incentives for training new employees, which made the increase less painful.

"If you own a restaurant or any small business, it's vitally important to be involved politically at the grassroots level," says Steven Anderson, president of the NRA. "We literally storm the Hill [Capitol Hill] during our public affairs conference in September. The legislators know when the restaurant owners are in town."

Anderson says thousands of small business owners belong to his group, since 70 percent of America's eateries employ twenty people or fewer and post annual sales of less than $500,000. While you may think you are too busy running your business to be active in politics, consider how state, local, and federal policies affect your bottom line. Health and safety regulations, environmental standards, labor laws, and the tax code all influence the way you manage your company's affairs.

"The key thing for a small business owner is to personalize an issue and explain to employees how a government action can affect the business, positively or negatively," says Amy Showalter, a Columbus, Ohio–based consultant who helps big and small companies become politically active. "Small business owners have a great advantage because they have a personal relationship with their employees. Once you inform them about an issue, help them get involved."

Showalter managed grassroots political efforts for Nationwide Insurance for about ten years before starting her own firm, The Showalter Group. "Many small or medium-sized companies don't have the financial resources to hire lobbyists," says Showalter. "However, you have a rich resource in your employees."

She says even the busiest entrepreneurs can quickly obtain current legislative information from their trade or professional association and pass it along to employees via e-mail, company

g/G

newsletters, meetings with supervisors, paycheck inserts, or bathroom stall posters. "Posters work really well, because you have a captive audience and people read that stuff," says Showalter. "You can also call a staff meeting and say there are things happening that will impact our business."

Showalter suggests building political awareness by hosting a voter registration drive for your employees. Or invite local politicians to visit your company. If you are located near the state capitol, organize a field trip for a few employees to meet with legislators. "The number one way to communicate with your legislator is face-to-face," she says. "Number two is a personal letter, and three, a phone call. E-mail and faxes are way down the line."

"The groups that get in front of the lawmaker eyeball to eyeball have the advantage over those who are sending e-mails," she says, adding that, "the key question a politician asks himself or herself when meeting with constituents is, 'who is more likely to vote against me?'"

For more information, contact the National Federation of Independent Business (**www.nfib.org**) and National Small Business United (**www.nsbu.org**).

gross lease A lease of real property in which all payments are included in the monthly or quarterly rental payment. (*See also* lease.)

When drafting or negotiating a lease of office space, retail space, or other real property, it is important to know what is included in the monthly or quarterly rent payment, and what must be paid to the landlord separately. In a gross lease, the landlord agrees to pay all expenses that are normally associated with ownership of real property, such as utilities, repairs, insurance, and (sometimes) taxes.

gross margin In accounting, the difference between an item's sale price and its cost of production. It warns you when increasing your sales will actually cost you money.

G/g

gross profit The difference between total sales and the cost of producing those sales. (*See also* income statement.)

This figure tells you how much you're making now and where to set prices in the future. Your gross profit will need to cover the costs *not* directly associated with the sales that produced it, that is, the operating overhead of rent, utilities, salaries, and insurance. Thus, unless your gross profit covers *all* your expenses, you'll eventually lose money no matter how great your sales.

gross-up clause A provision in an agreement that any payment will be net of federal and/or state income taxes. (*See also* Subchapter S corporation.)

In some employment agreements for key executives, and in some stockholders' agreements, the parties may want to agree that certain payments will be made net of any federal or state income taxes. In effect, the employer or corporation agrees to pay the recipient's federal and state income tax liability on the compensation or other payment made to the individual, as and when the same is due. Such a provision is generally referred to as a "gross-up clause," because the payment is being increased to a gross amount sufficient to cover the recipient's tax liability.

Gross-up clauses are commonly used in stockholders' agreements for Subchapter S corporations in which there are minority shareholders. In a Subchapter S corporation, the corporation's profits and losses flow through the corporation to the shareholders, who must report their pro rata share of the corporation's profits and losses on their federal Form 1040 each year. If there are minority shareholders, a situation may arise in which the individual shareholders must pay taxes on their pro rata share of income, even though the majority shareholders decided not to make a cash distribution of corporate income to the minority shareholders during the taxable year. This situation is known as the "phantom income" problem, in that the minority shareholders must report and pay taxes on income they never in fact received as cash. In such a situation, the minority shareholders will want a gross-up clause included in the shareholders' agreement.

g/G

harvesting A venture-capital term for cashing out of an investment. (*See also* exit strategy.)

health insurance A fundamental cost in maintaining your employees' health. (*See also* benefits.)

FINDING AFFORDABLE health insurance benefits for your employees is getting tougher every year. "Premiums have gone up tremendously," says John Kimbrell, an insurance agent in Orange, California. He said an aging population, increasing drug prices, and a backlash against managed care have all contributed to price hikes.

While it's tempting to give up the search for affordable coverage, savvy entrepreneurs know that providing good health insurance benefits can help retain valued employees and recruit new ones. And, as your business grows, you may find that offering health insurance is no longer optional under many state laws.

"The last time premium increases were this high, managed care was the answer," says Scott Lyon, executive director of group services for the Council of Smaller Enterprises (COSE) in Cleveland, Ohio (216-592-2245). "This time, I don't know what the answer is."

In California, the leading health insurance purchasing alliance for small businesses is a company called CaliforniaChoice (calchoice .com; 714-835-6752). If a California company enrolls with CaliforniaChoice, every employee can choose a different plan, even a different carrier, all under one account. Business owners can set their contribution levels, allowing their employees to make the final decision about which carrier they will use and how much more they want to spend for added benefits.

"Most employers decide [on a health insurance plan] by price," says Kimbrell, whose insurance agency has five employees. "They don't care about the employees. One of the selling points of this plan is that it's really a good way to make employees happy."

The founder of CaliforniaChoice said his company has received a warm reception from business owners. "Twenty-five years ago small business owners were asking for this product," said John Word, managing partner and cofounder of CaliforniaChoice. "They're tired of making these decisions for their employees. They'd say, 'can't I just give them the money, and let them choose?'"

If you don't live in California, there are comparable health plans in many other regions. In Ohio, for example, COSE offers a selection of health plans to its members in much the same way that CaliforniaChoice does. Lyon reports that several thousand of the 13,400 companies that offer insurance through COSE offer multiple plans to their employees.

Small businesses in New York City and nearby Westchester County can find coverage options through HealthPass, an initiative sponsored by New York City. Wisconsin is also developing an initiative for small businesses based on the CaliforniaChoice model.

Your local chamber of commerce can be a great resource in finding leads to purchasing alliances in your region, but be prepared to spend some time on the research process. Despite the convenience that these alliances can offer small groups, you will still want to devote time and thought to this purchase.

Lyon, who counsels business owners on many aspects of management, recommends that entrepreneurs approach a health insurance purchase with a goal in mind. "Don't just buy a plan to buy a plan," says Lyon, "Buy a plan to accomplish a goal. Buy a plan that will meet the needs of the company and its employees."

"The average COSE member spends $20,000 a year on health insurance," says Lyon "If you were buying a $20,000 machine every year, you'd want to do a lot of research before making the purchase. Health insurance deserves the same attention."

hiring Done well, the next best thing to firing. (*See also* affirmative action; Americans with Disabilities Act.)

Many small business owners make the mistake of hiring the first warm body that walks through the door. This is a real mistake. Hiring people is easy. Getting rid of them is not. Firing has become a complex legal process, requiring detailed documentation and record keeping. You don't want to hire people with the hope they'll work out. You will increase your success if you cast a wide net and force yourself to check references.

PERFECT HINDSIGHT

A professional background check costs between $65 and $500, according to George Scharm, a former police officer who is founder and president of TSS Consulting Group, in Gurnee, Illinois. You can take these actions yourself to avoid hiring a bad apple:

■ Obtain an applicant's permission to conduct a formal background check. If they refuse to sign the release form, don't hire them.

■ Require applicants to fill out a detailed job application form as well as submitting a resume.

■ Carefully check several references. If former employers are reluctant to answer your questions, try to speak to colleagues or vendors who dealt with the person at his or her former company.

■ If the job requires driving, check your state's Department of Motor Vehicles to confirm that the person has a valid license and the one required for driving commercial vehicles, if necessary.

H/h

Reference checking is time-consuming and bothersome, but it can keep you out of very hot water. A close friend who runs a consulting company didn't take the time to check the references before hiring a manager. Long story short: The woman had served time in prison for embezzlement and proceeded to steal $56,000 from my friend's business and personal savings accounts. She's back in jail, but my friend is still trying to get the bank to cover her losses.

We sort of checked references on an office manager we hired when SBTV was starting up. We confirmed that he had worked for an executive at a big company, but the fact that his last boss wouldn't return our calls should have been a red flag. Our new office manager not only suffered from wild mood swings and dressed like a Las Vegas magician, but also one day charged a personal real-estate agency fee to my company credit card. When I found the charge and fired him for theft, his excuse was a

■ Check public court records for civil and criminal lawsuits filed against the person. The records provide a wealth of information. Anyone can go into the clerk's office of the county, state, or federal court, fill out a form, and check the records. Some filings are on microfiche, others are now accessible by computer. You can search for information based the person's name. Try to get the full name, including middle initial and birth date. A Social Security number is helpful, too. If you have a completed job application, you'll have all the information you need to look for filed lawsuits, liens, and divorce or custody records. You have to be careful though about using the information wisely and not violating a person's privacy. Check with an employment attorney if you find out something that will dissuade you from hiring the person.

h/H

doozy: "Since I open the mail for you, I planned to pay the bill before you saw it."

Before you hire anyone, make sure they meet with the rest of your team. Chemistry is as important as skills and experience, especially in a small company with a handful of employees. Ask the usual questions about background, but add a few more offbeat inquiries to get a sense of how the person thinks or operates under stress, such as:

- How did you handle a crisis at your last job?
- What was your greatest challenge, and how did you meet it?
- Where do you see yourself in five years?
- Do people ask you for your advice at work?
- Do you ask other people for advice at work?
- What did you like most about your last job?
- What did you like least about your last job?

We often hire people on a probationary basis—for a month or so. We put a new employee on the payroll, but with the understanding that he is on trial. Because we are so small, we like to get a sense of whether someone fits in well at SBTV.

Imagine yourself seeing this new person every day. Would you like to see that face around the office, or would you dread it? Rely on gut instinct to a certain extent. Surround yourself with people who make you laugh. A sense of humor can go a long way when things get stressful around the office.

hitting the wall The way exhausted entrepreneurs feel when they are very close to giving up. (*See also* stress.)

Many times during your entrepreneurial career, you will feel like you just can't go on. This is a common feeling, so don't despair. Owning your own business can be fabulous and horrible at the same time. You may feel like you've hit the wall when you have no cash in the bank, when a major order you were counting on disappears, or when that big deal you thought was in place falls apart at the last minute.

It's OK—no, necessary—to allow yourself to totally wallow in your depression for a full twenty-four hours. Feel miserable. Cry.

H/h

Rue the day you started your business and quit your comfortable corporate job. Scream. Holler. Vent. Tear up your business plan and business cards. Then, get up the next day and get back to work. You know you wouldn't be happy doing anything else.

home office The place where your business never sleeps. (*See also* virtual office.)

Millions of Americans are working at home, doing all sorts of interesting things full and part time. Working at home has its advantages; it's cheap, it's convenient, and you can set your own hours. The downside is that you can't really see clients at home unless you are a doctor, therapist, or insurance broker; you'll probably gain weight because the refrigerator is close to your desk; and you'll feel very isolated.

I worked at home for several years, first in a small nook adjacent to our kitchen, then in a converted two-car garage across from a paddock and chicken coop. I don't think I could have accomplished much under those battlefield conditions if I hadn't been trained to work in a noisy newsroom. If you can concentrate when fifty people are talking on the telephone and rushing around on deadline, you can work anywhere.

Be disciplined about knowing when to stop working. It's tempting to work all the time, but your health and productivity will suffer. You need to take regular breaks and get out of the house at least once a day for a long walk or to run errands. The toughest thing is concentrating on your work when you know there are five loads of laundry to do or a messy kitchen to clean up.

Some people can't work at home and they shouldn't. You may do better renting office space from a friend or renting space in an office complex set up for home-based workers looking to leave the nest.

For more details on the work-at-home lifestyle, see books by Paul and Sarah Edwards, or Terri Lonier's *Working Solo* (John Wiley & Sons, 1998).

illegal alien (or illegal immigrant) A foreigner unauthorized to reside in the United States, and therefore unauthorized to be employed in the United States.

THE IMMIGRATION AND NATURALIZATION SERVICE (INS) uses the terms "illegal alien" and "illegal immigrant" interchangeably; many who consider those terms hostile prefer "undocumented alien." The 2000 Census found that the previous estimation of 6 million illegal aliens in the United States was understated, possibly by half, meaning there could be as many as 12 million illegal aliens residing in the United States and looking for work.

An employer is required to complete an INS I-9 Form for every new employee within three days of the hire. Reviewing an original document, such as a birth certificate, passport, or a driver's license and a Social Security card, is deemed sufficient to have made a good faith effort to verify the new employee's legal status.

The terrorist attacks of 2001 have resulted in more aggressive policing of airport jobs, even such humble ones as parking valet and janitor, because officials believe an illegal alien who may have gotten such a job with a false identity would be vulnerable to blackmail by a terrorist group. But no matter what industry your business is in, be sure to check the status of all new employees.

The penalty for employing an illegal alien ranges from $2,000 for the first offense to $10,000 for the third.

income statement A report reflecting all the income booked by your company. (*See also* balance sheet; financial statement; profit and loss statement.)

The income statement compares revenues and expenses to show how profitably (or unprofitably) a business is performing. It is also called a profit and loss statement, or P&L.

An income statement actually shows two kinds of profit: gross profit, or sales less the expenses specifically associated with them; and net profit, which is gross profit less all the unassociated overhead. Looking back in time, the P&L will show you whether your margins are growing or shrinking, and will help you pinpoint why. Looking forward it will tell you how to budget expenses and price your products to keep your margins healthy.

income tax Uncle Sam's share of your earnings. (*See also* Subchapter S corporation.)

Most business owners write off and expense everything they can to minimize their tax burden. This works well until you decide to sell the business and a prospective buyer wonders why you have so little cash and such high operating expenses. If you are planning to sell your business, talk to your tax adviser about leaving some money in the bank and aim for showing a profit, rather than breaking even or reporting a loss.

The type of business structure you operate under affects the amount of income tax you'll pay. At the time of this writing, corporations pay about 39 percent for income under $335,000 and 34 percent for income between $335,000 and $10 million. (Congress passed 404 amendments to the tax laws in 2002 so by the time you are reading this, the laws may have changed again.)

One big tax issue for privately held companies is the repeal of the so-called death tax. Family-owned businesses have had a tough time passing the business down to the next generation because federal estate taxes take such a huge bite. The death tax was repealed until 2010, but is due to return in 2011. At this writing, Congress was considering another amendment to kill it all together.

If you operate a Subchapter S corporation, the business loss or profits pass through to you as an individual. If you plan to pay yourself all or most of the profits, this structure may work best for you. Achieving the delicate balance between showing a profit to prove you are a strong business, and minimizing your annual income tax keeps many business owners and advisers up at night.

incubator An intensive care unit for start-up companies.

Incubators were all the rage in the late 1990s. Colleges, economic development centers, urban lofts, Silicon Alley in New York City, and Silicon Valley in northern California were loaded with companies packed into shared, low-rent space, working shoulder to shoulder in the dot-com salt mines.

Most of those high-tech incubators folded when the market crashed in April 2000 and venture money dried up, but incubators remain a viable option for companies on a budget that prefer not to go it alone. There are about 1,000 incubators across the United States, each home to an average of eighteen businesses according to the National Business Incubation Association in Athens, Ohio (**nbia.org**). Universities and public-service organizations operate many incubators; many also look for

---

AT CONCEPTION

Steve Massarsky, founder of the Business Incubation Group in Manhattan, has the following tips for businesses looking for incubation:

■ When you think you're done researching your market and the competition, research some more.

■ Incubator managers may want to change your idea. Be willing to listen.

■ Always follow your passion. Commitment is contagious.

SHELTER FROM THE COLD

Incubators offer a safe haven for many former corporate executives who find themselves suddenly on their own. Vanessa Freytag, former national director of the women's entrepreneur initiative at Bank One, left the corporate world in April 2000 to start her own marketing consulting business. She moved into a small office in the Hamilton County Business Center in Cincinnati, Ohio. It is a former paint factory about a ten-minute drive from her home.

"As a banker, I saw how important it was to get good advice," says Freytag. "I also didn't feel I had the discipline to work at home. Although we are all doing different things, we have a common bond—to be successful." Her incubator is home to about forty-five companies, ranging from a single person service business to a $3 million candy maker. She pays $150 a month for a cozy office complete with high-speed Internet access. The incubator offers free seminars on how to run your business better and a full office support center. She can meet clients in a conference room and host a seminar in a large conference room—all included in her rent. "I've made good business friends in here," she says. "It's isolating when you are the owner and so much rests on your shoulders."

The incubator also conducts a CEO roundtable discussion and has an arrangement with Cincinnati Bell to install high-speed Internet access and offer it at a discount to tenants. There is also a database of local companies available for marketing campaigns, a copy center, three parking lots, and security.

"I feel confident and proud to be working in this building," says Freytag, who consults with major financial institutions looking to tap into the women's business market.

i/l

profit by investing money, a team of managers, or both.

Business incubators have been around since 1957 when the first one opened in Batavia, New York. They offer entrepreneurs space, business and marketing advice, and the usual business resources such as desks, phones, fax machines, and computers. Some also provide seed funding. Steve Massarsky, founder of the Business Incubation Group in Manhattan, explains that his company naturally takes a bigger share of companies that require more management. "If it's a 'beach boy deal,' where a company has just the idea—they come to me and say, 'Wouldn't it be nice if there was ...' then I take 20 to 30 percent of the equity," says Massarsky. "If something major is already happening to the business, we may take 10 to 15 percent, and if the deal is almost hatched, we'll take 5 percent."

Massarsky says the entrepreneurs have to understand how he works before any arrangements are made. The business has to be a potential home run; the people have to be smart, dedicated, and nice; and the incubator team has to feel needed.

Dinah Adkins, executive director of NBIA, contends that if you tracked a group of small business start-ups for five years, 80 percent of those nurtured in an incubator would still be around.

indemnity or indemnification clause A clause in which one party agrees to protect the other parties to the agreement against his or her negligence or misconduct.

In most legal agreements, each party agrees to certain duties, obligations, and responsibilities. If they fail to perform those obligations, or do so sloppily or carelessly, not only they, but also the other parties to the agreement, may be sued by third parties.

Accordingly, in many types of legal agreements the parties will indemnify each other, or hold each other harmless (which is basically the same thing), by means of an indemnity or indemnification clause. In an indemnity clause, one party (the indemnifying party) will indemnify the other party (the indemnified party) against "any and all loss, claim, damage, liability, cost or expense whatsoever" which the indemnified party may incur as the result of the indemnifying party's acts, omissions, negligence, or willful misconduct.

The indemnifying party will also frequently extend its indemnity to the indemnified party's officers, directors, employees, and agents, in the event they are sued in their individual capacities because of something the indemnifying party either did or did not do. The scope of the indemnity and the wording of the clause will vary widely from agreement to agreement, and should be scrutinized carefully by your attorney to make sure you are not signing up for more than you bargained for.

Most indemnities are open-ended, in that they are indefinite in their scope and amount. Because the parties cannot anticipate exactly what types of acts or omissions may give rise to an indemnity claim, the language of indemnity clauses tends to sweep very broadly, in an effort to cover anything and everything that may possibly happen. If a small business is asked to give an open-ended indemnity, it may be possible to limit the amount of the business's indemnity obligation, or to limit the amount of time in which the indemnity clause may be invoked in order to limit the small business's exposure to indemnity claims.

independent contractor Someone who works for you but is not your employee for legal or tax purposes. (*See also* employee; subcontractor; work made for hire.)

Generally, anyone who works for your small business will be either an employee or an independent contractor. The distinction is critical, because when you have employees, you have lots of legal obligations. If workers are independent contractors, however, you merely have to pay them for their services, and that's it.

The line between an employee and an independent contractor is difficult to draw, and many small businesses err by classifying people who are functioning as employees as independent contractors. Generally, a worker is an independent contractor if

■ You do not direct or control how their work is done. You can set deadlines, goals, and objectives, but the worker determines how and when best to get the work done.

■ The worker has a direct financial interest in the work. For example, she is paid only if she succeeds, or upon completion of the task to your satisfaction.

i/1

GOOD FORM FOR INDEPENDENT CONTRACTORS

An independent contractor agreement should contain the following terms and conditions:

- a description of the services to be performed by the contractor (many businesses draw up a detailed scope of work and attach this as an exhibit to the agreement)
- the amounts to be paid to the contractor and when they will be paid
- whether or not the contractor will be entitled to reimbursement of out-of-pocket expenses
- a work made for hire provision
- a confidentiality or nondisclosure provision
- an acknowledgement by the contractor that he is an independent contractor and that it is his sole obligation to report as income all compensation received from your business
- an indemnification from the contractor for any liability you may incur as a result of the contractor's failure to report and properly pay taxes on the amounts you pay the contractor
- an equitable relief clause by which the contractor consents to your obtaining a court injunction or restraining order against the contractor prohibiting him from violating any term of the agreement (without this clause, you will have to prove to the court the necessity of an injunction or restraining order, thereby losing valuable time).

- The worker does not work exclusively for you, and derives his income from a variety of clients.
- If a worker truly is an independent contractor, you pay him only the amounts required by your agreement with him. You do not withhold income tax, Social Security, or Medicare taxes from, or pay Social Security and Medicare taxes or

federal or state unemployment tax on, amounts you pay an independent contractor.

Generally, if you pay an independent contractor more than $600 during any calendar year, you are required to deliver IRS Form 1099-MISC to each independent contractor no later than January 31 of the following year. You will need the contractor's Social Security number or federal tax identification number in order to fill out Form 1099. Always ask the independent contractor to complete IRS Form W-9, Request for Taxpayer Identification Number and Certification, before she begins work. Otherwise you must withhold income tax from each payment in an amount equal to 31 percent of the payment. This is called backup withholding.

The scope of work an independent contractor will receive, the amounts she will receive for her services, and the terms and conditions of her relationship with your business, will be specified in a written agreement between your business and the contractor. If you do business frequently with independent contractors, you should consider having an attorney draw up a standard-form consulting agreement that you can use as the starting point for negotiations with each new contractor.

initial public offering (IPO) Selling stock to the public with the hope of raising cash to expand your business. (*See also* direct public offering; exit strategy.)

When record numbers of businesses were going public in the late 1990s, everyone was excited about selling stock. But going public is a complex and expensive process. It requires a skilled team of accountants, attorneys, and investment bankers—all who need to be paid both before and after the deal closes.

Also, not every company can make an initial public offering. Because partnerships and limited liability companies (LLCs) have extremely informal management structures, they will likely have to convert into corporations in order to launch an IPO to sell their shares publicly. Because their assets "go home every night," and are difficult to value, service businesses will find it difficult to attract the marketplace's attention (unless they are franchised operations with outlets in many states).

The IPO process is extremely costly (the legal and accounting fees alone can run in excess of $100,000), and there is no assurance that the shares will sell. If an IPO is launched shortly after a major market downturn (such as those that occurred in 1929, 1987, and 2000), it may be years before the IPO shares will sell.

There may also be legal restrictions as to how much, when, and how the business owners can sell their shares. To avoid founders selling all of their shares right after the IPO is launched (thereby driving the share prices down and destroying investor confidence), investment bankers generally require the owners of an IPO company to sign standstill agreements. Under such an agreement, the owners will be prohibited from selling their shares for a period (usually six months or one year) after the IPO launch date.

Think carefully of the ramifications before you make any big decisions. Speak to other entrepreneurs who have gone through the process and ask them to tell you honestly what it was like.

Here are some questions you should consider before deciding to go public:

- Is your company profitable and growing? Investors want to invest in solid, profitable ventures with bright futures.

- Do you have a strong management team that can handle daily operations while you concentrate on raising money?

- Are you ready to be the spokesperson at the dog-and-pony shows necessary to raise awareness and interest?

- Do you have the financial resources to pay for lawyers, accountants, and investment bankers? The printing costs for materials required by the Securities and Exchange Commission can cost more than $150,000 alone.

- Can you manage in a fishbowl? Public firms must file detailed financial reports on a quarterly and annual basis. You'll have to answer tough questions from your board of directors as well as your stockholders.

- Are you prepared to resign if the company goes in a direction you don't agree with? Can you relinquish the power and control of the company you started?

■   Are you prepared to step aside if your management team thinks investors want new leadership? Operating a private business means you can keep all financial information private and you only have to answer to a few key board members and advisers.

insurance Protection you buy so you can sleep soundly.

Every business, no matter how small, needs insurance. If you have stuff, you need to protect it from theft and damage. If you have employees, you'll need workers' compensation insurance to cover them if they are injured on the job, state-mandated unemployment insurance in case you have to let them go, and possibly disability insurance, which provides benefits if they are unable to work.

The best way to buy insurance is to work with an independent broker who represents many different companies. The broker needs to understand everything about your business: what you do, what you sell, and all the risks involved. The broker needs to know exactly what your employees do, including whether they travel on business, lift heavy boxes, or stand behind a counter facing upset customers all day.

Be honest and explain all the ins and outs of your operations. Ask about key person insurance, which covers a top manager or employee you would have a tough time living without. Find out about business interruption insurance, which provides funds if your business is knocked out of commission by a fire, flood, or explosion.

You'll have to make some tough decisions to balance what you need and what you can afford. You might be able to save money with high deductibles on your vehicle insurance if you hire experienced drivers with clean driving records. But don't skimp on covering all your computer equipment and other valuable machinery. Pay your premiums on time and review all your policies every year. Insurance companies love it when you forget to cancel a policy on that old truck you sold or close an office and forget to reduce your coverage.

i/I

intellectual property Thoughts transmuted into assets. (*See also* copyright; invention; trademarks and service marks.)

Intellectual property (IP) includes trade secrets, patents, recipes, and secret formulas that set your company apart from the competition. In the software or entertainment business, IP can represent up to 90 percent of a company's assets. It's imperative that you do everything possible to protect it.

Written materials should be copyrighted. You can copyright something just by putting the copyright symbol © on the document. You can also file a form with the Copyright Office in Washington, D.C. (**www.loc.gov/copyright**).

Writers often register their manuscripts and scripts with the Writer's Guild of America (**www.wga.org**) or other professional associations. You can't copyright an idea, but you can copyright the description of the idea or premise. I recommend buying *The Copyright Handbook,* by Stephen Fishman (Nolo Press, 2000). Nolo Press, a Berkeley-based self-help publishing company, has a library of great books, many with software disks included (**www.nolo.com**).

A trademark protects product names and slogans used in interstate commerce. While you can register a company or product name in your state, it's best to have federal trademark protection. For that, you will have to prove to the U.S. Patent and Trademark Office (**www.uspto.gov**) that you are using the product name or slogan in commerce.

We have a trademark application pending on SBTV, the Small Business Television Network. We use SBTV and SBTV.com on our website, on all our promotional materials, tapes, CDs, and in everything we produce and distribute. Although I obtained trademark protection for "Succeeding in Small Business," (the name of my first book and column) by doing the paperwork myself, we retained a law firm that specializes in intellectual property to handle the registration of SBTV. We wanted to make sure every filing was perfect so there is no question about the validity of our trademark, especially because the name is so recognizable and says exactly what we do.

If no one tries to steal your trade name, you may think you've

wasted money on the legal fees to protect it. But, if you h
legally protected what is yours, you won't have a leg to stand on
if someone does try to infringe on it. It's pretty easy to prove
trademark or copyright infringement because you will have samples of the offending material. Defending a patent can be much
more expensive, especially if you have a hit product that people
are knocking off.

interference with contract Malicious intent causing someone to
breach a contract with a third party. (*See also* hiring.)

If you breach a contract with someone, you can be sued for
damages. But inducing someone else to breach a contract with a
third party can get you into even bigger trouble.

Let's say you want to get business from Company X, but you
know that they have an exclusive supply arrangement with one of
your competitors. You call the president of Company X and say,
"Hey, if you break off your agreement with our competitor, we'll
give you a better deal." Or, say you have just hired a leading scientist away from one of your competitors. He has signed an agreement saying he won't disclose confidential information of his
former employer, which you know about, but you still insist that
he divulge the competitor's secret formula for their best-selling
product. In either case, you have committed interference with
contract, and, chances are, your competitor is going to come
after you.

Because interference with contract is a tort (a legal term meaning a wrongful act done willfully but not involving breach of contract) in most states, your competitor will not be limited to a
recovery of actual damages when it sues. It will be able to seek
punitive and other damages that may have a crippling effect on
your company.

In order to commit interference with contract, there must be a
contract between your competitor and the third party, you must
know that the contract exists, and you must intentionally cause a
breach of the contract.

Hiring an employee who shows up on the first day of work
brandishing a non-compete agreement you didn't know about is

i/l

not interference with contract. Luring a senior executive away from your biggest competitor is not interference with contract if the executive's contract specifically allows him to quit his job at any time. Stealing a customer from one of your competitors is not interference with contract if the customer has no exclusive contract with the competitor, or if the exclusive contract expired a month ago.

To avoid liability for interference with contract when soliciting new business or hiring new employees, be sure to find out if there are any agreements that would prevent the other party from doing a deal with you.

Internet A global computer network of coherent anarchy.

What did we do before the Internet? Think back to fax machines, overnight deliveries, and face-to-face meetings. Ah, the good old days.

The Internet is fantastic for doing research and marketing. The Internet is also great for sending and receiving electronic mail and transmitting presentations, contracts, and documents in a few seconds around the world. We use e-mail to send contracts, distribute my newspaper column, and file forms.

Every business—no, every *person*—should have a website, even if it's just one or two pages, extolling their virtues and products. Why not? Our son Evan designed his first website when he was twelve. If he can do it, your son or daughter can create one for you, too.

Internet marketing The art of driving traffic to your website. (*See also* website.)

Internet marketing is back to the basics. Targeted marketing with a clear message delivered multiple times is what works, according to marketing experts like Nancy Michaels, president of the consulting company Impression Impact in Concord, Massachusetts (**www.impressionimpact.com**). Find your core customer group and sell to them. Then, treat them well, deliver the goods on time, and exceed their expectations. They will return to your website and become repeat customers.

We attract visitors through links from our big sponsors' web-sites. Our content appears on the Merrill Lynch Business Financial Services site (**www.businesscenter.ml.com**) and in MasterCard's Small Business Connections newsletter. In 2002, I started providing content to Sprint.

We tried print advertising, but that didn't work because people reading magazines are usually not logged on to the Web at the same time. We can't afford television advertising, but when our video segments aired on *Lifetime Live!*, a daily show that aired at noon on the Lifetime cable network and our Web address appeared on screen, our traffic spiked.

Your mission is to get your Web address out there in as many places as possible. Ask everyone you do business with to include your site whenever possible—online and offline. Reciprocal links (links from one site to another) cost virtually nothing to add to a website and help promote your business to potential customers and clients.

Whether your site is transactional or intended as a marketing tool, it should be viewed as an additional form of advertising for your business and not a primary advertising source. If you want your site to promote and advertise your business, you need to pro-mote and advertise your site, which will help increase traffic on your website. Here are some simple ways to get the word out:

- Print your Web address on brochures, business cards, fax cover sheets, press releases, mailing lists, letterhead, and pro-motional products like caps, mugs, and bumper stickers, post-cards to customers, forms, invoices, bills, receipts, labels, and stickers attached to product packages.

- Include your Web address in business directories, Yellow Page listings, trade publications, and chamber of commerce newsletters.

- Post your site to Internet newsgroups whose topics are rel-evant to your site.

- Register your name at **Verisign.com** or **Register.com**. Your Web address should be as close as possible to the name of your com-pany so customers make the connection.

- Own your server. Though more expensive than renting

space, owning your own server gives you more control over your site and its quality, and makes it faster for customers to access.

■ Register your site with as many search engines as possible. Use relevant keywords in your site's name and content to get a high ranking with search engines. Be sure to choose key words that directly apply to your business type, products, and services, not to its name or logo.

■ Provide a free service or activity to make your website a destination, not just a shopping tool. Consider providing updated useful information on a topic relevant to your product, a game, a referral service, or some other recreation or service activity. Serve as a bulletin board, cyber-gathering space, or resource center for people interested in a topic relevant to your business.

■ Let the site work as a catalogue. Show off your products with photos and detailed descriptions.

■ Track and chart traffic to your website, how long people stay, and at what point they exit the site. See what seems to interest visitors and alter your content to keep people at your site and to encourage them to visit the complete site.

■ Websites can appear different with different browsers. Test your site to make sure it appears properly with all the popular browsers, including their older versions.

■ Make sure your site also provides a name, address, phone number, and location of your company. Consumers want to know with whom they are dealing. A phone number with a human voice on the other end of the line is crucial.

invasion of privacy The law that spoils a gossip's fun. (*See also* defamation.)

If you say something bad about someone else that is patently false and designed to ruin the person's reputation, you may be sued for libel (if done in print) or slander (if done verbally) under most state laws. Even if what you say about that person is perfectly true, however, you may not be out of the legal woods yet. If what you said about the person discloses to the public something that most normal, ordinary people would keep strictly to themselves, you may be open to a lawsuit for invasion of privacy.

Invasion of privacy is designed to protect everyone's right to be left alone. Here are the most common types of invasion of privacy that can get you into legal trouble:

- **Disclosure of private facts.** Revealing private or embarrassing (albeit true) facts about an individual when there is no legitimate public concern can also be invasion of privacy. Let's say that in digging through some old newspapers you discover that a friend—a popular and beloved figure in your community—was convicted of possession of a small amount of marijuana twenty years earlier. Publishing this information may be an invasion of your friend's privacy unless justified by a legitimate public concern—for example, your friend is running for mayor on a strict antidrug platform.

- **False light.** Falsely portraying an individual in a highly offensive manner can get you into trouble—for example, taking a photograph of your competitor's head, pasting it onto the body of a convicted felon being hauled off to jail, and publishing the doctored photo on the Web.

- **Intrusion.** Intruding upon a person in a situation in which that person has a reasonable expectation of privacy—for example, digging through his garbage, peering into his backyard through a telescope, or wiretapping his telephone—may be an invasion of that person's property, and may be viewed in some states as criminal trespass.

Every state has its own set of rules for invasion of privacy, so be sure you contact a lawyer before using that wonderful, candid anonymous, person-on-the-street photo in your advertising campaign without the subject's permission.

invention A simple or revolutionary idea that spawns a new way of doing things. (*See also* copyright; intellectual property; knockoff; patent; trademarks and service marks.)

Of all the great ideas, the successful ones are due to the unrelenting determination of the inventor. A guy like Mark Juarez, founder and CEO of the Happy Company, is a perfect example of someone who talked his way through the patent process and ended up selling 10 million of his Happy Massagers and millions of other body-care products.

Juarez founded the company, a division of the parent company Tender Loving Things Inc., in Hayward, California, in 1992. Prior to becoming an inventor he was working as a massage therapist and hotel desk clerk in Berlin, Germany. Frustrated by how tired his hands became after a long day at the massage table, he made a funny looking, four-legged wooden gadget whose legs were designed to hit four key acupressure points at a time. When he couldn't afford to hire a patent attorney, he bought a do-it-yourself patent applications book, filled out the forms, and flew to Washington, D.C. He was so naïve, he showed up at the U.S. Patent and Trademark Office fully expecting to leave with a patent a few hours later.

He remembers the clerks laughing. They laughed until, as he tells it, he jumped over the counter and massaged a very grumpy clerk's back with the little wooden Happy Massager. The astonished clerk was so impressed he called the examiner who reviewed applications for massage tools and begged her to meet with Juarez to check out his invention. She was grouchy, too, but gave him five minutes. He skipped the explanation and gave her a back massage. Impressed, she told him how to do a patent search in three hours instead of three months. Juarez massaged his way around the patent office, getting the guy who made photocopies in the patent library to help him and persuading (through massage) the guy at Mail Boxes Etc. to keep the store open after hours to type up the final patent application. "I had my patent-pending status in three days," recalled Juarez. "Everyone at the patent office was so helpful."

Juarez continued working as a masseur and hotel clerk for a year to pay for the first 25,000 Happy Massagers. The Maine manufacturer had never filled such a small order, but Juarez persuaded the owner to take a chance. With thousands of units on the way, he manipulated his way into a Nordstrom department store by massaging the clerks and gift buyer. By demonstrating how the Happy Massager worked, he and the cosmetic department clerks sold 600

I/i

massagers during the big gift-buying weekend after Thanksgiving. He also sold massagers to thirty small gift and health food stores around the Bay Area. When all thirty stores immediately sold out their first orders, he knew he had a hit.

At its peak in 1996, Juarez says, the company had 300 employees and booked $20 million in sales. In recent years, sales dropped to under $10 million and he now employs twenty-five. He blames the dramatic drop on the fact that many companies are making knockoffs of his patented products. For information call 800-486-2896 or visit **www.thehappycompany.com**.

Whereas Juarez remarkably managed to patent the first massager on his own, he now relies on a patent attorney. Obtaining a patent is complex, and although you can do it yourself, it pays to hire professional help. The critical challenge is proving that your invention is *different* from what's on the market already. That's why the research process is so time-consuming and stressful for most inventors. You not only have to document in writing every step of the invention process, but you also have to convince a patent examiner that you have come up with something completely new.

inventory financing A form of financing based on the value of inventory, rather than receivables, assets, or purchase orders. (*See also* accounts receivable financing.)

For most businesses, inventory is dead capital sitting in a back room. But if your company generates orders faster than cash, you might look into working with a specialized lender that bases credit on inventory, rather than receivables.

"We like inventory, but not many lenders do," says Jeff Koslowsky, executive vice president of Gerber Trade Finance in Manhattan. Rather than financing individual transactions, Gerber provides a revolving credit line for businesses at about 2 percent more than the prime interest rate.

Gerber is unique in lending money based on inventory. (You can find other firms by doing an Internet search for "inventory finance.") These firms are not banks, but rather are companies that borrow money from banks to finance their clients. Gerber is a five-year-old firm owned by Investec Group, an investment bank traded on the Johannesburg stock exchange, and the Gerber Goldschmidt Group.

Gerber offers clients credit lines between $200,000 and $2.5 million. Clients use the credit lines to pay their bills and pay it back when they get paid. "The two stats we look at most closely are inventory days and receivable days," says Koslowsky. "A good trade cycle is thirty days," he says. "Shrimp is thirty days. Steel is thirty to forty-five days. Toothbrushes are more like ninety days."

Jeffrey Martinez-Malo, president of Ocean World Fisheries USA in Miami, Florida, imports shrimp and crab from Latin America. He turned to Gerber when he had a problem; he had orders for tons of seafood, but needed to pay for it when it was loaded into the containers in Latin America. He started with a $300,000 credit line that was increased to $600,000. Some of the money went to help his shrimp suppliers build more ponds for farm-raised shrimp. "I help them manage production, make sure quality is consistent, and help them package the product [for export]," says Martinez-Malo, who travels frequently to Latin America to meet with his suppliers. In 2001, he projected sales of 4 million pounds of mostly farm-raised shrimp, about twice what he sold in 2000.

Martinez-Malo attributes his sales increase to Gerber's willingness to finance him. "Our number one criteria for lending is people," says Koslowsky. "I'd rather be undercollateralized and work with people I trust than lend to people I don't want to do business with." Gerber Trade Finance can be reached at 212-888-3833.

inventory management A strategy to make enough of your product or products to meet demand and not be stuck with a warehouse filled with unsold goods. (*See also* back order.)

Managing inventory is one of the toughest challenges for a business. It's easy to figure out how to make your product; the trick is figuring out how to make enough for your customers without getting stuck with too much extra and having to dispose

I/i

of the excess. There are lots of inventory management programs out there. You can start with something simple like Intuit's QuickBooks Pro (**www.quickbooks.com**) that includes a module to keep track of inventory information based on the invoice. You can also spend hundreds of thousands of dollars on a customized industry-specific program, but I don't recommend doing that at the beginning.

Your challenge is to project how much stuff you'll need when you launch a marketing or advertising campaign and orders begin flowing in. Just-in-time inventory was invented by Toyota Motor Co. and perfected there around 1975; it remains the model for cost-effective manufacturing. A key aspect is to hold off production until you have a firm order in hand, but the challenge is to still have the proper inventory to start production at any time. You thus need to establish a network of reliable vendors who will ship the part you need on a timely basis.

If you make computers to order, like Dell, you know exactly how many boxes you have to build—and best of all, you've already charged the customer's credit card, so you have the money in your account before your workers start assembling Mr. Smith's new laptop.

If you are making small components for jet fighters, you'll probably rely on bar-coded stick-on labels to track the parts through the factory. If you make sweaters, you'll probably use bar-coded hangtags. (Retail stores, especially major ones, have very strict regulations and procedures for accepting merchandise from vendors. If you send an extra piece of tissue paper in a box, you can be dinged with what is called a "charge back." So, make sure your inventory system matches the needs of your customers.)

COSMI Corp., a Rancho Dominguez, California based-maker of value-priced software, tracks sales in retail stores and has the responsibility of shipping replacement software when it sells. Founder George Johnson said major retailers are putting more of the burden on their vendors to manage and control inventory. The company designs the programs, manufactures the disks, packs, and ships its software to major retailers like Staples and Office Depot.

"We have to be tremendously proactive," he says. "We get the sell-through information directly. Major retailers are going to what is called vendor-managed inventory or VIM. Eventually, vendors will be the ones responsible for creating purchase orders and pulling the items out of stock quickly."

Most software companies fail because they produce too many copies of a program that turns out to be a bomb. "They end up with a great amount of product that doesn't sell through the channels. That destroys most software publishers," said Johnson. "At our price points, we can't have many flops."

His other secret of success is to make only the products that are selling. "We don't maintain an inventory of finished goods, just raw materials. That means we don't have warehouses filled with mistakes." But their challenge is that they still have to ship a winner within forty-eight hours.

If a customer asks for a specific program, COSMI engineers can turn it around fast. For instance, after the September 11, 2001, terrorist attacks, a customer wanted a program to prevent identity theft. COSMI had it ready to go in eight days. It would have taken a larger company several years to do the same work.

inventory turnover The process in which your goods are sold and shipped. The number of times you "turn your inventory" is directly related to your profitability.

investment tax credit A credit against federal income tax. As of 2002, it has three components: the energy credit, the reforestation credit, and the rehabilitation credit.

Before you claim an investment tax credit for a business-related asset, speak to your tax adviser. According to Paul Gada, editor of the *CCH Business Owner's Toolkit Tax Guide 2002* (CCH Inc., 2002) you have to reduce the depreciable tax basis of the property. "The basis reduction would be equal to 100 percent of the rehabilitation credit you claimed, and 50 percent of the reforestation and energy credits."

investor relations Making sure the investors in your company are happy and well informed. (*See also* shareholders.)

If you are successful in building your business and ultimately sell shares to the public, you will have to hire a person or outside firm to do what is called investor relations, a function that is critical to the stability and prosperity of your company.

You can outsource this effort, but having a reliable, credible person on your staff whose sole mission is the care and feeding of your shareholders is a good investment. This person must be able to field tough questions, hold the hands of demanding stockholders, and tout your stock to the business press. Don't scrimp when it comes to hiring the best and brightest person for the job.

You, too, are the steward of your shares and should be kept up-to-date about the stock price every day or so. You don't have to live and die by the stock price, but you should know what's going on and make decisions based, in part, on how they will affect the public market for your stock.

investors People who provide you with money and advice while they wait to profit from trusting your management skills and judgment. (*See also* angels; venture capital.)

Small business owners admire investors. They have something we want—money. They often make us nervous and uncomfortable because they must be smarter than we are to be so wealthy.

During the dot-com boom, private and corporate investors were throwing millions of dollars—collectively, billions—at promising but risky ventures. We tried to scoop up some of that cash but missed the feeding frenzy. We were fortunate to find private investors in the form of my sister and brother-in-law. They believed in what we wanted to do with our company and provided essential cash and sweat equity—right when we needed it.

My sister, a scientist and venture capitalist in the biotech industry, spent nearly a year as our chief operating officer. She still hasn't been paid for her time but hopes to see her money someday. Her husband, Jeff, a physician and researcher, joined our advisory board and contributed hours of brainpower.

i/I

They were active investors because they were involved in day-to-to day management decisions. They showed up, read reports, organized brainstorming sessions, and helped pay the bills. Most investors are passive. They don't want to meet you or your team. They prefer to write big checks to an investment fund and read reports about their money every so often.

The best investors for small companies are folks involved in your industry or profession. Most of these angel investors are wealthy, semiretired entrepreneurs who know a thing or two about how to run your business. If you're lucky, they'll help you and provide the cash to grow.

The best way to find investors is to join your trade or professional association and be an active participant. Volunteer to work at the registration desk for a monthly meeting. Serve drinks. Schmooze. Make yourself known to the who's who of your world. Network like crazy and figure out who is likely to invest in your kind of company.

People invest in people, not companies. Remember that.

invoice Without a personal telephone call, the least effective way of getting paid within ninety days. (*See also* accounts receivable.)

The two most important things about invoices are to remember to send them and to verify that they have been received.

TOP BILLING

If your invoices aren't clear, your customers won't pay them on time. The Profit Advisors, Inc., a Rockville, Maryland–based consulting firm, says every invoice should
- List purchase order numbers
- Match the work order, contract, or packing slip
- Specify the quantities ordered, shipped, and back-ordered
- Include a contact name and telephone number to call if there is a problem.

I/i

We waited two months before calling an advertiser to pay an invoice, only to be told it had never arrived. Whether that was true or not, we should have followed up in two weeks, not two months.

Ask your clients and customers how they prefer to be billed. Some may want a hard copy faxed or mailed. Others might prefer e-mail. One big corporation insisted on our filling out a confusing online form. When it *never* seemed to go through or match the purchase order, I was told to send a hard copy via overnight mail so someone could walk it through the system.

Be a squeaky wheel. If people owe you money, confirm that they have received your invoice and that it is for the right amount. Remind them when it is due and don't do anymore work until they pay you. This isn't always easy, but it works.

i/l

job description The indispensable document for hiring, then for evaluating, every employee. (*See also* hiring.)

joint venture When two or more businesses join forces on a particular project and hope that they are not creating a legal partnership. (*See also* independent contractor; partnerships and limited partnerships.)

CONTRARY TO POPULAR OPINION, a joint venture is not a legally recognized type of business organization. The term joint venture is merely a business term used to describe the situation in which two or more businesses are joining forces on a particular project. For example, a jointly owned and managed factory in China is a joint venture.

Joint ventures between two or more companies may be organized in one of three ways—as a contract, as a partnership, or as an investment.

■ **A contractual joint venture** is when two companies act at arm's length as the independent contractor of each other. For example, Company A decides to buy all of its light bulbs from one supplier, Company B.

■ **A partnership joint venture** means that two companies

each contribute assets to the project and share in the profits and losses of the venture. An example would be a situation in which Company A provides investment capital, and Company B provides the facility, equipment, and personnel.

■ **An investment joint venture** occurs when two companies form a third, independent legal entity (usually, but not always, a limited liability company) that is jointly owned by the two companies and managed by employees of the two companies. An example is when Company A contributes $1 million to the capital of newly formed Company C in exchange for half of Company C's stock, and Company B contributes property worth $1 million to the capital of Company C in exchange for half of Company C's stock.

Unless the legal documents creating the joint venture specify the type of joint venture being created, or if third parties doing business with the joint venture have reason to believe the joint venturers are acting as partners, the law will assume that the companies intended to create a *partnership* joint venture. This means that each company will be 100 percent liable for the negligence and omissions of the other company and its employees, and this liability may not be limited to the joint venture business.

Joint ventures between competing companies may also give rise to federal and state antitrust concerns, especially if the appropriate authorities conclude that the joint venture business is likely to limit competition, raise consumer prices, or allocate market territories between the joint venturers.

i/J

Keogh plan A tax-deferred pension plan for the self-employed and their employees.

A KEOGH PLAN CAN BE either a defined benefit or a defined contribution retirement plan. Either way, the plan must meet the same requirements as any plan covering corporate employees, and if you have employees, they must be able to participate in the plan.

- **A defined benefit plan** provides a predetermined amount to employees or their beneficiaries. Rather than setting up individual accounts, the plan's assets are held in a pool. The down side of a defined benefit plan is that you still have to fund it, even if the company has no profit that year.

- **A defined contribution plan** is more flexible and less expensive to administer. Participants have their own accounts, and in 2001 the total amount that could be contributed to an employee's plan was the lesser of $35,000 or 25 percent of total earnings.

To qualify for tax deductions, your Keogh plan must follow a standard form and the details must be communicated in writing to employees. There are several forms that must be submitted with your tax return, so consult your tax adviser. Don't set one up without solid advice from a retirement planning professional.

Here are some good books to get you started:

RECOMMENDED READING

■ *You've Earned It, Don't Lose It*, by Suze Orman and Linda Mead (Newmarket Press, 1997)

■ *J.K. Lasser's Your Winning Retirement Plan*, by Henry K. Hebeler (John Wiley & Sons, 2001)

■ *The Wall Street Journal Guide to Planning Your Financial Future*, by Alan M. Siegel (Fireside, 1998)

kickback An illegal payment associated with giving or receiving a referral. (*See also* bribes.)

Kirton Adaptation Innovation Inventory A short test developed by a British psychologist to measure entrepreneurial tendencies. (*See also* entrepreneur.)

Everyone knows entrepreneurs are risk takers and innovators, but it may surprise you to learn that the tendency to start a business is believed by some industrial psychologists to be present at birth.

"We believe that this tendency is biologically predetermined," says John Eggers, Ph.D., an entrepreneur, industrial psychologist, and professor at the Richard Ivey School of Business at the University of Western Ontario, Canada. Prior to becoming a psychotherapist and academic, Eggers was a ski instructor and successful entrepreneur—he was the original worldwide distributor of Oakley Inc. ski goggles.

Eggers has given the Kirton Adaptation Innovation Inventory to graduate students, entrepreneurs, and corporate employees to determine whether they are "innovators" or "adapters." The simple written exercise takes about ten minutes to complete, but must be distributed and reviewed by a psychologist certified by its author, M. J. Kirton, a British psychologist and researcher.

More than 40,000 people have participated in Kirton's research, which found that age and ethnicity play a very minor role in determining whether or not you will be a successful

WHAT'S YOUR TYPE?

John Eggers, Ph.D., an entrepreneur, industrial psychologist, and professor, says that according to the Kirton Adaptation Innovation Inventory:

- **Innovators** love change, but have trouble following through. Innovators are the ones in a small group discussion who say, "This isn't the problem," or, "Oh my god, another meeting."
- **Adapters** accept problems as stated and don't throw out a lot of ideas. They are often perceived as not being on the team or not buying into a project.
- **Bridgers** don't show strong signs of either type so it looks like they are sitting on the fence. "They look wishy-washy," Eggers says.

entrepreneur. Women do tend to be more adaptive, but only slightly so, according to Kirton.

"There's a great deal of stuff on innovation, but a great deal of it has no basis," said Kirton in a phone interview from his office in Berkhamstead, England. "In the mid-1960s, I was asked to look at the term, 'management initiative,' which is used much like the term 'innovation' at the moment. These terms tend to be trendy. They tend to come and go. But, the notion that lies behind them is intriguing, so they keep returning."

Kirton says his inventory is not meant to pit innovators against adapters. "Clearly, this nonsense [about institutions killing initiative] was damaging because half the population quite enjoys working in large organizations," says Kirton. "And some innovators like working in big organizations because they find a niche."

While age doesn't affect the results of the inventory, women tend to be slightly more adaptive than men, according to Kirton. "This willingness to cooperate probably had its origins back in the 'hunter-gatherer stage' of human development when women were expected to be the nurturers," he says.

K/k

The thirty-three short questions on the self-scoring inventory ask about your work style, how patient you are, and how you like to manage projects. According to a pamphlet distributed with the test, adapters tend to accept problems as described and prefer structured situations. They are best at incorporating new information into existing policies. They also have a tough time accepting change. People who fall into a middle range are considered "bridgers."

Innovators tend to reject stated problems and refine them. They usually throw out many ideas when asked to solve a problem and aren't afraid to do things differently. They dislike structure and work well in a crisis mode, but usually have a tough time fitting into big organizations.

"Kirton discovered that large organizations tend to drive out the innovators," says Eggers. "Then, the company gets into trouble when they are left with only bridgers and adapters."

Big and small businesses should be concerned about losing innovators when they resist change, Eggers says. "Innovators crave change," he says. "They can't hold a job because of their preference for doing things differently. They can find solutions to problems, but generate lots of ideas that aren't very good quality. So, they get themselves into trouble, look flaky, and sabotage themselves."

Most people are surprised to learn a person's entrepreneurial tendency is not based on gender or ethnicity. "This information is based on the way your nervous system functions," Eggers explains. "Much depends on the gene pool you grew out of and how you respond to stimuli."

Eggers also points out that some entrepreneurial founders are adapters, but their companies look very different from most fast-growing ventures. "They usually start one company and keep it," he says. "Innovators tend to start three companies in a lifetime because they get bored and want to start over again."

Single copies of the Kirton inventory are available for $10 from Eggers. The test includes a brief telephone conversation after you complete the survey. Contact Eggers at jeggers@know-metrics.com.

knockoff A cheaper, unauthorized copy of an original item. (*See also* invention; patent.)

labor relations The respectful manner in which you treat your employees. If your employees belong to a union, you must adhere to strict rules and regulations affecting how and when they work.

labor union An organization entitled to represent employees in dealings with their employer. (*See also* independent contractor; union.)

A LTHOUGH THE MARKET SHARE of unions is shrinking (they represent fewer than 15 percent of U.S. workers in 2002 compared to 30 percent in 1946), labor unions remain potent in at least two ways: their bargaining agreements often set industry standards for wages and working conditions, and the threat of unionization is itself a barrier against the unfair treatment of nonunion employees. As an employer, you have the right to tell nonunion employees that you wish to remain union-free, but you cannot, by threat or coercion, violate their right to unionize. See the National Relations Labor Board website (**www.nlrb.gov**) for more information.

In 1998 some Microsoft permatemps—workers who had been employed for years through temp agencies—organized as the Washington Alliance of Technology Workers (WashTech), an affiliate of the Communication Workers of America. WashTech has no bargaining agreement with Microsoft, and it and the company dispute whether Microsoft improved the benefits of permatemps after WashTech's began trying to unionize them. Microsoft did, in 2000, pay $97 million to settle two lawsuits that claimed permatemps were shut out of a program allowing permanent workers to buy company stock at a discount.

The bottom line: Unionism may be in decline but even high-tech workers will fight back if they sense they're being treated unfairly.

lawsuit A court dispute that should be avoided at (almost) all cost. (*See also* alternative dispute resolution; collections; commercial liability insurance; Fair Credit Reporting Act; Fair Debt Collection Practices Act; legal costs or expenses.)

Americans are among the most litigious people on earth. There is one lawyer for approximately every 200 citizens in America, as opposed to one lawyer for every 5,000 citizens in Japan and one lawyer for every 100,000 citizens in the People's Republic of China. With such a glut of lawyers, it isn't hard for plaintiffs with even dubious claims to find a champion for their cause. Once a lawsuit is started, it takes a lot of time, money, and energy to achieve a settlement or to obtain a resolution. It is not an exaggeration to say that lawsuits can, and often do, kill businesses.

Let's say someone has failed to pay your company a large invoice on time, and you want to sue. Most lawyers will charge from $1,000 to $5,000 as an up-front retainer just to handle your collection lawsuit. Therefore, if the amount in dispute is $1,000 or less, filing a lawsuit may be simply throwing good money after bad, and isn't worth it. It may be a better idea to take more informal action such as hiring a collection agency, repossessing the merchandise sold (if it is legally permissible in your state to pursue a self-help remedy), sending a report to the major credit bureaus that will affect the customer's credit rating, pursuing the claim in small claims court (see below), or writing off the debt and insisting on payment in advance from similar customers in the future.

Consider also whether informal alternative dispute resolution (or ADR) mechanisms are available to help resolve the dispute

l/L

without the need of a protracted lawsuit. If arbitration and mediation are infeasible and the amount in dispute is relatively small
(generally below $5,000), the best approach is to take the case to
your local small claims court. Small claims procedure varies widely
from state to state, but generally, you file a summons with the
court, the two parties appear, and then the judge hears both sides
and renders an enforceable judgment. Most state court systems
publish a pamphlet describing, state by state, what you must do to
file a case in small claims court. This is usually available without
charge from your state court administrator, and can also be obtained from many local attorneys.

If all else fails, and the amount is too large to walk away from,
you are going to court. Most states have a statute of limitations
for different types of lawsuits, meaning that if you fail to com-
mence the lawsuit within that time period, you are forever barred
from bringing the action in court. In most states, commercial disputes will have a statute of limitations of between eighteen
months and three years.

A lawsuit is begun by the plaintiff's attorney filing a "summons
and complaint" against the other side (called the "defendant"),
who has a specified number of days in which to respond to the
complaint. If you are served with a summons and complaint, you
should seek the services of an attorney immediately, as the
response period in some states is quite short (fifteen to thirty days
from the date of service). At this point, it is too late to discuss the
matter informally, or to pursue mediation or arbitration. Your goal
is either to win the suit or to achieve a settlement in the quickest
possible time.

"The key to winning a lawsuit is that the judge has to like and
believe you," says attorney and small business legal expert Cliff
Ennico. "It certainly helps if the law is on your side, and the facts
are on your side, but if the judge just isn't buying what you have
to say, and thinks you are the one playing games in the lawsuit,
you and your attorney will have an uphill battle. So your case must
be compelling and convincing. If it isn't, you should consider
accepting the first settlement offer that's made to you and getting
out of there before things get ugly and expensive."

Under no circumstances should you ever consider acting as your own attorney in a lawsuit, whether as plaintiff or as defendant. While most states permit you to represent yourself (this is referred to as representation "pro se"), most judges strongly discourage you from arguing your case in court. Keep in mind that if your business is a corporation, limited liability company, or other legal entity, you cannot represent the business in court unless you are admitted to practice law in your state—representing even your 100 percent owned corporation is not considered representing yourself for legal purposes, because the corporation is distinct from you.

lawyer A highly misunderstood professional who can help you protect your business against lawsuits, the government, and other perils.

It's difficult for small business owners to admit they need a lawyer or to understand how lawyers can add value to their businesses. Most people don't even like lawyers in the first place, and even the best lawyer can't help you put money in your pocket. They are a business expense, not a revenue generator, and people hate to spend money on things they think they won't need right away. As a result, many small business owners look for a lawyer only after somebody has sued them.

This could be a big mistake, because by then, in most cases, the damage has been done. A single lawsuit can kill a struggling small business. Even if you are totally in the right, it will take years of your life and tens—if not hundreds—of thousands of your hard-earned dollars to get a judgment you may rightly deserve. Even then, the judge may not allow you to recoup your legal fees from the losing side.

What's worse, whenever someone sues a small business, they always go after the owners' personal assets, such as home, jewelry, stamp collections, and other valuables. Imagine trying to explain to your frantic spouse that the sheriff is removing furniture from your home and placing padlocks on all of the doors and windows because "something went a little wrong at the store."

One of the primary goals of any small or start-up business should be to avoid litigation at all costs. Believe it or not, your

L

NEED A GOOD ONE?

You probably won't find a good business lawyer by looking in the Yellow Pages, where you'll find a list of hundreds with no indication of their specialties. Here are
some better places to start you search:

■ **Word of mouth.** Talk to other small business owners in the area and ask who they use for business legal
advice. If the same two or three names keep popping
up, you're in business.

■ **Your local bar association.** Many times the local
bar association has a referral service. Ask for lawyers
who specialize in corporate law, business organizations, or business counseling.

■ **Findlaw.com.** Several excellent websites, including
www.findlaw.com, can help you search for lawyers by
both specialty and zip code.

■ **SCORE.** Your local SCORE (Service Corps of
Retired Executives) chapter will almost always know
one or two local lawyers who help them answer their
small business legal questions.

■ **Local resources.** Your local high school or community college probably offers a course in basic business law as part of its evening adult education
program. This course is usually taught by a local business lawyer. (Even if you don't like the lawyer, you
probably should take the course anyway to learn
more about your legal risks. It's a lot cheaper than
paying legal fees.)

best ally in avoiding lawsuits is ... a lawyer.

Some of the things lawyers can do to help protect your
business:

■ Forming corporations and other legal entities that will help
shield your personal assets from exposure to a business lawsuit

L/|

LEGAL MINDS AT WORK

What traits do all good business lawyers have in common? Here are some basics:

■ They should be able to form corporations and limited liability companies (LLCs), draft contracts and form letters, help you comply with government regulations, provide basic tax advice, and know something about the different ways small businesses are financed.

■ They work with a wide variety of small businesses in the same geographic area.

■ They work with lawyers in other disciplines and can help you find more specialized legal services (such as patent filings and immigration matters) on short notice.

■ They have worked with other clients in your business, but do not currently represent any of your direct competitors.

■ They are willing to charge flat fees for routine matters. When lawyers bill by the hour, they must be willing to give you a fee estimate up front and inform you immediately of circumstances that would increase the estimate.

■ They always respond to client telephone calls, faxes, and e-mails within twenty-four hours.

■ Drafting contracts and agreements to avoid misunderstandings with customers, suppliers, employees, and other key players in your business

■ Transferring assets out of your name to people or trusts that are not involved in your business

■ Complying with government regulations you didn't even know existed

■ Negotiating with difficult people and working out mediated settlements before a lawsuit breaks out

1/L

No lawyer, even one of the best and most expensive ones, can keep you from being sued. If someone hates you badly enough, you've given someone good reason to hate you, and you've got some juicy assets worth suing over, you may sooner or later be sued. With the help of a good lawyer, though, you can throw up so many roadblocks, booby traps, and force fields around your business that your enemy (or more likely, your enemy's lawyer) will say, "Yeah, there's a case here, but it's not worth pursuing it against these folks." A few hundred dollars in legal fees today can save you a fortune in legal bills tomorrow.

ON THE TABLE

Landlords and tenants commonly negotiate the following terms in leases:

- **Substitution.** Watch out for leases that enable the landlord to move you to a different space without your consent during the lease term.

- **Noncompete.** Some leases will require you not to engage in any business that competes with another tenant in the building. Make sure this is limited to current, not future, tenants and their current lines of business, and that this provision appears in the landlord's other leases as well.

- **Nondisturbance.** The landlord usually will want the right to sell the building or shopping center without your consent. This sale is fine, as long as the landlord makes reasonable efforts to ensure that any new owner will not disturb your quiet enjoyment of the leased premises as long as you are paying rent and otherwise being a good tenant.

- **Default.** Make sure you have the opportunity to cure any alleged defaults or breaches under the lease—rent checks do get lost in the mail sometimes.

L/l

leadership Declaring a vision, setting an example, and taking the heat.

lease A legal document by which a small business gets possession, but not ownership, of real property or equipment for a period of time. (*See also* double-net lease; gross lease; net lease; triple-net lease.)

Even if you operate out of a home office, it may be a good idea to have a lease between your business (the tenant) and yourself (the landlord) to justify deductions for monthly rent.

Every small business needs at least one physical location in order to conduct its business. A principal office or retail location is necessary, unless the business is one of those rare entities (such

■ **Termination.** If the lease terminates, the landlord may want you to continue paying rent for the balance of the lease term, or worse, pay all the remaining rent in a lump sum. Try to cap this obligation to a reasonable period, say, six to twelve months after termination. If the payment must be made in a lump sum, make sure you are only obligated to pay the present value of the remaining rent payments.

■ **Personal guarantees.** If you are personally guaranteeing the lease obligations of your corporation or LLC, try to limit your personal guarantee to the first few years of the lease term, or "for as long as I am a shareholder or owner of the tenant." You do not want to sell your business only to find yourself still personally obligated under your successor's lease.

■ **Space.** Make sure the space described in the lease is the same space the landlord showed you. If you need time to put in trade fixtures and spruce up the place, try to get the first one to two months rent-free.

as family medical or dental practices) that can sometimes operate out of residences. Most often, the location will be leased rather than owned outright.

Commercial leases of retail or office space come in two varieties: the gross lease and the net (or triple-net) lease. A gross lease is one in which the rent includes taxes, utilities, and insurance; a net lease is one in which you must pay for these separately.

In a lease of retail space (such as a storefront in a shopping center), you will have to make three types of payment to the landlord: fixed monthly or quarterly rent; a percentage rent based on your monthly or quarterly gross sales; and reimbursement of the landlord's expenses for property taxes, insurance, and maintenance of the common areas, such as sidewalks and landscaping. In an office lease, there is usually no percentage rent requirement.

Certain items of equipment can also be leased rather than purchased outright, and this may make economic sense, especially if the equipment easily becomes obsolete, such as computers and motor vehicles. Why take on the headache of finding a buyer for your out-of-date computers when you can simply give them back to the leasing company at the end of the lease term and lease new ones?

Like real estate leases, equipment leases come in two varieties: true leases and financing leases. In a financing lease, you are actually purchasing the equipment outright by leasing it for the full period of time during which it can be depreciated. The lease usually will give you the option of buying the equipment at the end of the lease term for a nominal amount, say $1.00. In a true lease, the lease term for the equipment is less than the depreciation period—the equipment is expected to have some real value at the end of the lease term, and you are expected to give it back at the end of the lease term, or buy it for its fair market value at that time.

If you use a corporation or limited liability company (LLC) to run your business, do not be surprised if the landlord asks you and all of your business partners to personally guarantee the corporation's or LLC's lease obligations.

leasing employees A way to let another company handle the payroll and benefits for your staff. (*See also* professional employer organization.)

There are more than 2,000 companies, often called professional employer organizations (PEOs), that handle all the paperwork and headaches related to having employees. Today's leasing companies have figured out how to handle the paperwork, provide good services, and make a profit.

Leasing may be an attractive alternative to direct hiring if you are growing fast and don't have time to solicit and screen applicants. In many cases, you just prepare a wish list of skills and experience and the leasing company heads out to recruit good candidates. You are involved in the hiring process, but after you give the nod, the employees are the responsibility of the leasing company. Their paychecks, health benefits, and retirement benefits (if needed) are managed entirely by the leasing firm. If the person turns out to be a dud, the leasing company terminates the employment.

The one drawback is the steep administrative fees you pay for all this service. The fees are based on a percentage of total payroll and usually range from 2 to 8 percent. The upside is that you write one check a month for everything, and the leasing company takes on the responsibility of seeing that your employees are paid and their human resources needs are being met. Because they represent lots of employees, leasing companies can often negotiate lower prices for insurance and other benefits.

You'll have to decide whether leasing employees make sense for your business. Be sure to carefully check references and speak directly to other clients of the leasing firm. If the firm collapses, you can be left in a lurch and still owing state and federal payroll taxes.

To verify that you are dealing with an accredited PEO, check with the Institute for the Accreditation of Professional Employer Organizations at **www.iapeo.org** or 501-219-2045.

l/L

legal costs or expenses One of the tolls that must be paid on the highway of entrepreneurial success. (*See also* lawsuit; lawyer; indemnification clause.)

If you are planning to start your own business, there are three painful but necessary "tolls" that must be paid, and budgeted for, along the way: taxes, accounting fees, and legal fees. Legal fees are probably the most painful of the three, because they usually must be paid on short notice, under deadline pressure, in unpredictable amounts, and at a time when the business can ill afford to make payments but must defend itself against a lawsuit.

Legal fees generally come in one of three varieties: the traditional hourly rate, the estimated (or capped) hourly rate, or the flat fee. Always insist on a written agreement, called a retainer letter, with any attorney you choose to represent you. The retainer letter, in a form prescribed by state law, will set out the lawyer's hourly rate, the estimate (if any) of the total fee that will be charged, the times the lawyer will invoice for his services, and any other important matters. Most attorneys will offer a retainer letter without your having to ask.

Traditionally, lawyers bill by the hour. You may be able to negotiate the hourly rate by asking that a junior attorney in the firm handle the matter. Younger or less experienced members of the firm will bill at much lower hourly rates than the senior partners with whom you will first meet. Rarely will lawyers agree to cap their fees, but they may sometimes agree to do so, especially in routine matters (such as real estate transactions) where the amount of time to be spent is reasonably predictable. Lawyers customarily will ask for a retainer or advance against their fees—in litigation matters this will usually range from $2,500 to $7,500, but may be lower for business transactions or contract matters. Where an advance is required, be sure to ask for a partial refund in the event you decide to withdraw or settle the matter quickly. In such a situation, the lawyer should charge for only the time actually spent on the matter (at the standard hourly rate), and refund the excess retainer amount.

Increasingly, lawyers are charging flat fees for routine business transactions such as incorporations, simple contract negotiations (such as consulting and employment agreements), and estate planning. When quoted a flat fee, be sure to ask if the fee includes all of the lawyer's out-of-pocket expenses, such as filing fees, Federal Express charges, and travel costs. Many attorneys add these to their flat fee quotes.

Even in situations in which lawyers charge an hourly rate, there are ways to manage and control your legal costs. Always insist on a detailed billing statement, in which the law firm describes each hour of work performed by each attorney in the firm assigned to the matter. This will force the law firm to review its time sheets carefully to avoid duplication of effort or excessive billing by junior attorneys. Also, the more preparation you can do yourself, the easier, and therefore less costly, the lawyer's work will be. Lawyers hate spending countless hours in routine preparation, assembly of documents, file research, and other tasks that could just as easily be performed by your staff, and at a much lower cost.

Finally, beware of contract provisions such as indemnification clauses that require one party to a contract to pay the legal costs of defending the other party against certain lawsuits. Unless capped or otherwise qualified, these can be blank check provisions creating a virtually unlimited liability for the indemnifying party. There is no guarantee that you will be able to recover your legal fees and expenses, even if ultimately you win a lawsuit. The awarding of legal fees in most states is entirely subject to the discretion of the presiding judge. In practice, most judges will award legal fees to the winner only if both parties had already agreed to that outcome (this is called an English Rule clause, because that's the way things are done as a matter of course in the United Kingdom) or if the lawsuit is won by the defendant and is considered by the judge to have been frivolous and a waste of the court's time.

lender A business partner, such as a bank, that lends money secured by an asset. Emphasize *partner*. (*See also* banker.)

I/L

letter of intent A statement of the principal terms of a business transaction designed to advance the transaction without committing either party to a contract. (*See also* due diligence.)

Most important business transactions, such as investments or strategic acquisitions, occur in three distinct stages:

■ During the first stage, the business people meet and work out the business and economic aspects of the transaction, the deal points that must be achieved for the transaction to proceed.

■ During the second stage, the business people of one party and their legal, tax and financial advisers perform due diligence on the other party to make sure that it is everything it was promised to be.

■ During the third and final stage, the lawyers and accountants for the parties draft and negotiate definitive legal documents that bind the parties to the transaction once the documents are signed and money changes hands.

At the end of the first stage, the parties often sign a short document known variously as a letter of intent, a term sheet, or a memorandum of understanding. This document is a short (usually two to three pages) letter, listing the important business points of the transaction. For example, a letter of intent for an investment transaction, where a venture capital firm is purchasing stock in a closely held corporation, may contain the following terms:

■ the amount of the investment

■ the percentage of the company's outstanding stock that the investor will receive

■ any special rights the investor will receive that are not enjoyed by shareholders generally (for example, the right to elect one member of the company's board of directors)

■ the investors' right to participate in any future public offering of the company's stock

A letter of intent does not legally bind the parties to proceed with the transaction. Nonetheless, your attorney should always review a letter of intent before you sign it. Lawyers who specialize in business transactions will be familiar with the types of matters that should be included in (and excluded from) a letter of intent, and can suggest additional business terms that should be covered in the letter before it is signed and the professionals start their clocks running.

leveraged buyout (LBO) The process of buying a company with short-term bank loans secured by the target company's own assets.

It's a neat trick, buying a company with collateral that you don't own yet. Obviously it's a risky arrangement, but where there's risk there's also the promise of big money. That's why public companies make the best targets for LBOs: Their shareholders can be bought with the promise of a bonus on top of the stock price. Being acquired in an LBO can feel like a win if you hold a lot of stock, but not if you're sentimental about the company. The buyers have big loans to repay, and they usually have plans to sell the company's choicest assets.

liability Being responsible for certain actions and behaviors.

license and license agreement A business relationship between two companies in which one company acquires the rights to use certain property (usually intellectual property) of the other. (*See also* indemnity and indemnification clause.)

A license is to intellectual property (patents, trademarks, copyrights, and computer software), what a lease is to real property (land, buildings, and office space). Like a lease, a license offers you the right to use certain property for a period of time in exchange for a periodic payment (called a license fee). You do not own the property and cannot sell it to a third party, although some licenses will grant you the right to sublicense the property, in the same way that a lease may permit you to sublease some or all of the rented space. If you fail to make payments on time or otherwise breach the license agreement, the company that owns the property (called the licensor) can take the property away from you and sue you in court for damages.

Depending on the nature of your business, you may agree to

L/L

TAKING LICENSE

Here are some important points for negotiation in a
license agreement:

- **License fee.** This fee may be paid up front in a single installment (called a paid-up license), or in several installments over a period of years. In the latter case, renewal terms should be negotiated.
- **Limitations.** The license may be limited to a particular geographic territory, to a limited number of personal computers, or to a limited number of locations.
- **Modifications and updates.** A provision can specify the user's right to future modifications, upgrades, or updates of the software or other intellectual property.
- **Infringement indemnity.** The owner of the intellectual property indemnifies the user against infringement claims brought by third parties.
- **Assignment and sublicense.** A provision can be added that either permits or prohibits assignment of the license or the granting of sublicenses.

license intellectual property from third parties. For example, a
manufacturing concern may license a patent from an inventor,
a distributor may license the right to use a manufacturer's
trademark or service mark in its advertising and promotional
materials, or a publisher may license a copyright from the
author of a book.

lien A legal claim on business or personal assets approved by the
court. Always check for liens before purchasing a business or signing
a deal with a potential partner.

life insurance A necessary evil for business owners about what happens to their families if they die.

> Life insurance is one of those things you hate to spe on, but if you don't you put those closest to you at risk. The amount of coverage you buy depends on how much your family or partner needs to keep going if they lose you and your future earnings. One formula used to compute the amount of life insurance to buy to cover a decade of lost earnings is to multiply by 8.5 your annual after-tax income. Term life insurance is cheap and offers pure insurance protection. Other forms of insurance, known as cash value policies, provide life insurance and function as an investment account. They usually cost about eight times as much as a term life policy because you are paying agent commissions and administrative fees, according to insurance industry experts.
>
> Try to deal with an independent insurance broker who represents many different insurance companies, rather than a person who only sells one kind of insurance. Tailor your coverage to your particular needs and pay those premiums on time.

LIFO (Last In, First Out method) A way to value inventory that assumes the last items to be purchased will be the first to be sold. You then compute the cost of the inventory based on the cost of the earliest purchases. (*See also* FIFO.)

limited liability company (LLC) A great way to limit your personal liability in business without all of the headaches of forming a corporation. (*See also* corporation; Subchapter S corporation.)

> Until the early 1990s, the only way for small business owners to limit their personal liability for business debts and obligations was to form a corporation. Corporations are complex and expensive, however, and were perceived as too cumbersome for small businesses that want to operate informally. The limited liability company, or LLC, was developed as an alternative to incorporation, to help most small business owners limit their liability for business activities without all of the headaches, expense, and complexity that go with forming and operating a corporation.

l/L

PROS AND CONS OF THE LLC

Pros:
- Owners enjoy the same limitation of their personal liability as stockholders in a corporation.
- LLCs are simple to operate, require little paperwork, and give you maximum flexibility in structuring the business any way you wish.
- Except in a few states, start-up costs are low.
- There is no double taxation of LLC income.

Cons:
- Because LLCs are taxed like partnerships, LLC members are required to pay federal and state income taxes on a LLC's net income, even though the income was never distributed to them but retained by the LLC for business purposes.
- If an LLC has employees, there may be restrictions on the LLC's ability to deduct the costs of certain compensation and employee benefit schemes.
- It may be difficult for an existing business to convert into an LLC.

The LLC provides its owners with limitation of their personal liability for business debts and liabilities—the same as with a corporation. So if an LLC is sued by anyone, only the assets that the LLC owners (called members) contribute to the LLC are at risk. The owners' personal assets are safe. Like a corporation, however, the owners of an LLC must make sure that suppliers, customers, and others who do business with the LLC know that they are doing business with an LLC and not with the owners as individual proprietors.

In most states, forming an LLC is much less expensive than forming a corporation. You can expect to pay between $200 and $800 in legal and filing fees, as opposed to the thousands of dollars it will cost to form a corporation in most states. In a few states (notably New York), however, you may be required to publish a legal notice of the LLC's formation in several local newspapers, and the publication fees may actually make an LLC more expensive.

More importantly, LLCs in most states are easy and inexpensive to operate. There are few paperwork requirements and no legal limitations on who can and cannot be an owner, as is the case with Subchapter S corporations. With an LLC, you and your business partners can operate as informally as if you were a partnership. If you are doing business overseas, you can set up your LLC so that it resembles the overseas companies you do business with (for example, you can give yourself the same management titles as your overseas counterparts use). You can even issue shares of stock (called membership interests) to the LLC owners so that your business more closely resembles a corporation.

An LLC's income is taxed in almost exactly the same way as a partnership's, in that profits and losses flow through to the LLC members in exactly the same way as partnership profits and losses flow through to the partners. There are, however, some differences between the tax treatment of partnerships and LLCs, particularly in the area of employee compensation and benefits. You may (but very few LLCs do) elect to have your LLC taxed as a corporation by filing IRS Form 8832 with your regional IRS office. The form is available as a free download from the IRS website at **www.irs.gov**.

Like a partnership, an LLC with more than one owner reports its annual income on IRS Form 1065 but is not required to pay taxes as a legal entity. If an LLC has only one member, the member files Schedule C on his or her personal tax return each year. Like a partnership, an LLC must use the calendar year; using a different fiscal year end will require IRS approval.

An LLC may be converted into a corporation at any time by a relatively simple procedure, but it is difficult for a corporation or Subchapter S corporation to convert into a LLC. For that reason, many small businesses start out life as a LLC and then convert into a corporation once the success of the business model has been proven.

The biggest disadvantage of an LLC is its perception in the business community as a "mom and pop" business. If you are operating a small retail or service business that services a local or regional market, is run by a stable team of family members and personal friends, and is not expected to grow big anytime soon, the LLC in most states will be the ideal way to organize the business, at least in the beginning. A fast growing, high-technology business that serves a national or worldwide market, that is run by a growing and ever-changing management team, and that expects to seek outside capital within the first two to three years of operation is better advised to organize as a corporation. Corporations are generally taken more seriously than LLCs by the venture capital community and other institutional investors.

limited liability partnership (LLP) A form of partnership, used mostly by professional service firms, that ensures some degree of limited liability for all partners. (*See also* limited liability company.)

A growing number of states are allowing partnerships—particularly those engaged in rendering professional services—

PROS AND CONS OF THE LLP

Pros:

- LLPs are easy and inexpensive to form.
- In some states, LLPs may be the only way allowed for professionals to limit their liability for the acts and omissions of their partners.
- LLPs are not taxable entities. All income, gain, profit, and loss passes through directly to each LLP partner, who reports his or her pro rata share on Form 1040 each year.
- An existing professional partnership that converts into a LLP can continue to use its existing partnership agreement, with only slight changes.
- Using an LLP permits a professional practice to open branches in other states with a minimum of accounting and legal hassle.

L/l

to provide some measure of limited liability to all of their members. In a limited liability partnership, each partner enjoys limited liability (i.e., liability is limited only to the amounts contributed to the partnership) for the acts or omissions of the other partners, but remains personally liable for his own acts or omissions. In addition, in some states, partners in an LLP enjoy limited liability for contracts which the LLP signs (such as a lease of office space).

The LLP was created at the behest of certain large professional service firms that operate branches in several states. Because certain states prohibit professionals—such as doctors, lawyers, engineers, and architects, from incorporating—these firms were required to maintain separate organizations in different states. In State A they would be a corporation, in State B a partnership, in State C a limited liability company, and so forth, with all of the attendant accounting and legal headaches. The LLP allows professional service firms to grant their partners some measure of limited liability without having to incorporate within the meaning of

Cons:
■   An LLP partner who acts negligently in a state that does not recognize the LLP may subject his or her partners to personal liability for his or her negligence.
■   Some states provide that only professional service firms can use the LLP vehicle.
■   Some states refuse to limit the liability of LLP partners in breach of contract cases where the contract was signed on behalf of the LLP.
■   Some states limit the liability of LLP partners in breach of contract cases to each partner's pro rata share of the contract damages, an amount that may be substantially greater than the partner's total contributions to the partnership. For example, a partner who contributes $1,000 for a 10 percent interest in an LLP may be socked a year later with 10 percent of a $1 million damage award.

those state laws that prohibit professionals from incorporating.

An LLP is formed by filing an application or registration form with a state government agency (usually the secretary of state's office), and will be required to file annual or biennial reports to the state in order to continue in existence. These forms may require the LLP to list the names and addresses of all partners as of a certain state.

Except for professional service firms, the LLP has not been a popular vehicle for organizing small businesses in most states, which continue to prefer the limited liability company.

line of credit An unsecured loan that operates like a checking account. You use what you need and try to repay it as fast as you can to keep your credit solid and the lender happy.

Savvy business owners should apply for a commercial line of credit as soon as they begin experiencing steady cash flow. A line of credit, even one of a few thousand dollars, can help you weather the lean times between payments from clients and customers. Most banks offer credit lines but usually charge a steep application fee of several hundred dollars. I would recommend joining Costco as an executive level member just so you can apply for a preferred, low-interest line of credit from Key Bank (**www.costco.com**).

You will have to personally guarantee the line of credit even if you are incorporated, so start with a small amount. Use your credit line only for real emergencies. In many cases, the rate is much lower than a credit card, so you might use the line to pay off a high-interest credit card. Paying off the credit line balance is the first step to establishing good credit. In many cases, your limit will be increased immediately after you pay off the balance as a reward for prompt and full payment.

liquidity The amount of cash readily available to your company by selling its assets.

loss leader A product or service that attracts new business, but costs you money. Often a low-cost, impulse item displayed in the front of a retail store.

management buyout (MBO) A process in which the managers of a company raise or borrow funds to buy the controlling interest. This is often used to sell a division of a bigger company to a group of loyal employees.

manufacturing extension partnership (MEP) A federal program that provides technical assistance and consulting services to small manufacturers. (*See also* starting a business.)

MEP IS A NATIONAL NETWORK of about 400 nonprofit centers organized in 1986 by the National Institute for Standards and Technology. The program has at least one center in every state and territory, and helps more than 20,000 small manufacturing businesses a year. Most of these businesses have fifty or fewer employees. Eligibility for participation in Manufacturing Extension Partnership varies by region. You can check to see if you're eligible in your region by contacting MEP at 800-637-4634 or visiting their website at **www.nist.gov**.

Kevin Carr, director of MEP, says it typically helps business owners adopt the best manufacturing business practices to minimize costs. It also promotes new and better methods to mass-produce products. "Business owners usually call a center when they have

HIGH TECH AND LOW

Melissa Trombley took a recipe she had for all-natural dog biscuits and launched The Barking Bakers Inc. in Syracuse, New York. "I rented some space in a commercial bakery and started churning out 1,300 biscuits a day," she says. She went to MEP center, Technology Development Organization in Syracuse, New York, when she needed more production capability. "I didn't want to buy the equipment to produce a huge amount of biscuits," said Trombley. "So they helped me find a good alternative in outsourcing." Trombley now relies on workers managed by the Association of Retarded Citizens to help her bake biscuits in their commercial kitchen.

Carol Latham started a business manufacturing thermally conductive adhesives and encapsulants that prevent electronics like computers from overheating. "I think it's pretty unusual for women to be in the manufacturing world, but I don't think about it," said Latham, president of Thermagon, based in Cleveland, Ohio. Latham began developing the products in 1989 after she left a job at British Petroleum. "At BP, I was working on devices that had heat problems," said Latham. "That's when I realized heat was a big problem for electronics." After three years of working on her own, Latham hired two employees and then took the products to the market. She now employs 105 people and has annual revenues approaching $20 million. With MEP's help, Latham received help from the Great Lakes Manufacturing Technology Center when she needed to set up a new computer system.

a problem with quality or overall output," says Carr. "We go in and look for the bottlenecks in their process and see where things could be streamlined." There is no fee for the initial assessment, but if the company decides to go further with the recommendations, there is a consulting fee based on the specific project.

markdowns Discounts on merchandise that retailers need to move out of their stores in order to bring in cash.

marketing A strategy designed to let current and potential customers know what you have to sell and why they should buy it from your company. (*See also* advertising; advertising specialties; sales force.)

Many business people are confused about how marketing differs from advertising and public relations. Advertising is purchased time or space that you completely control because you've paid for it. Public relations is based on sending information to reporters and producers in hope that they will write or produce a story about your company. If they do, you benefit from what is called third-party endorsement. Any positive, accurate television segment, magazine story, or newspaper story about your company is priceless in terms of raising awareness and shining a spotlight on you and your products.

Marketing, however, is the overarching plan you create and implement to let people know what you have to sell and, more importantly, why they should by it from your firm. A solid marketing program relies on a combination of advertising and public relations. It may also include a variety of initiatives ranging from promotional items with your logo to passing out free samples of food or drink in a supermarket (in-store promotion), to sponsoring a local Little League team by providing jerseys with your company's name emblazoned across the back.

Through the years, we've used acrylic fortune cookie key chains, laminated bookmarks, postcards, posters, flyers, e-mail newsletters, and video segments to promote my books, conferences, and television projects. We've put promotional logos on T-shirts, sweatshirts, and button-down collar shirts. We've produced radio commercials and promotional loops to play at trade shows. The marketing plan you develop has to be highly targeted and resonate with your customers and clients. Whether you go upscale, downscale, or mass depends on your specific marketing goals. To get started, read any of Jay Conrad Levinson's guerrilla marketing books. He's written dozens, and they are good places to start if you can't afford professional marketing help.

marketing, multilevel A means of distributing and selling products through a casual sales force paid by commission.

Because managers are usually paid a commission on the sales of their subordinates, multilevel marketing is open to abuse when low-level salespeople are recruited willy-nilly. But done properly, multilevel marketing is a proven means of tapping the latent energy of home-based entrepreneurs.

Case in point: Tastefully Simple. This fast-growing company sells gourmet foods at home parties and was founded in 1995 by Jill Blashack of Alexandria, Minnesota. Blashack, who loves food but hates to cook, based her business on the idea "small indulgences for busy lives."

She researches an ever-changing line of party foods that require no more than one or two extra ingredients to prepare. Classic Beer Bread requires a can of beer or soda; best-seller Nana's Apple Cake needs chopped apples and eggs; Simply Salsa is mixed up with chopped fresh or canned tomatoes. Prices range from $4.95 for Belgian Truffle Brownie mix to $36.95 for a large gift pack (tastefullysimple.com, 320-763-0695).

Blashack pays home-based reps about 10 percent of gross sales. A rep hosts a sales party at home, or in someone else's home, and earns about $30 on $300 worth of food. The rep pays about $200 for a training kit, which includes instructional videotape, catalogues, and samples.

Between 1998 and 2000 sales nearly tripled, from $1.4 million to $4 million. In October, 2000, *Inc.* magazine ranked Tastefully Simple the fortieth fastest-growing privately held company in America. The company buys back all unsold food, less a 20 percent restocking fee, offers a money-back guarantee on every product, and allows reps to sell anywhere: at trade shows, expos, and even to corporate accounts as gifts. Because the inventory goes to the home party, buyers take home what they have tasted and purchased, so there is no waiting, shipping fees, or delivery delays.

"I knew if this was popular in a town of 8,000 people in upstate Minnesota, it would sell anywhere in the United States," said Blashack, who stored her inventory in the trunk of her Pontiac when she was on the party circuit.

She still relies on word-of-mouth to attract new consultants because she believes "these type of businesses fail if they grow too fast."

markup The profit margin you build in to every sale price. Most retailers double the price they paid for an item to determine the retail price. This allows them to discount the price if the merchandise doesn't sell.

meeting A waste of time until it's your turn to speak.

The fewer meetings you schedule or attend, the more productive your business life will be. Before you set up a meeting, think carefully about whether you can accomplish the same goals with a conference call, group e-mail, memo, or after-hours voice mail message. The most effective meetings have a very narrow purpose and should be focused on making a group decision. Meeting to discuss whether or not to do something is usually a waste of time. Meeting to decide whom to hire, whom to fire, or with whom to form a strategic alliance make sense.

If you have to call a meeting, limit the attendees to the absolute minimum number of people. Send out an agenda ahead of time and specify who speaks when and how much time they have. State the purpose of the meeting and what you expect to accomplish. If background materials are required, send them out a day or two in advance and ask people to read them before they gather to save time. Someone should take notes and verify who is doing what to move the project along.

Setting a meeting right before lunchtime is a good way to speed things up. Insist on promptness and start without latecomers to show respect for people who showed up on time. Don't set meetings for late Friday afternoons unless you deliberately want to make decisions by yourself.

mentor A person who helps another to solve problems, make connections, and live up to his or her full potential. (*See also* Service Corps of Retired Executives.)

Many successful entrepreneurs credit their success to the help and support of personal mentors. Being able to set your ego aside and ask for help is essential to good decision making. I've turned to many mentors through the years, beginning with my college law and media professor, who encouraged me to enter a student writing competition that I won, to a high-level government official who encouraged me to stick with my business during rough times.

No matter what you do or who you are, you should have a least one mentor in your life. Twenty-four years ago, when she was fourteen, Lena Fafard's fate seemed sealed. The eighth-grader rarely attended school and hung out with a dangerous crowd in Pasadena, California. If they met her today, none of her old friends would believe she was the same person they knew then. In the late 1990s, Fafard and her two partners successfully sold their recruiting and employment agency, one of the top ten in Los Angeles, with revenues of $4.5 million.

Fafard attributes her personal achievements to having a series of mentors who steered her in the right direction and drastically changed her life. Mentoring is widely supported and promoted by nonprofit organizations, social service programs, and corporations. "It is the first time in history that we are preparing a generation of girls to start businesses," said Joline Godfrey, CEO of Independent Means Inc., a firm that provides economic empowerment and educational programs for young women, based in Santa Barbara, California. Godfrey's company offers camp programs that teach young women business skills and works with the Girls Scouts of America and corporate clients to provide financial education skills.

Mentoring has also created new consulting opportunities, such as personal coaching and mentors-for-hire. Roz Relin, president of Dial-A-Mentor in New York City, was working as a communications, marketing, and public relations consultant when she realized she was also providing clients with strategic career and life planning advice. "What I bring to my clients is not my success, but what I've done wrong, what I've learned from my mistakes," said Relin, who uses her expertise in building client relationships and customer service to mentor small business owners.

Relin has been mentoring Ellen Sills-Levy since 1983. Sills-Levy, founder, president, and CEO of Strategic Surveys International in Manhattan, said she considers the fees she pays Relin to be "not an expense, but a huge investment in growth."

"I always call her for advice on business and personal matters," said Sills-Levy, whose firm provides competitive intelligence and market research for clients. She said the most important thing a mentor offers is a different perspective on life and business.

Whereas Sills-Levy pays for help, Fafard's first life-changing mentor belonged to the Big Sisters of Pasadena. She said her volunteer Big Sister showed her the possibility of a better life she never knew existed. "They kind of slapped me in the face and said make changes, or you are going to wind up dead," Fafard recalls.

At sixteen, she enrolled in Job Corps, a federal program in Phoenix, Arizona, modeled on military boot camp. There, Fafard earned her high school degree in eleven months and received basic clerical and business training. A chance meeting back in Los Angeles led to a job as a salesperson and personal assistant to Nancy Lee, owner of Mother Goose Distributors, whose family owned Lee's Press-On Nails.

Fafard used her experience with Lee to enter the executive recruiting and personnel field, where she flourished. "People need to know that mentoring does work," says Fafard.

Although not billed as a mentoring program, the Service Corps of Retired Executives (SCORE) provides small business owners with free expert consulting, while the SBA also provides a mentoring program for women entrepreneurs. Contact SCORE through your local SBA office or visit its website: **score.org**.

merchandising The creative display of goods in windows, on counters, and on shelves with the sole purpose of encouraging shoppers to buy. (*See also* point of sale.)

Retailers live and die on the success of their merchandising skills. They spend thousands of dollars hiring window dressers and designers who must figure out a way to attract the eyes of shoppers. Once inside the store, the merchandise must be displayed in a way that is appealing, easy to peruse, and easy to try on or examine. Your merchandising strategy depends on what you are selling, whether it is clothing or Lladro collectibles. The display cases, lighting, aisle space, counters, and shelving are critical to merchandising success.

Years of sales experience are reviewed to determine what works and what doesn't in a cosmetics store. Estée Lauder, for example, hires interior architect Debra Orlando to design stores around the world. The heights of the counters, shelves, storage cupboards, and cash registers are fairly standardized from store to store. But the height of the mirrors, stools, and display racks are carefully calculated in each individual store design.

If you are a novice retailer, this is one area where you should pay for professional help. You only get one chance to make a positive first impression on each customer who walks into your store.

mergers and acquisitions (M&A) How small businesses change hands in hope of getting bigger and better. (*See also* buying a company; exit strategy; selling a business.)

No matter how a small business is organized, it can be bought, sold, or merged into another company at any time. Generally, there are three ways for a small business to be bought or sold:

1. The business may be merged or consolidated into another business.

2. The business owners may sell their ownership interests (stock in a corporation, partnership interests in a partnership, or membership interests in a limited liability company) to another person.

3. The business may sell all or substantially all of its assets to another person.

The method chosen will depend on the tax consequences to the buyer and seller.

In a merger, two or more businesses essentially combine their balance sheets and income statements, becoming one company in the process. The owners of the business that is to be merged out of existence (called the merging company) swap their ownership interests in the merging company for ownership interests having an equal value in the company that survives the merger (called the merged company). Generally, a merger is a tax-free transaction, and the selling business owners will not be required to report or pay taxes as the result of the merger. In most states, a merger will require a supermajority vote of two-thirds or more of the owners of each company (the merging and the merged).

In a stock sale, the owners of a business sell their ownership interests to another company, either for cash or for ownership interests in the buying company. If the selling business owners receive only ownership interests in the buying company, they will not be required to report or pay taxes. If the selling business owners receive cash or property (other than ownership interests in the buying company) from the buying company, they will have to report and pay capital gains tax on the difference between the value of the ownership interest they sold and the value of the cash or property they received in return.

In an asset sale, a small business sells all or substantially all of its assets to another person, either for cash or for ownership interests in the buying company. If the selling company receives only stock or securities of the buying company, the transaction will be tax free to the seller. If the selling company receives cash or property (other than ownership interests in the buying company) from the buying company, it will have to report and pay capital gains tax on the difference between the value of the assets sold and the value of the cash or property it received in return. In addition, if the selling company dissolves or liquidates shortly after selling off its assets, the selling company's owners may have to pay capital gains tax on the amount they each receive in the liquidation process.

The seller and buyer in an asset sale may be required to report the transaction to the Internal Revenue Service on IRS Form 8594. The form is available with instructions as a free download from the IRS website at **www.irs.gov**.

In a merger or stock sale, the buyer acquires the entire balance sheet of the acquired company—both assets and liabilities. So if there are any hidden liabilities that are unknown to the selling business owners, the buyer will have to deal with them when they

BEFORE YOU BUY

A small business for sale may have some hidden costs. The following are some things you should do to make sure you know what you're getting when considering a merger or acquisition:

■ Find out how long the business has been on the market and why the owner wants to sell.

■ Learn the neighborhood buzz. A business owner who is a little too eager to sell may know something you don't know (like a major competitor is moving in down the street).

■ Review the seller's federal and state tax returns, along with the internal books and records of the business.

■ Spend some time in the business to see if cash receipts actually match what is reported on the seller's books.

■ Ask the state tax authorities for a tax clearance letter relieving you of any liability for sales, use, and payroll taxes that accrue before the business changes hands.

■ Make sure the seller is willing to indemnify you for any surprises that may crop up after the business changes hands and that he or she will be around to help should you become liable for things that happened before you bought the business.

■ Make sure that any important contracts necessary to run the business (such as an office lease or an exclusive agreement with a key customer) do not expire or terminate once the business changes hands.

arise. In contrast, the buyer in an asset sale acquires only those liabilities he or she wishes to assume. So if there are any hidden liabilities that are unknown to the selling business, the seller will have to deal with them when they arise. Because of this, almost all purchases and sales of small businesses are asset sales.

No matter how the merger or acquisition takes place, certain tax liabilities (such as those for sales, use, and payroll taxes) may survive a merger or acquisition and come back to haunt the buyer of the business at a later time. In many states, the buyer(s) may be personally liable for these taxes, even if a corporation or limited liability company makes the acquisition.

microloan A small loan offered to novice entrepreneurs with poor credit to enable them to start a small business. (*See also* capital, raising; Small Business Administration.)

Many microlending programs are managed by economic development or nonprofit associations and require borrowers to sign up for training or educational programs.

The concept of making small loans to borrowers in a group with their peers took hold initially in Third World countries like Bangladesh. In the past fifteen years, the practice has been gaining support in the United States. The Aspen Institute based in Washington, D.C., estimates that there are about 2 million low-income entrepreneurs who could benefit from a microloan. "There are sectors of the world awash in money and venture capital," said Bill Edwards, executive director of the Association for Enterprise Opportunity (AEO) in Arlington, Virginia. "But, if you are a woman with a minimum wage job who has been catering birthday parties for supplemental income, the world is not awash in capital for you." AEO is a trade association representing about 430 organizations that make microloans. AEO defines a microloan as being under $25,000. The average microloan is $12,000 and made to companies with fewer than five employees.

In 1997, the 283 programs tracked by the Aspen Institute's microenterprise directory served 57,125 individuals, lending about $33 million to microentrepreneurs. The average loan amount was $10,000. Maine tops the list of states with the most microloans outstanding. Arkansas, New York, North Carolina, Minnesota, California, Florida, Massachusetts, Illinois, and Ohio complete the top ten list, according to the Aspen Institute.

There are hundreds of microloan programs operating in the United States, some offered through government agencies like

m/M

the Small Business Administration, others operated by nonprofit groups and private foundations. The challenge for U.S. microlenders is that while a $500 loan makes a huge difference in El Salvador, it hardly helps someone start a business in El Paso, Texas. John Hatch, founder of the Foundation for International Community Assistance (FINCA International) said U.S. entrepreneurs require more cash and more sophisticated business skills to launch a successful business. "In the Third World, you don't have the regulations we have here in the U.S.," said Hatch. "A woman with $50 can move a table out on the sidewalk, buy vegetables, and get into business right away."

FINCA has made about 55 loans to 150 U.S. borrowers. One success story is Beulah Williams, owner of B.B. Designs in Olney, Maryland, a suburb of Washington, D.C. In 1994, Williams borrowed $500 from FINCA and used the money to buy a professional sewing machine. Williams sews choir robes, makes custom clothing, and does alterations in her home. "When I went to the bank, I couldn't get a credit card," says Williams "I didn't have bad credit, I just didn't have any credit at all."

Across the country in the San Francisco suburb of Marin County, about a dozen women meet weekly at Tamalpais Bank to learn basic business skills. At the end of the fifteen-week program, sponsored by Community Action Marin, they can apply for microloans. Linnea Kilgren makes collectible porcelain dolls; Andrea Harris runs Little Darlings Child Care in her San Rafael apartment; and Susan Price charges clients $30 an hour to run errands and organize their lives. "Before I started this class, I wasn't thinking big," said Harris, a single mother of two. "I was just a day care provider. Now, I'm the owner of small business."

Military Spouse Entrepreneurial Readiness Program

A program designed to help military spouses start new businesses. (*See also* starting a business.)

The wife of a U.S. Navy anti-submarine expert, Rhonda Mollenkopf grew accustomed to moving every few years, but became tired of constantly looking for a new job. "Every time we would move, I would have to start out fresh," says Mollenkopf.

Finally she started her own home-based business with the help of the Military Spouse Entrepreneurial Readiness Program (MSERP), a pilot program run jointly by the Department of Defense and the Small Business Administration's Office of Women's Business Ownership. The program offers classes and counseling on starting a business.

"The number one [business] issue for military spouses is portability," said Molly Haley, program director of MSERP in Norfolk, Virginia. (The program also has an office in San Diego.) After Mollenkopf enrolled in the course, she founded Halcyon Hills Studios, a Chesapeake, Virginia, company that makes prairie lamps inspired by Frank Lloyd Wright's designs. Mollenkopf sells the lamps through her website: **www.prairielamps.com**.

"The class I took made me feel more bold," says Christine Spano, founder of Horztails in Virginia Beach, Virginia. Spano makes and sells hand-crafted saddle pads, horse quilts, horseshoe racks, and other horse-motif gifts for horse lovers. Spano, whose husband is a Navy engineer, says the program gave her the skills to build up local business at craft fairs and trade shows. "Before the class, I couldn't walk up to somebody and speak to people at crafts shows. It taught me not to be afraid."

minority-owned business An enterprise eligible for preferred standing in the award of certain contracts and financing. (*See also* certification.)

mission statement A written, memorable sentence or short paragraph that summarizes the purpose of your business. The statement itself forms the basis for all decisions made about how to operate the company.

Business owners pay consultants and facilitators lots of money to help them come up with a mission statement. It's not easy. I participated—along with fifty other people—in drafting one for a professional association I'm involved with and it was a very painful, head-banging process because too many cooks do spoil the planning process.

Your mission statement doesn't have to be prize-winning poetry, but it should clearly reflect what your business is all about. Disney's mission statement is "To make people happy." Boeing's is "To push the leading edge of aviation, taking on huge challenges doing what others cannot do."

It's best to recruit a few key employees to help you craft your statement. Spend some time thinking, discussing, and writing down ideas. Focus on the solutions you provide to customers as a way to get started. When you come up with the statement, post it on company bulletin boards and include it in the employee manual and other printed materials you use to promote the company.

morale, employee The way your employees feel about working for you and your company.

Poor morale erodes the foundation of your business. If your employees are unhappy day after day, it will affect their productivity and, ultimately, your profitability. I'm not saying everyone has to whistle while they work, but people should feel appreciated, fairly compensated, and be told that their efforts make a difference. Corny "employee of the month" programs with plaques and special parking spaces aren't as effective as a sincere "thank you" and a company culture based on expressing appreciation.

When someone does something great, tell them right away. Don't wait until the end of the year performance review. Send notes or e-mail messages with quick feedback, even if it's not entirely positive. Just feeling like your boss is paying attention to what you are doing every day can boost employee's morale.

naming your company A nerve-wracking process that can help or hurt your financial success.

G EORGE JOHNSON, founder of COSMI Corp., a value-priced software maker in Rancho Dominguez, California, said some of the most successful business names have six letters that spell nothing, such as Exxon, Xerox, and Compaq. While big companies can afford to pay consultants millions of dollars for making up names like Lucent and Accenture, most small companies have to rely on family and friends to do the work.

When I left my job at the *Los Angeles Times* to form my own communications company, I called it The Applegate Group. At first, the group was comprised of just my cat and me. My husband, Joe, came up with our best business name, SBTV, which stands for small business TV. The name of the streaming video network we launched in 2000 told viewers exactly what they would see when they logged on to our free multimedia website.

Your business name should be memorable, clever, and not too cute. Through the years, I've conducted contests to find the best and worst small business names in America. Some of my favorites were a massage therapy center in Burbank, California, called Nice to Be Kneaded and a clinic in White River

Junction, Vermont, named Twin Rivers Urology.

If you are just starting out, make a list of names you like and run them by a group of friends and business associates. You might also organize an informal naming party. Ask four or five smart, creative people to give you an hour of their time. Tell them what you plan to do at your business and ask them to brainstorm for a while. A few heads are better than one, and you might end up with a great name.

net lease Sometimes called a *closed-end lease,* a lease in which the tenant agrees to pay all expenses which are normally associated with ownership, such as utilities, repairs, insurance, and taxes. (*See also* lease.)

net profit The money left over when you have paid all the expenses associated with producing your products or services. (*See also* pricing strategy.)

Net profit is what really counts when you are measuring business success. It is the true bottom line, what's left in your business bank account after you have provided the products or services you've sold to customers and clients. Every cost associated with delivering the product, from inception to shipping, must be accounted for in your net profit calculation. What you charge for your products depends on the industry norms, but generally you should be building in a 30 to 40 percent profit margin to provide a cushion for unexpected increases in raw materials, delays, or price increases.

networking Making important connections with other business people who can help you meet new people, generate new business, and keep an eye on your competition.

Going to the local chamber of commerce mixer to catch up with fellow business owners used to be the extent of networking. Now, smart business people have a clear networking strategy. The meetings and conferences they attend are carefully chosen based on the people they expect to meet. One attractive, newly licensed real estate broker I know volunteered to work the registration desk at several benefit galas, just so she could pin carnations on some of

N/n

New York's richest men. The contacts she made by passing out place cards and pinning flowers served as the foundation for her real estate business.

A few times a year, I invest in a ticket to a fund-raiser or professional meeting just so I can meet the industry leaders I need to know. You can't be too pushy or aggressive in a social situation, but you can introduce yourself, mention what you have to offer, and ask the person if you can follow up with a phone call or e-mail.

Making it known that you are open to making introductions to other people is a great way to build your own network. People know I know lots of people through my work as a producer and journalist. So, I'm usually happy to make a call or an introduction if it opens a door or two. This creates enormous goodwill and pays off when I need someone to make an introduction for me.

noncompete agreement A document by which one party agrees that he will not work for, or deal with, a competitor of the other party. (*See also* hiring; interference with contract; nondisclosure agreement.)

How would you feel if one day your key employee—the one who knows all of your sensitive, confidential information quit on short notice and took a job with your biggest competitor? Guaranteed, you would not be happy about it.

Yet unless you have a written noncompete agreement with the employee, you may not be able to prevent such a thing from happening. While most states have laws that prevent employees from stealing their employer's trade secrets, this term is defined very narrowly by the courts and may not protect your company against leaks of valuable information.

In a few states, most notably California, noncompete agreements with employees are illegal if they extend beyond the term of employment. In most states, however, a noncompete agreement with an employee may be enforceable if it is reasonable in scope, in geography, and in time—in other words, if it doesn't deny the employee the right to earn a living. An agreement stating that "you will not work as a typesetter anywhere in the world for five years after your employment here is terminated" probably will not be enforced. An agreement stating that "you will not

n/N

Companies X, Y, and Z in an executive capacity for one
your employment is terminated," or that "you will not
ny of our direct competitors within a radius of twenty-
or one year after your employment is terminated," both
stand a good chance of being enforced.

Generally, the courts are hostile to noncompete agreements,
especially those involving employees. They may, however, be used
as a threat to keep an otherwise disgruntled employee honest. A
better way to protect your company is to require your employees
to sign confidentiality agreements in which they agree to keep all
information learned during their employment strictly confidential.
You can also have them sign nonsolicitation agreements in which
they agree not to contact customers, suppliers, employees, and
other key relationships for a period of time after their employment
is terminated for any reason. The courts are much friendlier to
these agreements, as they do not interfere with the employee's
freedom to seek work, and you generally can protect your sensitive
information for longer periods of time than you can with noncompete agreements.

nondisclosure agreement (NDA) A document by which one
person agrees to keep strictly confidential another's proprietary information and trade secrets. (*See also* confidentiality agreement; interference with contract; noncompete agreement.)

Generally, the law prohibits you from improperly disclosing or
using the trade secrets of another person. The term *trade secret* is
narrowly defined, however, and may not protect you from disclosure of all of the information you consider proprietary to your
business. For example, while the secret formula for your hot new
energy beverage would almost certainly be considered a trade
secret, your Rolodex card with the name of the key contact person at your best customer and her favorite brand of single malt
Scotch probably would not.

If employees, customers, or others have regular access to your
proprietary and confidential information, the only way to protect
against disclosure is to require them, prior to disclosure, to sign a
nondisclosure agreement, or NDA.

We sign NDAs all the time before we meet with prospective clients and sponsors. They are often required if you are looking at investing in another company or dealing with outside investors looking at your firm. Whereas most venture capitalists usually refuse to sign NDAs, angel investors are often more open to signing such documents. Many contain restrictions that affect future investments or activities. For example, it may preclude the investor from investing in similar companies or similar industries.

Timing is important. If you have to sign an NDA, push for it to expire as soon as possible. And, more importantly, if you decline to make an investment, be sure the NDA is terminated when the discussions end.

Angel investors tell me if you really want to take a look at a deal involving proprietary technology, you may not be able to find out what's what without signing the NDA. That's the trade-off; sign the agreement and promise not to disclose what you're told, or don't sign it and possibly miss the greatest investment of your career.

An NDA can be a formal legal document or an informal letter, but should contain at least the following provisions:

- **A confidentiality clause** by which the person promises to keep all information disclosed in the course of your business relationship strictly confidential

- **A nondisclosure clause** by which the person promises not to disclose any of your confidential information to third parties.

- **A nonuse clause** by which the person promises not to use any of your confidential information for his own purposes, or otherwise to your detriment, in any way

- **An equitable relief clause** by which the person consents to your getting a court injunction or restraining order preventing him from making unauthorized disclosures if the need arises. Without this clause, you will have to prove to the court why an injunction is necessary, wasting valuable time in the process.

Most attorneys have several forms of NDAs, which they routinely use for their business clients, and you should not have to pay for more than two hours of an attorney's time to have an NDA prepared for your business.

n/N

Occupational Safety and Health Administration (OSHA)
A federal agency designed to provide standards for reducing or eliminating health and safety hazards in the workplace.

IN 2002, OSHA EMPLOYED about 1,200 inspectors to monitor and promote safety in the workplace. Since the agency was created in 1971, workplace fatalities have been cut in half, even while U.S. employment has doubled from 56 million to 111 million.

The federal Occupational Safety and Health Administration, or OSHA, was created in 1971 to provide standards to identify and eliminate health and safety hazards in the workplace. OSHA's directives are aimed primarily at private sector employers who bear the brunt of the responsibility of maintaining a safe working environment.

Virtually every type and size of private employer in the United States is subject to OSHA's requirements, including many classes of employers that are not subject to other federal laws. The term *employer* includes virtually all categories of endeavor. OSHA has been construed to apply to nonprofit and charitable organizations, professionals such as attorneys and doctors who employ at least one person, and, in many circumstances, independent contractors hired by an employer.

OSHA inspections and investigations are the areas of compliance that most concern employers. Understandably, employers fear that routine inspections will uncover workplace violations, the abatement of which will entail costly modifications and/or result in expensive litigation. There are four types of inspection, listed in order of decreasing urgency and priority:

- Catastrophe or fatality investigations
- Employee complaint investigations
- Target industry program investigations
- General inspections

Catastrophe or fatality investigations are OSHA's top priority. Under OSHA regulations, an employer must promptly report to the nearest OSHA office any employment-related fatality or any accident that results in the hospitalization of three or more employees. These reports must be made within eight hours of the accident's occurrence.

The second category of inspections covers those arising from employee complaints. Inspections are not limited to the matters being complained of, so it's a good idea to accompany the inspector yourself. Third, target industry program or TIP inspections are conducted in selected industries that have been determined to have high rates of injury. Last, general inspections are conducted as agency time and manpower permit and are based on the general frequency of reported injuries for various industrial classifications.

Penalties for violations of OSHA regulations are quite severe, up to $70,000 plus $7,000 for uncorrected violations. Criminal penalties include six months' jail time.

office manager A person who functions as the air traffic controller around your office; a skilled administrator worth his or her weight in gold for a busy company.

The best office manager we ever had was a young woman on her way to medical school who was working for a temp agency to earn money. She was computer-literate and had excellent phone skills and a brilliant mind for details. She handled all the logistics for a ten-city conference tour we produced, including the venue and travel arrangements, and shipping.

When you start your business and are wearing all the hats, you will reach the point where you will need an office manager to free you to focus on more important work. You might start with a part-time person, perhaps a retired executive secretary who is looking for a steady, half-time job. You might get lucky if you call a temp agency and ask them to send someone over. (The best thing about temps is that if they don't work out, they can be gone and replaced in a few hours.)

Remember, experience counts more than looks or personality when it comes to managing an office. You want someone who sees to all the details of day-to-day life, so you can focus on motivating and managing your employees, bringing in new business, and thinking about the future.

office romance The original desktop interface. (*See also* sexual harassment.)

An office romance provides good material for a sitcom, but in reality, it creates a big headache for you the owner and other employees. I experienced this firsthand when my husband, Joe, went out to the garage-turned-office to borrow some tape and came running back into the house, flustered.

"What's going on between Bob and Janice?" he asked me, eyes wide. (Names have been changed to protect the guilty.)

"What do you mean? They are working on a marketing project," I replied.

"The sexual tension out there is so strong you can feel it," he said.

I remember sitting there, dumbstruck. Sexual tension in my tiny company based in a remodeled garage in Sun Valley, California? I was afraid to go to the office after Joe's discovery, but I couldn't sit in the house all day. I spoke with them separately and when they admitted to having a relationship, I had to do something. Since Bob was a consultant and not my employee, I couldn't stop them from dating, but I could keep him out of the office. So, I started meeting with Bob outside my office. It was inconvenient because he lived far away, but we met in the

O/o

middle and worked in restaurants and hotel lobbies.

You can institute a no dating policy for your employees, but it's very tough to enforce it if people are attracted to each other. You have to be careful, too, when it comes to restricting behavior. You don't want to be accused of discriminating against one employee as compared to another. You can outline in writing a prohibition against a supervisor dating an employee, which is pretty standard in the work world. You can also discourage flirting in the office by setting the tone and speaking up if the atmosphere is getting too friendly or casual.

No matter what kind of business you operate, at some point you'll probably end up dealing with an office romance. Just don't let yourself fall in love with an employee, which could lead to sexual harassment charges, which are not to be taken lightly.

online talent agencies A way to recruit temporary and full-time workers via the Internet. (*See also* employee; independent contractor.)

Freelancers rarely have to knock on doors looking for work anymore. Online recruitment, a $100 million industry in 2001, is expected to grow to $1.7 billion by the end of 2003, according to analysts at Forrester Research. About 20 million of the 131 million workers in the U.S. civilian labor force have ditched their real jobs to work independently from home or in the field.

"More than anything, the advantage of using an agency is the speed," says Liza Ahearn, vice president of human resources for X;drive, based in Santa Monica, California. Ahearn said the company liked one freelance Web designer so much, it offered him a full-time job after only one day.

"When you need a freelancer, you usually needed them yesterday," said Leslie Berliant, general manager of Etalent Agency which places designers and artists in many dot-coms (**www.etalent agency.com**). Berliant says many small businesses make the mistake of posting job openings only on their company's website. "Unless freelancers have heard of your company, no one's going to find your ad," says Berliant.

Companies are willing to pay a premium for talent that has been prescreened, reference-checked, and tested on specific soft-

o/O

HIRING TIPS

Here are some timesaving (and headache-saving) tips for recruiting and hiring employees via an Internet talent agency:

- Before you call an agency or recruiter, list the technical skills and job experience you require for the project.
- Ask employees who will be working with the temporary employee what kind of skills they need help with.
- Determine the scope of the work you need done. Be as specific as possible.
- Determine how long you think the project will take.
- Ask the agency to provide a range of hourly costs so you can prepare a budget.
- Make a list of internal and external contacts the temporary worker will need to get the work done.
- Explain any company policies or rules that may affect their work.
- Make sure a staff person is available to welcome temporary workers, show them, around the office, and introduce them to colleagues.

ware skills before they show up for work. If they like the freelancer enough to hire them full-time, they pay the agency a finder's fee of 25 to 35 percent of the first year's salary.

Etalent's parent firm, Artisan, which has offices in Chicago and New York, was founded in 1987. Prior to launching its website, Etalent worked offline, using advertising, direct mail, and meetings to connect candidates with companies. "Our website is a great resource for us now, but in this business, especially at the high-end creative level, we still have to connect people one-on-one," says Berliant.

O/o

online training Internet-based instruction, usually in the use of business software programs.

Anyone who has waited on hold for live tech support will appreciate the advantages of online training. Thanks to the Internet, there are thousands of affordable courses available twenty-four hours a day, seven days a week.

Response from business people has been so strong that revenues from Web-based training is expected to reach $7 billion a year in 2002, according to International Data Corp., a respected research firm. And, online training industry experts say that about one-third of that money will be spent by small- and medium-size businesses.

Busy people can gain more experience with financial and accounting software programs, brush up on management skills, or better understand how to use their contact management database. Online training is extremely affordable; monthly subscriptions for one course begin at about $10. The annual subscription for most courses is about $100. Even the most complex course in HTML or other computer programming languages is available for less than $200 a year at many online training sites.

Online training has another subtle, but significant benefit: employees consider any kind of training to be a valuable benefit. Here are some websites worth checking out:

- OnLine Training Institute, **www.oltraining.com**
- Freeskills, **www.freeskills.com**

operating expenses *See* expenses.

option An alternative to buying something outright; often used to give employees the option to purchase company stock at a set price.

organization The art of keeping track of your papers, files, and other materials that you need to run your business.

Here's a scary thought: the average executive loses six weeks a year retrieving misplaced information from messy desks and missing files. If you pay yourself $75,000 a year, that wasted time adds up to more than $8,000, according to professional organizers.

"I also think people lose business on a regular basis based on what their offices look like," said Mary Lou Lundberg, owner of Chaos Cancelled, a Denver-based consulting firm. Lundberg says 80 percent of clutter is the result of disorganization, not a lack of space. And disorganization, whether it's a filing system gone haywire or office management procedures that have collapsed, is often the result of poor time management.

So, if you're embarrassed to invite clients to your office, it's time to deal with the mess. Vowing to clean up your office is as popular as swearing off fattening foods on New Year's Eve. But, like a too-strict diet, staying organized rarely lasts more than a week.

The key to successfully organizing your office, said Lundberg, is planning and scheduling time for organization and filing as diligently as you schedule meetings and appointments. "It always takes longer than you think, and the mess gets worse before it gets better, so when you see open time, plug organizational tasks into it," advises Lundberg, whose system begins with buying a weekly planner and writing everything down.

Lundberg says managing paperwork is the most daunting task. "The fear of letting go of paper is second to almost no other fear," said Lundberg. But, if you immediately record contact information in your address book or your contact management software program, you can toss those piles of business cards and documents.

"Eighty percent of paper files are never referenced again," said Lundberg, who offers these filing tips:

- Purge files at the end of every year.
- Retire current files as soon as possible, separating and retaining your tax and financial material.
- Use different color folders for different topics or subjects.

"You can be organized if you're serious about it," says organizational expert Barbara Hemphill, author of *Taming the Paper Tiger at Work* (Kiplinger, 1998) and *Taming the Paper Tiger at Home* (Kiplinger, 1998). Hemphill and Lundberg agree that no matter how computer illiterate you are, you must incorporate some kind of software into your life. "Three programs are essential," said Hemphill. "You must have a contact management pro-

THE HARDWORKING CALENDAR

Mary Lou Lundberg, owner of Denver-based consulting firm Chaos Cancelled, offers these tips for making sure that your planner or calendar is working to your advantage:

■ Write a stream of consciousness list of tasks that must be done for the year, including those things you personally want to accomplish.

■ Set aside time for planning; and, when planning, schedule time for organizing.

■ Plug organizing tasks into blocks of time between appointments.

■ Group similar tasks together in the same time slots.

gram, a financial management program, and a paper file management program."

She says being organized is "not about being a neatnik, but about finding the information you need."

outsourcing Obtaining labor or expertise outside the company in order to save money, improve operations, or reduce liability. (*See also* independent contractor.)

overhead The day-to-day costs involved in operating your business, including rent, utilities, payroll, marketing, telephones, advertising, cost of materials, manufacturing, packaging, shipping, and so on. (*See also* expenses; slash and burn.)

Overhead includes any recurring costs that you have to pay no matter how slow or busy things are around the office. Sharing space is one good way to reduce your overhead. Many business owners who outgrow their home office rent a spare office from another business owner or move into an executive suite or incubator to keep costs down. Executive suites are great if you want to work in a classy office building and need conference space and a professional receptionist. Don't try to hide the fact that you are sharing space and paying for the service. Your clients will appreciate that you want to work in a professional environment. If you have extra space, you can reduce your overhead by renting it out to an independent businessperson who doesn't require a big office.

If your business fluctuates or is seasonal, you can reduce overhead costs by hiring temporary workers for just the time you need their help. Once you hire someone and put them on the payroll, they can become a financial burden, especially if sales are dropping.

You can reduce overhead by cutting down on the number of business phone lines you install, by calling other companies on their toll-free numbers and using the U.S. Postal Service's Priority Mail instead of private overnight delivery services.

O/o

partnership agreement A written agreement among the partners of a general or limited partnership. (*See also* partnerships and limited partnerships.)

IN MOST STATES, the partners of a general partnership are not required to have a written agreement. The partnership statute in virtually all states, known as the Uniform Partnership Act (UPA), acts as a partnership agreement that binds the parties unless they agree otherwise in writing. A partnership is often an informal or temporary arrangement, and may be created unintentionally.

Nonetheless, many attorneys consider it malpractice to advise their clients to enter into partnerships without having a written agreement. This is not just because the lawyers want to line their pockets. It is because the Uniform Partnership Act may not reflect the informal, verbal agreement of the parties, which will not be acknowledged by the courts in the event of a dispute among the partners.

Let's say that you and your partner decide to split the profits and losses from the business 75 percent to you and 25 percent to the partner. You decide to forego a written partnership agreement in order to save legal fees and start up the business. A year later, the business is doing great and your partner decides that he or she deserves 50 percent of the profits because "I'm doing the lion's share of the work here and, after all, that's what we agreed a year ago, right?" Except that's not what you agreed to do. You take your dispute to court and the Uniform Partnership Act in your state says that without a written agreement partners are presumed to have equal shares of the profits and losses from the business. Your partner wins, even though he doesn't deserve to.

A written partnership agreement helps to avoid disputes before they happen, and settle them when they do happen. If the partnership doesn't work out, it can also provide for a neat and orderly breakup of the business, without the nasty haggling over items of partnership property that can lead to costly litigation.

It will generally cost $500 to $1,000 to have an attorney prepare a standard partnership agreement for your business, and it is money well spent. Some of the items your partnership agreement should contain are:

- The names of the partners, and the procedure to be followed when admitting new partners
- The business of the partnership, and whether a partner may conduct a similar business outside of the partnership (you and your partner do work for a client, for example, and the client tells you of a little consulting job that needs to be done, but they want to work only with you)
- The percentage share of profits and losses for each partner
- A contribution and indemnity clause providing that if one partner is hit up for more than her fair share of a partnership obligation, the other partners will chip in and contribute their fair share
- Who will get what items of partnership property if the partners determine to shut down the business

Unlike a general partnership, a limited partnership in virtually all states is required by law to have a written partnership agreement. These are generally more complex documents, and will cost between $1,000 and $1,500 on average.

P/p

partnerships and limited partnerships Two or more individuals who pool their resources and share profits and losses from a small business. (*See also* sole proprietorship; corporation; limited liability company; limited liability partnership.)

A partnership is formed when two or more individuals agree to pool their resources and—this is the key—share profits and losses from the business. For example, if two or more lawyers share office space and refer clients to each other but render separate bills for their services, such that each lawyer keeps what the client pays him or her, this is not a partnership. If, however, the lawyers render a joint bill for their services and split the profits by an agreed-upon formula, that is a partnership.

PARTNERSHIP PROS AND CONS

Pros:

■ Partnerships are easy to form, and there are few if any startup costs.

■ Partnerships are not taxable entities—profits and losses flow through to the partners based on their percentage ownership of the partnership business.

■ Partnerships are easy to operate—there is little paperwork, and no need for formal meetings or resolutions to document the partners' activities.

Cons:

■ Partners have unlimited personal liability not only for their own acts and omissions, but for those of all of the other partners as well.

■ Partners are required to report their percentage share of the partnership's net income on their personal tax returns, whether or not the partnership actually paid them their share in cash (the so-called "phantom income" problem).

---

p/P

FINDING THE PERFECT PARTNER

"People will interview receptionists more carefully than they will a potential partner," says Dr. David Gage, founder and director of Business Mediation Associates, a Washington, D.C.–based firm that helps partners resolve conflicts.

Gage and his associates came up with an idea for a Partnership Charter, a sort of prenuptial agreement that clearly spells out the roles and the expectations for each partner. It details many aspects of the initial relationship to put things on the right track. The charter can also help the parties and attorneys involved unravel things if the partnership has to be dissolved.

Gage says partners most often squabble about issues of fairness and expectation. Usually, one feels that he is putting in more effort or more hours than the other, or that the other is just in it for the money. And although clear agreements between partners can establish the ground rules, Gage warns that "documents won't fix a troubled relationship."

He recommends asking yourself these questions before taking on a partner:

- If I'm looking for money, would applying for a loan make more sense?
- If I'm looking for expertise, should I hire a consultant?
- Am I afraid to operate the business alone? Why?

Gage reminds business owners that when their businesses become successful, they may not want a partner to be involved. "It's much easier to get rid of a loan than a partner," he says.

P/p

A partnership may be formed entirely by accident. If the lawyers in our example do not share profits and losses from their respective practices, but conduct their business in such a way that clients have reason to think they are doing business as a partnership (for example, the lawyers all use business cards or stationery that say "Moe, Larry, and Curly, Attorneys at Law"), the law will hold them liable as partners, even though no partnership was intended or created.

There is no legal requirement that a partnership agreement be in writing. Of course, any attorney worth her salt will say you are crazy to enter into a partnership without a written agreement. If you do not have a written partnership agreement, the partnership statute in your state (called the Uniform Partnership Act, or UPA) will be invoked to decide disputes between you and your business partner(s), and you may not like the result the UPA will reach. A simple partnership agreement will generally cost between $500 and $1,000 in legal fees, and is well worth the expense.

A partnership is not considered a legal entity for tax purposes; profits and losses flow through to the individual partners based on their percentage share of the partnership. If Tom and Bill are fifty-fifty partners, and the partnership has $100 in profits each year, Tom must report $50 as income on his personal tax return and Bill reports the other $50 as income on his personal tax return. What, however, if the partnership decides to keep the $100 in its checking account and not pay the money out to Tom and Bill? Under current federal tax law, Tom and Bill must still each report $50 on their personal tax returns. This is referred to as the "phantom income" problem, and effectively prevents partnerships from retaining earnings from one year to the next. To avoid unhappy partners who will have to pay taxes on income they never actually received, partnerships are usually forced to pay all net income to the partners at the end of the business year.

A partnership reports its annual income on IRS Form 1065 (available with instructions as a free download from the IRS website at www.irs.gov), but is not required to pay taxes as a legal entity. A partnership must use the calendar year as its fiscal year; using a different fiscal year-end will require IRS approval.

p/P

The biggest disadvantage of the partnership is that each partner has unlimited personal liability for the debts, obligations, and liabilities of the partnership business. There is no legal separation between the partner's personal and business assets, as would be provided by a corporation or a limited liability company. What is worse, a partner's liability is "joint and several," which means that the partner is fully liable not only for his or her own mistakes, accidents, and bad behavior, but for those of each other partner as well. If Partner A makes a bad judgment call, Partner B may end up losing his or her house even if Partner B took no part in the decision.

A variation of the partnership is the limited partnership, in which some of the partners (those not participating in the day-to-day operation of the partnership business), agree not to take part in the partnership business in exchange for a limitation of their personal liability to the amounts they actually contribute to the partnership. Unlike a general partnership, a limited partnership must have a written partnership agreement and will be required to file periodic documents with a state government agency stating precisely who the limited partners are. A limited partnership must have at least one general partner with unlimited personal liability for anything that happens.

Since the advent in the early 1990s of the limited liability company or LLC, partnerships and limited partnerships are fast becoming a thing of the past. Some attorneys even consider it malpractice to help people form partnerships when for the same amount of money they can obtain the protection of an LLC.

Because partnerships can be formed by accident, however, it is very important when doing business with other people to make sure you are not conducting your business in such a way that third parties (customers and suppliers) might think you are partners. If you feel you are in that situation, you should notify each customer, supplier, or third party (preferably in writing) that you and the other person are not partners.

P/p

part-time or seasonal employee A person who legally is your employee, but only for some of his or her time. (*See also* employee; independent contractor.)

The Bureau of Statistics of the U.S. Department of Labor defines a part-time employee as someone who works less than thirty-five hours a week for your company but is still an employee for legal and tax purposes. In contrast, an independent contractor or contract worker is someone who may work long or short hours for your company, but is not an employee for legal and tax purposes. Whether or not an individual is your employee depends on how much control your company exercises over how the person performs their work.

For example, let's say you own a landscaping firm. You have a small permanent staff, but between the months of May and October each year you hire and fire an additional twelve laborers to help you cut people's lawns. If you have the ability to tell these laborers what to do and when to do it during the time they are working for you, and they do not work for anyone else during this period, they are your employees for legal and tax purposes, notwithstanding the fact that they only work for part of the year. Similarly, someone who comes into your office one day a week on a regular schedule, during which time you tell them what to do and when to do it, is a part-time employee and must be treated as such.

Even if employers are careful to define part-time employees as nonpermanent, casual, or seasonal workers in employee handbooks, employment contracts, and other documents, your actions can affect whether a person will be classified as an employee or contractor for legal and tax purposes. If you provide a person with tools, define how their work is done (versus what is to be accomplished), provide them office space or training, give them business cards, or set hours of employment, they are your employees. You should consult with your attorney or tax adviser if you have any questions about the legal classification of a particular individual who works for you.

Do you have to provide part-time employees with the same benefits, such as medical plans and stock options that you make available to your full-time employees? The law in this area is somewhat

p/P

murky, but a number of recent court cases are providing at least some guidance for employers, at least in the area of retirement plans such as 401(k)s and pension plans.

Generally, the IRS requires that all eligible employees be included in a company's retirement plan. However, it is permissible to exclude certain classes of employees, such as employees under the age of twenty-one and employees who have not yet met the plan's minimum service requirement. Other categories of employees, such as leased or part-time employees, may be excluded from a retirement plan if doing so does not present other compliance issues. For example, under federal law if highly compensated employees are allowed to participate in a company's retirement plan, the plan must include at least 70 percent of the non-highly compensated employees of the company. Passing the coverage test is an annual requirement, and a company that excludes an employee group, such as part-time employees, from its retirement plan, must pass the test every year. So, if a retirement plan excludes part-time employees, and part-time employees constitute 30 percent or less of the eligible employee group, the plan should be permissible under federal tax law. There are many other requirements under the federal laws governing retirement plans, however, and competent tax counsel should be consulted whenever you are designing or amending a retirement plan for your employees.

patent A legal monopoly that protects inventors and other developers of technology from being ripped off … at least for a while. (*See also* invention; patent application; trademarks and service marks.)

A patent is a government-granted monopoly, for a fixed number of years, to encourage inventors to disclose their inventions to the public by permitting them to prohibit anyone else from making, using, or selling their inventions. After the grant has expired, the invention as described and claimed in the patent is dedicated to the public, at which time anyone can make, use, or sell the invention as described in the expired patent. A U.S. patent runs for a term of seventeen years from the date it is granted, or twenty years from filing. A patent may not be renewed.

A patent gives the patent holder (and people who license the patent from the patent holder) the right to stop others from using the work. However, the patent does not automatically give the inventor the right to use the invention. Other considerations, such as implication of use to humans, animals, and the environment as well as ethical, moral, or other issues may have to be resolved before a patented work can be put to use.

The U.S. Patent and Trademark Office (**www.uspto.gov**) uses the following criteria in deciding whether to grant a patent:

- **Novelty.** An invention is novel if it has not previously been described and there is no prior record that it has been publicly disclosed in any form.

- **Not obvious.** A patentable work cannot be an obvious "next step" extension of another work as judged by someone who is an expert in the field.

- **Sufficiency.** The work that is to be patented should be described in detail so that it can be reproduced by someone else who works in the field.

- **Industrial applicability or utility.** The inventor should demonstrate the applicability and utility of the patentable work (such as by clinical trials or animal studies).

Most patent applications are filed on a country-by-country basis, so your United States patent will not protect your invention in Canada, for example. Under the Patent Cooperation Treaty of 1978, which is administered by the International Bureau of the World Intellectual Property Organization (WIPO) in Geneva, Switzerland, inventors can submit a world-wide patent application for the seventy-nine nations that currently subscribe to the treaty, while paying the fees imposed by only ten of those nations (**www .wipo.org**). You may, however, be required to file a separate application within each participating country within eighteen months after the worldwide patent application.

It is very difficult to obtain a patent without the assistance of a competent patent lawyer or patent agent who is registered to practice before the United States Patent and Trademark Office. Patent claim drafting is a highly precise art, and as a result most patent lawyers also have engineering degrees. (However, some entrepre-

p/P

neurs, including the inventor of the Happy Massager, profiled in the "invention" entry, do manage to do it themselves.)

The cost of filing and prosecuting a patent application in the United States, including the cost of a thorough patent search to ensure that your invention does not infringe on any previously filed patent, can run anywhere from $2,500 to $10,000. The cost depends on the complexity of the invention and the number of objections or concerns raised by the patent examiners to which you or your attorney will need to respond.

patent application An invention's first fight for survival. (*See also* patent.)

"Ninety-five percent of patent applications to the U.S. Patent and Trademark Office are appealed [questioned by examiners]," says Sharon Zumm of Rochelle, Virginia, a single, working mother of three, who succeeded in patenting her invention, the Bottle Bunny.

Years ago Zumm tried to find a baby-bottle holder that an infant could grasp, so she could free up one arm during mealtime. In 1991, after a futile search, she invented a plush stuffed toy that holds a bottle in several positions. Almost ten years later, her company, Smile Time Inc., began marketing her Bottle Bunny on the Internet at **www.bottlebunny.com** and in gift stores.

Like all inventors, Zumm's greatest challenge in bringing her new product to market was not creating a prototype or finding a manufacturer, but obtaining a patent. Before you start the process, which can be lengthy and expensive, you have to determine whether or not your idea belongs to someone else.

"Because the Bottle Bunny had a function, I had to get a utility patent, which is the most difficult to get," says Zumm, who hired an attorney to assist her with the patent search and application process. The search revealed several baby-bottle holders, and Zumm and her attorney had to explain to an examiner why her design deserved its own patent.

The United States Patent and Trademark Office (USPTO) receives about 3,300 applications every week and registers 200,000 patents and trademarks every year. For new inventors and small

P/p

business owners, the risk of unwittingly infringing on an existing trademark or patent is considerable, and the consequences can be dire. Having to cease production or change the name of your company can be financially disastrous.

Mark Search Plus, a service of MicroPatent, an East Haven, Connecticut company that publishes patent and trademark information on CD-ROM, was designed by Alan Davidson, a former USPTO examiner and patent attorney. The service costs $35 for unlimited searches during one 24-hour period and prompts users through the logic of evaluating conflicts and provides tech support from trademark experts. Mark Search Plus files are updated weekly, giving users access to about 1 million more files than are available on the USPTO database. It also provides obsolete records that the USPTO does not.

Entrepreneurs should keep in mind that while Mark Search Plus is an alternative way to search for registered patents and trademarks, it is not a substitute for the USPTO application process. And, while the service may be cheaper than paying a lawyer to do multiple searches, you will probably need an attorney as the process continues. Zumm's attorney knew to include in her application all bottle holding stuffed animals, not just bunnies, and variations like musical animal holders.

Finally, the biggest mistake entrepreneurs make in this area is the common misconception that the USPTO is a policing organization. It is not. It is up to you to monitor the market place for illegal uses of your name or product and take the necessary legal action. For more information, go to the USPTO website at www .uspto.gov.

payables *See* accounts payable.

payroll The salary and taxes paid to employees.

payroll taxes A variety of state and federal taxes paid to cover employees who are injured on the job, heading toward retirement, or heading toward unemployment. (*See* employment taxes.)

p/P

pension plan A method for employees and employers to share in the cost and responsibility of providing for retirement. [*See also* 401(k).]

When your business is stable and growing, it's time to consider establishing ways for you and your employees to set money aside for the future. Retirement benefits are very attractive to employees and can be instrumental in recruiting and retaining good workers.

A pension plan is not to be taken lightly. Pension plans are strictly regulated by the federal Employee Retirement Income Security Act of 1974, known as ERISA. The law requires employers to provide a plan with strict investment guidelines, to select funds into which employees can invest this tax-deferred money, and to communicate investment-related information to participants. For help with this section, I turned to Ginger Brennan, a top sales person with ING U.S. Financial Services for help in sorting out this often-confusing topic. (ING has been a client of SBTV; we do not have any retirement programs managed by ING.)

Most employee pension plans are defined contribution plans, which means the contribution level is set and regulated by law. Your challenge as an employer is putting together a plan that recognizes that people's needs are different and that every employee has a different tolerance for risk. A thirty-something worker has a different view of the future than an executive in her late fifties.

These different investment goals are addressed by allowing the employees to select the funds in which to invest their money. In order to comply with ERISA, you need to select at least three diversified investment funds. Participants have to be able to change funds or redistribute money at least once every three months, although some plans allow access on a monthly basis. It is essential that all plan participants are able to exercise control over their assets in their individual accounts. You must give them clear deposit and transfer instructions, in writing, and a detailed list of the fees involved.

No matter which plan you choose, or which firm you hire to administer the plan, communicating with employees is critical to the plan's success. Setting up a pension plan is a time-consuming and serious business. You should work with a qualified broker or

P/p

financial adviser. This is not something you can do by yourself, no matter how financially savvy you may be. Here's a checklist developed by ING U.S. Financial to get you started:

■ Evaluate your plan participants based on age, projected retirement age, risk tolerance, and income levels. Make investment choices based on these needs.

■ Evaluate the setup and monthly costs for the pension plan. A payroll service working with a brokerage, for instance, charges $1,500 to set up the plan, $100 a month as a service fee, and about $5 per person per month to administer the plan.

■ Decide where to invest the pension funds and document how you made those decisions.

■ Evaluate the funds with the help of a professional and document which funds you selected.

■ Use these materials to base an annual review of the plan and fund performance.

The following are some plan options to consider:

SEP-IRA (Simplified Employee Pension). This type of individual retirement account works well for a self-employed entrepreneur with a few employees. Both employers and employees can contribute 15 percent of their annual compensation up to about $30,000. (Check with your tax adviser for the amount.) Contributions are deductible for the employer. The plan can't discriminate in favor of highly compensated employees. You also have to make sure your contributions to your SEP-IRA are proportionate to contributions made by employees. The plan is flexible in that you can vary the amount you contribute every year or even skip a year.

You can roll over a SEP-IRA into another SEP-IRA, a traditional IRA, or other retirement accounts (check with your tax adviser for details).

SEP-IRAs are easy to set up and you don't have to register them with the Internal Revenue Service. They are easy to administer because you need to report only annually. The contributions are tax deductible as a business expense.

SIMPLE IRA. The simple stands for Savings Incentive Match Plan for Employees. A simple IRA works well for business owners

p/P

with up to 100 employees. The employer is required to contribute a 3 percent match or a 2 percent nonelective contribution. The maximum salary deferral has been about $6,500 per year. (Check with your adviser for the current amount.) The accounts are easy to set up and do not have to be registered with the IRS. You have to report to employees on contributions made to their accounts once a year and meet other employee notification requirements. Your employees will benefit from tax-deferred earnings on the contributions you make to their accounts.

SIMPLE 401(k). Congress established this plan in the 1990s to encourage small business owners to set up easy-to-manage pension plans. This works for businesses with fewer than 100 employees that don't have any other type of pension plan. Contributions must be 100 percent vested. Maximum salary deferral is $6,000 per year and the employer is required to make a 3 percent contribution. A SIMPLE plan requires some reporting to the government, but it is easy to administer and may allow loans and hardship withdrawals.

401(k). Named after the section of the tax code that created it, these plans are more complex to set up and administer. You must report to the IRS about who is in the plan and that you did not discriminate against employees who qualify for participation. The employer can match contributions but doesn't have to. Participants have been able to contribute up to the lesser of $35,000 or 25 percent of their compensation each year. (Check with your adviser for the current amount.) A 401(k) also permits employees to make tax deferred contributions.

"Finding the right plan for your business means asking yourself these questions," said Brennan. "What degree of responsibility do you want for contributing to your employees' retirement plans? How much do you and your employees wish to contribute? How much does each plan require you to contribute?"

No matter what kind of plan you intend to offer, get all the facts and rely on a professional to establish and maintain it. You don't want to get into trouble with Uncle Sam when it comes to pension issues.

P/p

RECOMMENDED READING

■ *The Complete Idiot's Guide to 401(k) Plans* by Wayne G. Bogosian, et al. (Prentice Hall, 2001)
■ *A Commonsense Guide to Your 401(k)* by Mary Rowland (Bloomberg Press, 1997)

percentage lease *See* lease.

performance review A periodic report on a manager's or employee's professional accomplishments. Equally dreaded by employees and supervisors. (*See also* online training; firing employees.)

Some employees believe performance reviews were invented by a sadistic management consultant who thought that at least once a year, employees should stay awake worrying the night before their boss reviews their work. The real purpose of a performance review is to measure and monitor professional achievement and use the information on which to base merit raises and promotions.

Rather than wait until the end of the year to do an annual review, I recommend semi-annual or even quarterly reviews. Evaluating an employee's achievements and failures on a more frequent basis makes sense. If they are in trouble, you may be able to help them avert a disaster. If they are doing well, you may want to promote them faster or pay them more so they aren't tempted to look for a better-paying job.

A good performance review explores several areas: whether your people are doing the job you hired them to do; how well they do the job; their overall attitude toward work; and how well they get along with customers, colleagues, and vendors.

Too many managers get tangled up in long, wordy evaluation forms. You can find a software program with a template for a review, but I think it's best to create your own review to fit your specific company.

The most important part of the review is the part where you make suggestions for improvement. Be as detailed and specific as possible. If customers have complained about customer service,

p/P

SHOULD YOUR EMPLOYEES EVALUATE YOU?

Your employees are probably still recovering from their year-end performance reviews, so cheer them up by asking them to evaluate your management skills. You don't have to make a big deal about it. Draft a simple, anonymous questionnaire to gather information about the way you communicate, encourage, criticize, and motivate your employees.

Collect the surveys, read them carefully, and determine what changes are possible. Schedule private meetings with each employee to collect feedback. While some people may be reluctant to criticize the boss, if you explain that you are really interested in what they think, they should open up. When I asked my employees to evaluate me, it came back that I was driving them crazy by micromanaging them. I would give out assignments and projects and then hover over them, wanting to know how things were going. This was not only hurting morale, but preventing them from actually *doing* the work. Once I backed off, the work was completed faster, morale improved, and I learned a powerful lesson: Good managers give direction and encouragement, but should never tell people how to do their jobs.

ask them for examples so you can tell employees, for instance, that their telephone skills need improvement. Stress that weaknesses hamper their advancement, whereas improvements may lead to more money and a more challenging position. If complaints are coming from coworkers, outline specific incidents rather than just saying they need to be more cooperative with other departments. Put a positive spin on your recommendations and emphasize why the employee should be making these changes in behavior or performance.

P/p

If the problem is a lack of experience or training, you'll need to provide the resources if the person is willing to make the effort. Online training is one way to help employees polish skills without breaking the budget.

Before you finish the review, ask the employee to read and sign it to acknowledge receipt. This written proof of receipt is important if you later decide to terminate the employee. You'll need to document this interactive counseling process to protect yourself from losing a lawsuit claiming unlawful termination. Be sure to set clear deadlines for improvement, especially if you are trying to get someone to improve attendance or reduce tardiness. It's more work, but it's important to hold them accountable to the promises they made during the review.

Finally, ask your employees to evaluate you at least once a year with an anonymous questionnaire. Ask them to rate your communication and leadership skills, and to suggest what you can do to improve your management techniques. You may benefit from their candor and specific suggestions.

Rating Employee Performance
Here are some sample questions for you to answer prior to the meeting:

- How well is this person performing daily tasks?
- Does the employee manage time well?
- Does the employee solve common problems in a timely fashion?
- How well does the employee communicate with colleagues? With customers? With vendors?
- Does the employee show up for work on time?
- Does the employee have good work habits? Are reports well written or proposals well thought out?
- Does the employee keep the work area tidy?
- Does the employee make an effort to do more than the minimum required for a project?
- Does the employee go beyond the call of duty without being asked?
- Does the employee have a positive attitude at work?

■ Does the employee show up on time and leave when they are supposed to?

■ Does the employee speak respectfully to colleagues and clients?

■ Do other staff members enjoy working with or complain about the employee?

■ How can this person improve work habits? Be specific.

■ If the employee improves, would you offer a promotion or expanded responsibilities?

Questions for Employees

Here are questions suggested by Barry Schimel, founder of The Profit Advisors, Inc., in Rockville, Maryland. The company helps clients improve profitability by crafting profit-enhancement strategies:

■ During the review period, what were your five major accomplishments?

■ In what areas do you feel you can improve and how?

■ What skills or knowledge would you like to further develop or gain to improve your performance?

■ What are appropriate performance objectives for the next review period?

■ What specifically will you do during the next thirty days to pursue those objectives?

■ What are your long-range career objectives?

■ What does your supervisor do that you find helpful?

■ What else could your supervisor do to help you achieve your goals?

■ What changes could be made to improve your effectiveness related to the work environment, equipment, procedures, or communication?

Questions for Employees in Supervisory Positions

■ What were your department's five major accomplishments?

■ What aspects of your team's performance fell short of your expectations and why?

P/p

■   What specifically will you do during the upcoming review period to develop and train your staff?

■   What will do you do help your staff achieve their individual career objectives?

perks *See* benefits.

personal finance Taking care of the money you don't want to mix with your corporate money for any reason.

personnel *See* employee.

piracy *See* copyright; intellectual property; knockoff; patent.

point of sale A computerized system that adjusts inventory based on cash register transactions.

premiums Small gifts given to clients and customers to promote your company. (*See also* advertising specialties.)

pricing strategy Aligning the price of your products with your company's goals. (*See also* break even.)

You're thinking: That's simple, my goal is to make money. But pricing is complex: Low prices will attract more customers; high prices will establish an image of quality. Some of your investors will want to capture market share and postpone their payoff until your company dominates its niche; others might favor prices high enough to produce a profit right away.

Start by knowing your break-even price: the cost of producing a product, plus all other overhead costs, divided by the number of units to be produced during a given period. Anything below this price will result in a loss, no matter how many units you sell.

private investors *See* angels.

p/P

professional employer organization (PEO) A company set up to hire, fire, pay, and provide benefits for "your" employees, for a fee usually based on a percentage of the total payroll. (*See also* benefits; leasing employees.)

Most business owners hate to keep track of employee-related paperwork, including filing of quarterly and payroll tax forms, performance reviews, finding affordable health insurance, and setting up retirement plans. In fact, the U.S. Small Business Administration estimates that business owners spend between 7 and 25 percent of their time on employee-related paperwork. So, outsourcing these day-to-day duties can be an attractive alternative, although it could cost you between 2 percent and 25 percent of your payroll, according a spokesman for to the National Association of Professional Employer Organizations.

PEOs gained momentum in the late 1980s as overworked entrepreneurs sought out alternatives to dealing with employee-related paperwork. A good PEO will provide you with a slightly customized employee policy manual, sexual harassment policies, and all the paperwork required to keep you out of trouble with state and federal tax authorities. A PEO actually hires your employees, puts them on its payroll, and leases them back to you. So, instead of qualifying for the poor benefits available to companies with a few employees, your workers are part of group that represents thousands.

If you don't want or can't afford the deluxe services of a PEO, consider using a payroll service. It's worth every penny to have someone else issue paychecks, pay state and federal payroll taxes, and file the complex tax returns. We've had good and bad experiences with payroll services, but I would never go back to doing it in-house.

Outsourcing human resources administration frees entrepreneurs to concentrate on growing their business. Best of all, knowing employees are well taken care of and that your company is complying with all rules and regulations helps you sleep better. "We bring big company benefits to small companies," says Thomas Hall, president and CEO of Automatic Data Processing, based in Roseland, New Jersey. "We have 75,000 work site employees.

P/p

When we go to Blue Cross-Blue Shield, that gets their attention," he says.

The PEO industry was tarnished when large companies began leasing out their lower paid employees to boost the pension benefits paid to higher paid employees. It is still crucial to carefully check references before signing up with a PEO—not only the financial strength, but check with current clients to determine whether the company provides reliable service. (Go online to a search engine and put in "professional employer organization" or "employee leasing" to find a number of companies in the field.)

Though a new and improved industry is emerging, the concept remains largely unknown to many small business owners outside of Florida, where the concept is very popular. Tom Strasse's forty employees at First-Weigh Manufacturing in Sanford, Florida, might not work for a large corporation, but they receive the same kind of insurance benefits and human resources services available to workers at a Fortune 500 firm. Tom Strasse admits that many of his managers were apprehensive about the changeover. But PEO experts say the process is "blind" and does not affect the employer's control over day-to-day hiring, firing, and management.

"Once we went through the initial training, no one knows, realizes or cares (who is handling the paperwork)," Strasse says. "The actual production and supervision of people has not changed. We have the ultimate power to hire and fire."

Small employers should think of PEOs as an added level of protection and service for both their employees and themselves. "To attract and retain key employees you need to offer top benefits comparable to the Fortune 500," says Sarah Stevens, the Manhattan regional manager for HR Tech, based in Columbia, Maryland.

"You may think, my little company will never have a sexual harassment case or a wrongful termination, but it can happen," Stevens says, adding that HR Tech attends all state legislative hearings and is part of a Washington, D.C., group working to clarify the IRS rules affecting PEOs. "Small business owners are overburdened with wearing so many hats," Stevens says. "With a PEO, you can transfer or share the liability."

p/P

profit Revenues minus expenses. The profit remains after you have paid for everything related to your products or services. (*See also* return on investment.)

profitability The reason you should be in business.

"Most good companies have already cut costs," says Gary Kravitz, accountant and partner in The Profit Advisors, a Rockville, Maryland–based consulting firm that helps big and small companies boost profits. "We teach firms to be able to step back, look at their company, and identify things that increase sales and improve margins," says Kravitz.

Millions of small businesses are not very profitable for several reasons, according to Kravitz: They don't maximize revenues from their existing customers. They don't treat their employees as importantly as they treat their customers. They don't know exactly where they are financially on a daily or weekly basis.

Jim Sweet, president of Smokey Glen Farms, hired Kravitz a few years ago to help his family-run catering business make some significant changes. "When you have a family business like I do, with such longstanding traditions, it's very difficult to make changes on your own," says Sweet, head of the company that caters special events on its ninety-one-acre Gaithersburg, Maryland, property. "My vision of the future was quite different from my brother's, which was also different from my mother's," he says. Like many savvy business owners, the Sweets set their egos aside and hired an outsider to help put the company back on track.

Kravitz and his partner, Barry Schimel, initially met with the family and its fifteen full-time and 220 part-time employees. The changes made ranged from including more managers in the decision-making process to offering guests a vegetarian meal. They also dealt with more mundane issues like the fact the company was spending too much money on spare ribs.

"Through the discussion process, we noticed that the case weights of the spare ribs we order were increasing," says Sweet. "We thought we were ordering thirty-pound cases, but in actuality, we were receiving cases that were thirty-five pounds or more.

P/p

PROFIT POWER

Trimming costs is only one aspect of boosting profits. Kravitz offers these tips for maximizing profitability:

■ Review your customers and ask yourself, "Are they buying everything that they can from us?" Even a 5 percent increase in your customer retention rate can have an enormous impact on your level of profitability.

■ Establish key measures of operations beside your financial statements. Make it easy for the average employee to know exactly how well your company has done at the end of the day.

Send invoices out promptly. Make sure that they are understandable and accurate.

■ Eliminate the "profit fumbles" in your company. Profit fumbles are identified by words that start with "re," "mis," and "un." Examples: redundant, redo, miscalculation, unavailable, unnecessary.

We saved money by correcting the order."

Another Profit Advisors's client, The Davidson Companies, a wholesale beauty supplier selling a variety of salon products, hired the firm to help with a major overhaul of their business. "Large things were our concern," says Ken Gilman, president of the Laurel, Maryland–based company. "We didn't need to save money by buying cheaper pencils."

The consultants helped Gilman identify which products were most profitable and which employees were most critical to the company's success. Gilman, who declined to release financial details, did say he expects to save around $1 million based on the advice he received. "Our initial cost, with everything implemented, was about $30,000," says Gilman.

Consulting fees vary from firm to firm and often from region to region. Schimel and Kravitz charge fees depending on the size

p/P

of the company and the depth of the service. A profit audit for a small company with fifteen to twenty employees costs $7,500; a large company with 200 employees pays $100,000. A profit audit entails a series of interviews and surveys that are given to both employees and customers.

profit and loss statement (P&L) A way to measure the results of business operations during a certain period of time. The P&L represents all of the revenues collected with all of the operating expenses subtracted. The resulting figure is what is left: profits or losses.

profit margin The difference between what it costs you to make your product and what you can sell it for.

profit ratio Net income (profit minus taxes) divided by sales revenue.

The profit ratio, like a coin, is valuable on both sides: as an expression of net income divided by sales, and as an indicator of what percentage of $1 in sales falls all the way to the bottom line:

net income/sales = profit ratio

Thus, net income of $5,000 on $100,000 in sales yields a profit ratio of 5 percent, or $5 profit on $100 in sales. Stand the number on its head, dividing sales revenue by net profit and the result tells you how many dollars have to come in the door before you earn a profit:

sales/net profit = income

Dividing sales of $100,000 by net income of $5,000 yields a figure of 20, meaning that for every $1 in profit you have to sell $20 worth of stuff.

profit sharing *See* employee stock ownership plan.

promotion *See* advertising; merchandising; publicity.

P/p

publicity A strategy aimed at raising public awa.
products, services, or management style.

Every business can benefit from publicity—even negative pu
licity if it's not too awful. Publicity is tough to get because you
have to convince a reporter, editor, or producer to tell your story
rather than someone else's. Most business owners rely on public
relations professionals to craft their message and pitch it to the
press. If you have the time or interest, you can make a list of
reporters who cover your industry and send an introductory letter
offering to serve as a source for a future story.

Position yourself as an industry expert, rather than pushing
reporters to write a story about you or your company. If you've
recently attended an industry trade show or professional meeting,
tell the reporter what happened and how you can provide insights
into the trends and issues affecting your industry. Your goal is to
be quoted by the press and you'll have a much better chance if you
speak about your industry than if you hope to get a single story
written about your company.

public relations (PR) The process of influencing one's image at
large and in the media. (*See also* crisis PR.)

Public relations is an art, not a science. There is no secret formula to good public relations, although businesses spend thousands or millions of dollars a year on public relations campaigns.
The PR department at a big company may handle everything
from deciding which local events the company should sponsor to
entertaining reporters at a trade show. Most smaller firms can't
afford an in-house PR person, so they rely on outside consultants
to provide PR services.

If you read or hear something positive about a company, call the
owner and ask who they worked with to get the press attention.
It's cheaper to work with a sole practitioner than a big PR firm.
You should be prepared to work with someone for at least ninety
days. It takes time for the PR person to get to know you, develop
your story, and make the appropriate pitches to the media.

Doing something good for the community, whether it be sponsoring a clothing collection drive for a homeless shelter or provid-

p/P

TIPS FROM THE TOP

Rick Frishman, president of Planned Television Arts and coauthor of *Guerrilla Publicity* (Adams Media, 2002), is credited with having pioneered the morning radio drive-time publicity tour in 1990. In these radio (and now television) tours, the author, executive, or celebrity merely sits in a studio and conducts back-to-back interviews with ten, fifteen, or sometimes even more stations. The stations schedule two- to five-minute windows of time and the interview is beamed via satellite into their newsrooms.

The best bookers will push for live interviews because the person paying for the tour can say just about anything they want to in an unrestrained manner. A taped interview can always be edited, or worse, not aired at all. (Disclosure: PTA has handled two tours for my clients and me.)

"I'm no genius, but I've been doing this [PR] for twenty-five years," said Frishman. "It's great if you have other people's money to spend on promotion and publicity, but if you don't, you can use elbow grease instead of dollars."

Frishman said that the chance of getting on the air somewhere is actually pretty high since about 10,000 guests appear *every day* on America's 4,000 radio and TV stations. "Americans watch an average of seven hours and fifteen minutes of TV a day and 80 percent of us rely on television for international and national news," he said. So, if you have an interesting story to tell or a great new product to promote, your chances of getting some coverage are actually pretty high.

For more information, check out Frishman's website, **www.rickfrishman.com**, where he offers all sorts of great tips for reaching producers, editors, and bookers.

P/p

ing your parking lot for a high school car wash, is a good way to get a small mention in the local paper. A good PR person will help you figure out where you want to be mentioned. If you only sell locally, being in a national magazine may be great for your ego, but won't really boost sales.

p/P

quick ratio The lean, mean number that indicates your company's ability to survive a rush by creditors.

S OMETIMES CALLED the "pounce ratio" (think tiger, stalking), the quick ratio takes only your most liquid assets (cash and receivables) and divides them by total current liabilities (short-term notes and other immediate debts). Anything greater than a ratio of 1:1 is solvent.

liquid assets/total current liabilities = quick ratio

real estate For many businesses, the asset least convertible to cash, and thus in the short term an unattractive use of capital. (*See also* lease.)

No BUSINESS SHOULD RUSH to buy real estate unless the owner is a developer and knows what she is doing. In the nineteenth century, many small merchants lived over their stores, so it made sense to buy a building. During an uncertain economy, buying real estate becomes more attractive.

The same rules for buying a home apply to commercial real estate: location is everything. You want to be in a place that's easy for employees and customers to reach. If customers or clients will visit your building, put more emphasis on the curb appeal and reception area when you start looking for space. Interior lighting, the number of windows, and exposure is important, especially if you have people working long hours at their desks. Decide how much warehouse or storage space you need and how many restrooms are appropriate. Fire sprinklers and other safety issues should also be on your list of considerations.

Buying commercial real estate is serious business. Hire an experienced commercial broker who not only understands your industry but also knows the neighborhoods you are interested in. Ask the delivery people who serve the area if they are aware of any buildings for rent or space available. If your business is stable and growing, meet with your financial and tax advisers before you consider buying a building. If you are struggling to meet the payroll and worry about the stability of your current clients, keep paying those rent checks.

receivables Assets owed for products or services already sold. (*See also* accounts receivable; barter.)

Receivables are almost always money owed by customers, although they could be goods promised in a barter transaction. In any case, they're technically an asset, but one that you want to keep as small as possible.

record keeping Tracking anything and everything that will help your business thrive.

State and federal taxing authorities, of course, require accurate accounting of income. But don't fall into the trap of keeping records just to satisfy the IRS. Like the dashboard instruments on your car, your daily record keeping will tell you exactly how your business is running, and where your focus should be today and tomorrow. Sometimes the simplest numbers can be surprising. I know a smart business attorney who analyzes his client list periodically. He was astonished to notice that 80 percent of his clientele was female. Imagine how one number like that would affect your business.

For more information, download IRS Publication 583, Starting a Business and Keeping Records, at **www.irs.gov**.

recruiting The process of introducing your company to good potential employees. (*See also* hiring.)

Big companies have entire departments filled with trained professionals devoted to recruiting new employees. They travel to job fairs and college campuses and set up glitzy exhibits to woo the best prospects. But most small companies don't have the budget to manage such a formal recruitment effort. Small business owners tend to hire the first warm body that walks in

R/r

the door and that often ends up being a big mistake.

Casting a wide net for talent increases your chances of landing a great employee. Your current employees are the best referral source of future employees. I always ask my writers and producers if they know any great people looking for jobs. Don't be shy about asking your vendors, suppliers, and even your competitors for referrals. Often a competitor has met someone they liked but can't hire and may be willing to pass along a job seeker's resume or phone number.

Help wanted ads are OK, but it's better to advertise in your industry newsletters and trade journals where your chances of finding someone with the right experience are better. If you have the money to move someone, advertise nationally. Online ads have a very wide reach, but only post one if you are willing to screen lots of applicants and consider an out-of-town candidate. When you narrow the field to a few candidates, be sure to check their references and introduce them to others on your management team. Chemistry is important, but a detailed reference check can save you untold grief.

referral The lifeblood of a business for bringing in customers and employees.

Word of mouth is still the most powerful form of advertising for small companies. Generating a positive buzz among your customers and clients is essential to your long- term success. However, it's up to you to ask your happy customers to refer new business to you. Then, make it worth their while.

Offering discounts on your products or services in exchange for a referral is a powerful incentive. Sending out a personal thank-you letter with a gift certificate to a local restaurant or movie theatre is also a very affordable way to reward a referring customer.

Big companies use referral programs all the time. For example, if you refer a new customer to Speakeasy, an Internet service provider based in Seattle, Washington, the company thanks you by providing a discount on your service.

If you have a retail store, take pictures of your best customers and post them on the walls. Veterinarian offices do this all the time, posting snapshots of happy cats and dogs on waiting room bulletin boards. Pediatricians also feature photos of smiling babies on their walls. If asking your customers for photos isn't appropriate to your business, ask them for testimonial letters. When we produce a promotional video for a client, we ask them to write a letter praising our efforts. We use these happy client letters to help woo new prospects.

Customer service experts say that an unhappy customer complains about your business to at least ten people. So, your mission is to encourage your happy customers to recommend your products or services to at least ten people—and make it easy for them to do so.

retail The first cousin to detail, the last in a chain of transactions that delivers to the buyer goods or services that he or she finds useful.

Small retailers always complain about being crushed by the superstores, but after dealing with big, impersonal superstores, many people prefer to shop close to home and support their friends and neighbors. I'll go out of my way to buy a birthday card at Ginger's Pelhamville Stationery. Why? Because, even though she doesn't make deliveries, she delivered forty-eight blue, white, and gold helium-filled balloons for our son Evan's bar mitzvah after working a long Saturday at her store.

If you are a retailer, you must love what you do. Retailing is tough. The hours are long. Many storeowners have little or no help. They wear every hat: buyer, window dresser, manager, and custodian. They're not in it for the money—most retailers operate on a very thin margin and often lose money. Still, retailing allows creative people to express themselves in many areas. They keep their doors open because they enjoy serving people. Their store fits their lifestyle. They like being able to create a pleasant little retail world around them.

You can learn retailing in school, but most successful retailers learned on the job. They learn to stock what their customers asked for, anticipate needs, keep up with trends, and make every visit to their store a pleasant experience. They serve coffee and cookies.

R/r

They have good candy on the counter. They offer free gift-wrapping services or free local delivery. They'll keep the store open late if you are stuck in traffic and help you pick out the perfect present for your sister.

Retail consultant Edgar Falk says smart retailers make sure they have good signs; one that says OPEN and displays the hours of operation and, if local sign regulations permit, a red neon sign that says OPEN. This old-fashioned eye-catcher acts like a magnet for foot traffic.

retention The ability of your company to overcome the attractions that lure good customers and employees away.

Too many business owners lose great customers and employees because they didn't pay attention to strong and obvious signals of distress. Unhappy employees are easy to spot. They start coming in late and leaving early. They seem distracted at meetings. They stare out the window and don't pay attention when you are talking with them. Their work suffers and they miss deadlines.

You may think you are too busy to deal with these warning signals, but you can turn things around if you make the effort. Saving a good employee is a lot less stressful than replacing one. Sit down and ask straight out what's wrong. Many times, this simple inquiry will trigger a flood of information. You'll find out what soured the working relationship and whether it can be repaired. Sometimes the unhappiness begins with a very small slight, such as a sarcastic remark or an exclusion from an important meeting or trade show. If they have been passed over for a promotion or not given a place on a prestigious project team, spirits can be crushed. Sometimes people just outgrow a job or have personal issues pulling them in a different direction. It's OK to let go if there is no hope. Why pay someone a full salary for half-hearted work?

A detailed exit interview is painful, but valuable. It's important to know what you did right and wrong in this particular working relationship. If an employee enjoyed working for you, but has been offered $20,000 more in salary by a competitor, there isn't much you can do. But if someone is leaving because she is unhappy

r/R

or feels unappreciated, consider this information and try to make some changes. Listen to her complaints and concerns and take them to heart.

Customer retention is similar to employee retention in that you have to pay attention to the signals. If long-time customers haven't been in the store for a while, make an effort to contact them. Many unhappy customers find it easier to walk away and take their business elsewhere than to complain, especially if they consider you a friend. Be proactive. Ask them what went wrong and what you can do to repair the relationship. Most people will give you a second chance if you are sincere in your desire to make amends.

Ask them what you can do to make things right. Don't beg, but be sincere. If they refuse, you have to let them go and learn from your mistakes.

retirement What every exhausted entrepreneur looks forward to experiencing and must plan for. (*See also* pension plan; succession planning.)

Most entrepreneurs dread thinking about retirement, but smart ones look forward to the time when they won't be working seven days a week. Even serial entrepreneurs, those who start more than three companies, should be making plans for a comfortable retirement. No matter how small your company is or how tiny your profit margin may be, you should be setting money aside in an IRA or SEP-IRA. A certified financial planner, who understands many different products, is usually the best person to work with when it comes to setting up your retirement funds.

You need to make plans for yourself, your family, and your employees. Grooming a successor should start a few years before your planned departure. If you aren't sure who the best candidate is, try a few people out. If you have family members in the business, consider hiring an outsider to avoid a major power struggle.

While it's honorable to say you'll work until you fall over, why should you? Every retired person I know fills their days with rewarding activities and a whirlwind of social activities. They all

R/r

wonder how they ever found time to work since they are
I look forward to joining the ranks of the retired sooner ra.
than later.

retreat, company-sponsored A break from routine that often
results in thinking big thoughts and solving small problems. (*See also*
brainstorming.)

Think of a retreat is an investment in the future of your company. You don't have to fly twenty people to Hawaii or Bar-
bados. You can host a retreat close to home by renting a private
room in a restaurant or hotel. We held a very productive daylong
meeting in an upscale Manhattan restaurant and spent about
$1,100 on a gourmet meal and meeting room with a big round
table. The waiters also provided cold and hot beverages
throughout the day.

Getting out of the office for a day or two is liberating. Hire a
temp to answer your phones, or just change the voice-mail greeting to tell callers you are attending a retreat and will get back to
them later. Your customers and clients will appreciate that you are
taking some time to actually *think* about your business.

Ask a staff member to handle the meeting logistics while you
focus on the agenda. Think about what you want to accomplish.
Do you want to establish long-term goals? Solve a prickly problem
with a client? Dream up a new slogan or product name? Focus on
improving customer service?

Planning is critical. You don't want a free-for-all. You may want
to hire an outside facilitator so you can participate in the discussions. Our retreat was facilitated by Dr. Jeff Tobias, one of our
angel investors who provided great advice to SBTV during its
start-up. With his help, I could participate in the exercises and
other fun things he had planned for the group. Another person
took detailed notes, which were summarized into a report and distributed to everyone a few days later.

If you are a small enough group to get everyone together in
one room, that's best. If you have more than twenty or thirty
employees, you will probably have to break up into groups and
have several facilitators managing the discussions.

r/R

Bring along plenty of colored index cards, all kinds of marking pens, white erase boards, flip charts, and spiral notebooks. The main challenge is to listen to everyone without throwing cold water on seemingly stupid ideas. Reserve comments and judgment. Just let people brainstorm and share their ideas in a neutral environment.

Follow the agenda and keep the discussions on track. Take several breaks during the day, but allow people to slip out for bathroom breaks. Ban all phones and pagers. No one should be excused to make or take a phone call.

You should leave the retreat feeling renewed, refreshed, and ready to work hard to achieve the goals you set as a group. Plan a retreat at least once a year; twice a year if you are growing fast and need to tap everyone's brainpower more frequently.

return on equity (ROE) Net income or profit, calculated as a percentage of the owners' capital. (*See also* balance sheet.)

ROE tells the original owners and shareholders, anyone with a direct stake in the company, how their investment is performing. Take owners' equity (capital plus any profit that's been set aside for reinvestment) and divide it into the net income.

owner's equity/net income = ROE

Say the result is 15 percent: That's a lot more than you'd get by putting your money in a savings account and going fishing. If, on the other hand, you've been working at your business for five years and find that your ROE is only 3 percent, the number is telling you (and your shareholders) that government bonds are a better investment than your own company.

return on investment (ROI) The ratio of net profits to total assets.

The ROI is obtained by simply dividing a company's assets by its net income:

total assets/net profits = ROI

The bottom line: ROI is a critical number, especially if you have outside investors. Venture capitalists are known to be ruthless when it comes to ROI. They usually want ten times their money and they want it fast. Angel investors may be less aggressive, but they, too, will be watching what their investment is generating and will want to know why the ROI isn't higher.

What you decide to pay yourself in salary, bonuses, and perks affects both the ROE and ROI of your business.

reverse merger The creation of a new company inside the nearly defunct shell of an existing corporation.

Merging a privately held company in the shell of a publicly traded one has certain benefits. The main one is speed—the merger often allows a company to sell shares to the public in weeks or months, rather than years. If the merger is approved, you will have to file quarterly and annual reports with the Securities and Exchange Commission.

Piranha Inc., a high-tech firm based in Dallas, Texas, develops

---

LOOK BEFORE MERGING

If you are interested in a reverse merger:

1. Do your homework to determine the existing public company is not saddled with debts, liens, or pending lawsuits. Check court records and credit reporting agencies.

2. Contact the SEC office near you or go online to SEC.gov to learn more about the company's trading history and records of any previous infractions.

3. Work with a skilled mergers and acquisitions team, including a veteran CPA and an experienced securities lawyer.

4. Prepare a detailed budget so you know exactly how much the merger process will cost.

products to manage compressed digital data. In 2000 it merged into Chicago-based Classics International Entertainment Inc. (CIEI), which retailed T-shirts, board games, and comic books via a network of twenty-two stores in five states.

Piranha CEO Ed Sample had been a technology executive at JC Penney, and was familiar with the problems faced by the printing industry in transmitting large amounts of data online. Every year under Sample's guidance, Penney produced and distributed sixty-five different catalogs to 20 million people.

Sample connected with a team of scientists who were developing new ways to compress huge amounts of data and was convinced they had a marketable technology. "We had a theory that better ways to compress data would have a big impact on many industries, including video streaming, online entertainment, and printing," says Sample.

He and his colleagues wrote a business plan and by November 1999 they went looking for capital to launch Piranha. "We validated the market for our technology. When we found it was there, we wanted to become public immediately," Sample recalls.

Sample met CIEI's chief executive, Richard Berger, through business associates. Four years earlier, Berger had terminated the remaining 144 workers at CIEI and had stayed on to deal with what was left—mainly pending lawsuits and unhappy creditors. "I was the last man," he recalls. "But, I was very concerned about trying to give our 2,700 shareholders something for their investment."

Instead of filing for bankruptcy protection or moving to dissolve the defunct firm, Berger started looking around for an entrepreneurial venture that wanted to go public fast by merging its operations into the empty public shell of CIEI. Although securities industry analysts and mergers and acquisitions experts believe hundreds of small companies go public every year using the reverse merger, surprisingly, the SEC does not keep statistics on them.

Sample and Berger decided to merge Piranha Inc. into the shell of CIEI with the help of a securities lawyer and other advisers. The once-prosperous company had a stock price of one-half penny per

R/r

share, but it was still a publicly traded company, with 20 million shares outstanding and seventy-five broker dealers and twenty market makers keeping an eye on it. When it resumed trading, Sample, Berger, and their management team raised about $10 million from investors.

risk Opportunity without a safety net.

No opportunity is real unless the chance of failure is real, too. My nephew Jeff was the stunt coordinator for the action movie *Spider-Man*. He's about the calmest person I know. Jeff creates the illusion of risk by hiding all of the safety measures that are so meticulously built into every stunt. As an entrepreneur, you strive to reduce risk, but, finally, you must accept the fact that a safety net cannot be built in as it is in the movies. That's real life, and it's only in that world that your dream can become reality.

risk-reward ratio A method of judging whether a deal is worth doing.

Traders and hedge fund managers use complex formulas to figure out whether to buy, sell, or hold. Business owners rely on a less scientific approach to decide whether or not to do a deal. You can measure the risks and rewards by listing them in separate columns and attaching financial projections to them, according to John D'Aquila, a CPA who works with many entrepreneurial companies. "You have to determine if the benefits outweigh the risks, and that's often not easy to do," he says.

Most business matters do have some hard numbers attached. If you open that new branch office, you need to figure out how much you'll spend on rent, personnel, and utilities. That has to be weighed against the potential revenue generated by new customers.

After you crunch some numbers, try the sleep factor. If the deal is keeping you up at night, you might reconsider. You should also discuss various scenarios with your staff and outside advisers whose opinions you trust before making a final decision.

Sometimes the money isn't the driving factor. We produced an online chat between presidential candidates George W. Bush and

Al Gore Jr., for America Online at no charge. While some of our management team thought I was crazy to do all that work for no compensation, I knew it would establish a very positive relationship. We went on to produce several projects for AOL Time Warner after that initial pro bono project.

R/r

sales Offering merchandise or services at a discount to bring in additional revenue. (*See also* loss leader; mark downs; markup.)

E VERYONE LOVES A SALE. Just the word *sale* gets people excited. Deciding when to hold a sale and what merchandise to put on sale is critical to its success. Retailers thrive on seasonal sales such as the spring white sale for moving lots of linens and towels; the back-to-school sale for fall shoes and clothing; and the year-end sale to get rid of aging inventory.

Every sale is different; there is no cookie-cutter formula for success. Two for one sales work well if you are selling low-cost merchandise like plastic housewares or greeting cards. That sale wouldn't work for someone selling diamond engagement rings. A sale with a sliding discount is often effective for higher-priced merchandise. For example, you can offer a 5 percent discount on goods worth under $100 and 20 percent off goods worth $1,000 or more.

sales and use taxes State taxes that must be paid on some, but not all, sales transactions.

Almost every state has a sales tax and a use tax on the retail sale of goods. In many states, these taxes also apply to certain types of services, usually those that involve the delivery of a document or other physical product, such as the preparation of a tax return or a written consulting report.

A sales tax is a tax on retail sales. So, if you sell an item to a consumer for $1 and your state sales tax is 6 percent, you must charge the customer an additional six cents (or eat it yourself), and pay the six cents to your state taxing authority. You will fill out a sales tax return, usually on a quarterly or annual basis, and pay the tax due along with the completed return. Many states have exemptions from sales tax for certain types of goods such as food and clothing up to certain specified dollar amounts.

Note that sales taxes apply only to retail sales. Unlike some foreign countries (such as Canada and the United Kingdom), there are no taxes on wholesale transactions anywhere in the United States. So if you are selling taxable goods to someone for resale, you should request an exemption certificate, in which the customer certifies that the goods are being purchased for resale and therefore no sales tax should be collected. Similarly, if you are buying taxable goods for resale, you should give an exemption certificate so your supplier can avoid having to pay sales tax. The form of exemption certificate is usually prescribed by your state's taxing authority and should be available as a free download from your state taxing authority's website.

Sales taxes apply only to in-state retail sales. So, if your business is located in New York, and you sell taxable goods to a customer in New York, you must charge New York's state sales tax and any regional or local sales taxes that have to be collected. If, however, your business is located in New York and you sell taxable goods to a customer in California, under current law you do not have to charge either New York's or California's state sales tax.

You must charge another state's sales tax, however, if:

■ You have a physical location in that state, such as a retail outlet or catalog store.

■ You have employees residing in that state who use their home offices to meet with customers and otherwise conduct your business.

■ The sale physically takes place in that state—for example,

S/s

if, while attending a trade show in Texas, you sell taxable
goods on the trade show floor to a Florida resident, you will
have to charge Texas's sales tax, no matter where your business is located.

■   Your state has an agreement with the other state providing
for the mutual collection of each other's sales taxes—for example, New York and Connecticut have such an agreement.

A use tax is the opposite of a sales tax. You pay this whenever
you buy taxable goods from a vendor outside your state that you
or your business consumes in state. So, for example, if your business is located in Connecticut and you buy a personal computer
from a mail order vendor in Ohio that you use in your business
(i.e., the computer is not bought for resale), you will not have to
pay sales tax but you will have to pay Connecticut's use tax on the
price of the computer. Usually, but not always, a state's use tax
rate is the same as its sales tax rate.

So what about goods sold on the Internet? An act of Congress
prohibits states from charging sales and use taxes on Internet
commerce until October of 2006. So until then, the same rules
apply on the Internet as would apply in a real world transaction.

If a company based in Maine sells taxable goods over the Internet to a retail customer in Maine, sales tax should be charged; but
if the same company sells taxable goods over the Internet to a
retail customer in New Jersey, no sales tax should be charged.
Similarly, if a company based in New Jersey buys taxable goods
over the Internet for its own consumption from a vendor based in
Maine, no sales tax should be paid, but the buyer may have to pay
New Jersey use tax on the purchase.

sales force The soldiers who promote and market your products or
services to current and prospective customers. (*See also* sales reps.)

For many small businesses, the owner is the chief cook, bottle
washer, and salesperson. You first become a salesperson when you
have to sell people on your business concept. To raise money, you
sell your idea to a banker or angel investor. If you're lucky enough
to raise millions, you've successfully sold yourself (and often your

soul) to a venture capitalist. And, if your business is prospering and growing, you've sold your employees on the benefits of working for you rather than someone else.

Selling to customers and clients is another aspect of selling. Tim Smith, author of *Loyalty-Based Selling* (AMACOM, 2001), says successful sales are based on the customer's answer to one simple question: "What will it take to provide you with the best service you have ever received?" That's it. "This step is so simple and the results so profound, yet it is rarely used," writes Smith. Providing great products or services based on what you *think* your customers want is a common, but misleading approach to selling. "You may believe you are on target, but undoubtedly sometimes you are not," says Smith. "You may be going a hundred miles an hour for your customers, but down the wrong street."

The secret to initial and repeat sales is making each individual customer happy. It sounds simple, but of course, it isn't. The good news is that small business owners have a big advantage over big companies—we usually know our customers personally. Our customers are not just another number or name in a database but real people we know on a first name basis.

If your company is big enough to have its own sales staff, your mission is to use them to find out exactly what your customers need and then to make sure every salesperson is properly trained and totally familiar with your products and services. Too many salespeople, ranging from the guy selling hamburger buns to the diner to the woman selling high-end video equipment, have limited knowledge of their products. They may be attractive and charming, but they won't inspire confidence in your customers if they can't answer basic questions intelligently. The more training you provide to your sales team, the more sales they'll book.

Most small companies rely on commission-based salespeople or work with a distributor who represents multiple product lines. No matter how small your business is, try to provide a small draw to cover expenses in addition to a fair commission on each sale. Since every industry has different rates, check with other business owners or your trade association for the specifics on commission-based sales.

S/s

Finally, remember that everyone in every department is a salesperson for your company. The person who answers the phone or answers the door is on the frontlines. Remember that corny but true advertising slogan for deodorant: "You never get a second chance to make a first impression."

sales reps The foot soldiers of your marketing army. (*See also* distribution; sales force.)

The people who represent you and your products must be carefully chosen. It's not easy for small companies to attract skilled sales people because they are in demand and can command generous compensation. A better approach may be to develop sales reps from within. Look for bright, energetic employees who get excited about what they're doing every day. If they really understand what sets your products or services apart from the competition, they can become great sales people.

Everyone who works for your company should be able to answer basic sales questions about price, availability, sizes, and shipping information. If they can't answer the basic questions with confidence, don't let them answer the phone.

sales tax A local tax on finished products, paid by consumers and collected by merchants. (*See also* sales and use taxes.)

The tax does not apply to purchase of inventory, or, generally, to goods sold outside the taxing jurisdiction, so long as the goods are also consumed or used outside the taxing jurisdiction. Hence many Internet sales are exempt from sales taxes if the customers buy and use the goods in another state. Your new business will need a vendor's certificate or similar document from your state tax department, which will detail which sales are taxable.

SCORE *See* Service Corps of Retired Executives.

S corporation *See* Subchapter S corporation.

s/S

search engine A ready-made Web-based marketing tool.

Search engines are the workhorses of the Internet. A few years ago there were scores of search engines, sorting, categorizing, and directing users to specific websites. At the end of 2001, the dot-com collapse left fewer, bigger search engines; Yahoo.com, Google .com, and Lycos.com remained the dominant players. In 1998 and 1999, online companies were throwing cash at search engine operators, begging for a more prominent placement in their search results. By 2001, it was easier and cheaper to get top billing on a major search engine. For example, SelectWinesLLC.com, a small Harrison, New York–based company selling imported wines, moved up several notches on all the major search engines when Wine.com went under, according to CEO John D'Aquila (who is also SBTV Corp.'s CPA).

Many business owners invest an enormous amount of time and money in building a website but forget to register their websites on every search engine available. Big mistake. It doesn't take much time to fill out the registration forms online. There is usually no cost to submit your site to the basic search engine. But if you want your site to come up high in the rankings, you will pay for the privilege. At this writing, Google.com is the number one search engine. It's reputable, updated frequently, and the one most business people use. Assign a staff person to search out all the search engines and make sure your site is listed properly. Check your position on the search engines frequently. If there are mistakes, go deep into the Contact Us area of the site to fill out a form to correct your listing.

security A commitment to put customer and employee's safety first. In e-business, the added promise of anonymity and secured financial transactions. (*See also* computer security.)

Good security measures keep the bad guys out of your business and protect the good guys inside from harm. But sometimes, the inside guys turn out to be the bad guys. In September 2001, the *Wall Street Journal* reported that Jerome Jacobson, a former police officer who worked for a marketing firm Simon Worldwide Inc., allegedly masterminded a scheme to defraud

S/s

McDonald's out of $13 million in sweepstakes prizes.

Jacobson was supposed to make sure the winning game pieces created by Simon Worldwide Inc. for McDonald's Monopoly and Who Wants to Be a Millionaire games were randomly distributed to the restaurants. Instead, according the FBI case file, he allegedly gave the winning pieces to friends and others who claimed more than $13 million in prizes over six years. The recipients then allegedly kicked back to Jacobson a portion of their cash prizes.

Alert receptionists can be your best frontline security. They should be familiar with frequent visitors, including the U.S. Postal Service delivery person, overnight delivery people, suppliers, vendors, and customers. They should question unknown visitors, especially those bearing small packages. If you are in any sort of controversial or high-risk business, you might consider installing an X-ray screening device for packages. Scanning packages for bombs may seem extreme, but better safe than sorry.

Any suspicious package should be taken outside the office. Call your local police department for help if you receive a fishy looking package or a visitor refuses to leave your lobby until they see a certain person. Your receptionist should also be wary of process servers delivering subpoenas for civil or criminal proceedings.

Locking the supply room and warehouse and limiting access to storage areas is also a smart practice. Limit the number of keys you make available and change the locks when you let a troubled employee go. A few dollars for a new deadbolt cylinder is a small price to pay for peace of mind, especially if you have terminated someone under stressful circumstances.

seed money No more than you need to get your business up and running. (*See also* microloan; Small Business Administration.)

The beautiful thing about seed money is how little you will need, given your ample supply of desire and determination. What amount do you need for that one plane ticket, one laptop computer, or software suite to get you started? Work a second job. Borrow it from your mother or brother. Tap your credit cards. Go for it. You may surprise yourself and become a success.

I sold candy in a movie theatre, wearing a turquoise and orange

s/S

miniskirt (not a pretty sight) to raise $700 for an IBM Selectric typewriter. It was a fortune in 1974; I could afford only one alternative typeface. Yet with that machine I felt invincible. Though I lived in the backwater of San Diego, I felt equipped to be the best correspondent *Newsweek* ever had. Soon I had bylines in *Newsweek* and the *Washington Post*. I was in business.

self-employment Working for yourself by serving everyone else. (*See also* entrepreneur; Kirton Adaptation Innovation Inventory.)

Not everyone is suited to be an entrepreneur. Why? You'll never work harder than when you work for yourself. I strongly recommend working in a business similar to the one you want to

---

A GREAT LOW-COST BUSINESS

The gift basket business continues to be one of the most popular, easy to start, often home-based businesses. The initial investment is usually hundreds, not thousands, of dollars. And, it's easy to test market your baskets to local clients. If you have a gift basket business that you would like to expand, or a similar home-based small business, here are some simple ideas:

■ Include a discount coupon for another gift basket with every basket you sell. This will encourage the happy recipient of your basket to order another one for someone else. Word of mouth is still the most powerful form of advertising, but coupons are also very effective.

■ Contact local groups, including arts organizations, and donate a lavish basket to a charity auction, especially a silent auction where your work will be displayed for a while during a high-profile event. You can also promote your business by serving as an expert for a how-to article or on a local television show around the holidays.

■ Take some close-up, color photos of your baskets and put together a press kit, featuring your brochure and business cards. Write a press release outlining some interesting tips about gift giving, possibly relating to an upcoming holiday. Send the release

---

S/s

start *before* you quit your day job. Take a part-time job in the field to learn the basics; attend the next big industry trade show to get a feel for the products and people. Speak to as many business owners as you can. Ask them to tell you the truth about owning a small company. They'll be happy to share their war stories.

The Right Stuff

Based on my encounters with thousands of business owners, I've found these qualities essential to being a successful entrepreneur:

- **Persistence.** You must be able to take rejection over and over again and not give up even when you are discouraged and exhausted.

---

inside a small gift basket to the feature editors of the local newspapers, radio, and television stations. You can digitize the images and post them on your website, if you have one.

■ Send a special basket to a high-profile local celebrity who has just had a baby. Ask her for a short testimonial about how much she liked your work. Since there is so much competition in your industry, you have to work hard to set yourself apart. Get to know birthing coaches, midwives, and pediatricians. Market your services to them because they are working closely with expectant mothers. Set up a special baby shower registry, where several friends can chip in to buy one fabulous basket.

■ Sign up to teach a one-session basket-making class at the local community college or adult education center. Smart entrepreneurs position themselves as experts to raise their profile and build credibility. Even if you share some design secrets, you know people will still want to buy professional baskets from your company. Make sure you have plenty of flyers and coupons at the class to distribute. And, hold a drawing to give away the basket you make during the class.

s/S

- **Stamina.** You need enormous physical and mental strength to keep going under adverse conditions.
- **Confidence.** It takes a lot of self-esteem to keep going when everyone tells you that you are crazy and will lose everything.
- **Open-mindedness.** You have to be able to set your ego aside and ask for help. Listening to advice and following what makes sense is a key to success.
- **Passion.** You have to be passionate about what you do and allow yourself to feel proud and energized when things are going well.
- **People-oriented.** People do business with people, not companies. You have to be a true people person to succeed in business.
- **Realistic view of life.** If things are not working, no matter what you do, you have to be realistic and know when the game is over.

Running your own business is like riding a thrill ride twenty-four hours a day. It feels great most of the time. But to really enjoy the entrepreneurial roller coaster, you'll need a strong stomach and a crash helmet.

selling a business The final step in resolving the problems of failure, success, and everything in between. (*See also* buying a business; exit strategy; valuation.)

Three reasons prompt most entrepreneurs sell their companies: they want to cash out, the company is failing, or the company is booming and needs new ownership in order to grow. While some dot-com companies sold for pennies on the dollar in the early 2000s, traditional small businesses selling metal components, electronic parts, plastics, printing, and information-technology services easily continue to change hands.

"Small to medium sized transactions are typically not as affected in a downturn," says John Mack, CEO of USBX, a business-sales brokerage in Los Angeles. "The debt financing that's difficult to come up with is [in sales of big companies] not typically used in

YOUR BUSINESS ON THE BLOCK

Selling tips from USBX.com, a business-sales brokerage in Los Angeles:

■ Never let your ego get in the way. Don't make excuses and don't confuse the failure of the business with personal failings.

■ Allow the buyer to focus on the upside: unrecognized potential, room to reorganize, and ways to rebuild.

■ Ask the seller to indemnify you to protect you against lawsuits filed after you sell the business.

■ Keep your employees informed throughout the negotiations. You don't want unfounded rumors to circulate and hurt morale. Your staff is often a significant part of what you are selling and you need them to stick around.

small transactions. Most businesses are sold with secured financing or the sellers taking back a note."

Although the number of business sales is not recorded, Mack believes about 250,000 businesses worth $50 million or less change hands each year in the United States. Of that total, about 50,000 businesses sell for between $1 million and $50 million.

In addition to outright sales, many small companies merge or acquire each other. About 9,200 business combinations involving deals in excess of $1 million took place in 1999, according to Mergerstat, which tracks private deals. The price of small companies is also increasing, from five to six times earnings before interest expense and taxes (EBIT) in 1992, to six to nine times EBIT in 1997, according to a landmarked report issued by the Arthur Andersen Center for Family Business.

"We'll continue to see a big turnover as the baby boomers sell out," Mack predicts. In considering a sale, the first step is to buy an objective assessment. Customers of USBX pay a $20,000 retainer,

s/S

which includes the valuation report. USBX also sells a simple valuation for $2,500 and a fifty-page version for $10,000. Sellers pay a small fee to list their business on the USBX site, usbx.com.

If the buyer, or acquiring company, is significantly larger, selling the company improves the chances that the business will grow into a much larger entity down the road. There are, however, some significant disadvantages in selling your business. The "fit" between the two companies must be appropriate, you will have to report to executives in the acquiring company (who may not have the same entrepreneurial spirit you have). There is no guarantee that you will be allowed to continue running the company, and the corporate identity of the company may disappear, becoming a small cog in a very large wheel.

Ronald Speyer, CEO of the brokerage Emerge Corp., based in Costa Mesa, California, works with privately held businesses in transition. Emerge has about 1,500 businesses listed online and collects a fee only when the deal closes.

"Many people use the sale of a business to solve a problem," Speyer says. "Some entrepreneurs realize they are better in the start-up phase and admit, 'I'm not the guy to build the business to the next stage.'"

Speyer advises daily attention to putting your balance sheet in order, documenting all systems and procedures, building a strong management team, recording all contracts, and hiring top talent. You want to be ready if and when someone knocks on your door with an interesting offer. "People think their buyer is across town, when in reality they may be far away, or above or below them in the production or supply cycle."

RECOMMENDED READING

■   *Keep or Sell Your Business ... How to Make the Decision Every Private Company Faces*, by Mike Cohn with Jayne Pearl. (Dearborn Trade, 2000). A readable, comprehensive guide to the sales process.

■   *How to Create a Buy-Sell Agreement and Control the Destiny of Your Small Business* (includes PC disk), by Anthony Mancuso and Bethany K. Laurence. (Nolo Press, 1999). All the facts and forms you need to sell your company to insiders or outsiders.

S/s

■ *How to Sell Your Business—and Get What You Want!,* by Colin Gabriel (Gwent Press, 1998). Anecdotes and tips from fifty-seven real business owners and managers.

SEP-IRA *See* pension plan.

service business *Serve* says it all. (*See also* retail.)

Any business that provides a service to a steady clientele has a better chance of success. Service businesses also require less capital to get started. If you know how to do something people will pay for, then you have a shot at starting a service business. Professional organizers, makeup artists, barbers, concierges, painters, caterers and dog sitters are all good service businesses. Think about providing services to other business owners, such as graphic designing, word processing, bookkeeping, delivery, gift-wrapping, personal shopping, or plant maintenance.

The best thing about a service business is that you can start very small, even working on nights and weekends to test the market. When you land clients, ask them to refer you to others who might use your services. Word of mouth is the most effective way to market a small service business.

Service Corps of Retired Executives (SCORE) Free, SBA-supported consulting services for small business owners.

For more than thirty-five years, thousands (11,500 in 2002) of retired business executives and owners have been providing free confidential consulting and advisory services to millions of business owners across the United States. In the late 1990s, SCORE went online with a deep and extensive site: **score.org**.

Business owners who prefer to work online can be connected with a veteran business owner familiar with their industry. You can e-mail your questions and receive answers directly from a SCORE counselor. SCORE also sponsors numerous free and low-cost workshops, seminars, and events. SCORE offices are often located in the local U.S. Small Business Administration (SBA) office or in a Business Information Center (BIC) or Small Business Development Center. You can find one quickly online or by calling: 800-634-0245.

s/S

sexual harassment Any kind of sexual behavior that is unwelcome or inappropriate for the workplace. (*See also* zero tolerance.)

It could never happen in *your* business because you set the proper tone and listen for complaints. Right? *Wrong.* "Too often employers, large and small alike, feel that no harassing behavior is occurring in their workplace just because they haven't had any complaints," says Dolores Ennico, a human resources expert who is currently director of employee relations for Olin Corp. in Norwalk, Connecticut.

"Quite often, the opposite is true—employees may be too fearful of losing their jobs, or of suffering retaliation from coworkers, to come forward with their complaints until the harassment reaches an intolerable level," say Ennico. "This is what you want to avoid at all costs. Most sexual harassment lawsuits start out as minor incidents. If you nip those in the bud and demonstrate your intolerance of harassing behavior, however inoffensive it may seem to some, you stand the best chance of avoiding the costly and demoralizing effects of a sexual harassment lawsuit."

Sexual harassment is a form of sex discrimination that violates Title VII of the federal Civil Rights Act of 1964. Sexual harassment can include verbal harassment, such as derogatory comments or dirty jokes under certain circumstances; visual harassment such as unfavorable or embarrassing posters, cartoons, and drawings; and physical harassment such as sexual advances and demands.

Sexual harassment can arise in two different contexts. The first involves the situation in which an employee with supervisory authority over another employee uses that authority to try to extort sexual favors. This is called quid pro quo harassment, and occurs when a supervisor makes the unwelcome demand in return for some kind of promised employment gain which the supervisor can give, such as a raise or a promotion, or when a supervisor threatens an employee with adverse action if he or she does not submit. Even if the harassed employee refuses the unwelcome demand and nothing else happens, harassment has occurred.

S/s

BASIC PROTECTION

Some steps to avoid sexual harassment lawsuits:

■ Adopt a sexual harassment policy that communicates the company's zero tolerance approach toward sexual harassment.

■ Provide multiple routes that employees can take to file complaints such as calling a hotline, contacting their supervisor, or contacting a designated employee.

■ Give employees the option of talking with a male or female company representative.

■ Conduct periodic sexual harassment training for all employees, even if it is only reading material or watching a video. Something is better than no training at all. Document the training given to each employee.

■ Conduct yearly meetings with your supervisors to review the sexual harassment policy.

■ Conduct a yearly sexual harassment survey among your employees.

Sexual harassment also occurs when a supervisor, coworker, or even a nonemployee behaves or acts in a way that creates an intolerable work environment for another employee. This type of harassment also occurs when a person is made uncomfortable because of his or her race, age, disability, religion, or some other characteristic that is protected under federal or state law. This is called hostile work environment harassment. The victim as well as the harasser may be a woman or a man; the victim does not have to be of the opposite sex.

Prevention is the best tool for eliminating sexual harassment in the workplace. Employers should establish an effective complaint or grievance process and take immediate and appropriate action when an employee complains. Your sexual harassment policy and the steps you take to make sure you comply with that policy

s/S

should be spelled out in your employee handbook. If you offer any sort of employee assistance programs, be sure your provider has information about sexual harassment so they can help your employees make an informal or formal complaint.

shareholders People who believe in you enough to buy shares in your company. (*See also* angels; investor relations; investors.)

shares Stock in a closely held corporation, or membership interests in a limited liability company. (*See also* corporation; Subchapter S corporation.)

The owners of a closely held corporation are said to own shares in the enterprise, meaning shares of stock. Shares usually are evidenced by printed stock certificates, which are registered on the books of the corporation.

It is important to distinguish between shares and the percentage ownership of the company that they represent. When a corporation is formed, the board of directors is authorized to issue up to X shares to investors. These are called the authorized shares, and constitute the maximum number of shares that may be issued. When shares are actually delivered to an investor in exchange for cash or property, they are considered issued shares. The board can keep issuing shares up to the point at which they have exhausted all of the corporation's authorized shares, in which case they will need to amend the corporate charter or articles of incorporation in order to increase the number of authorized shares (this will require the approval of the existing shareholders).

Together, the owners of a corporation's issued shares own 100 percent of the corporation; the authorized shares that are not yet issued do not count in determining a corporation's ownership until they are actually issued. To determine the percentage of the corporation owned by any one shareholder, you simply divide the corporation's total issued shares by the number of shares the shareholder owns. So far, it's pretty simple, right? Yet it can become complicated in a hurry, because the board can always issue new shares that reduce, or dilute, the percentage ownership of existing shareholders.

S/s

Say Investor A owns 100 shares of stock and the corporation has issued 1,000 shares, so that Investor A owns 10 percent of the corporation. The board of directors issues 100 new shares to Investor B. Investor A still owns his 100 shares, but his percentage ownership of the corporation has been diluted to 9.09 percent (1,100 divided by 100). If Investor A had antidilution rights and wanted to continue owning 10 percent of the corporation, he would have the right to buy 11 additional shares at the same price per share that Investor B paid for his shares.

Note that if a corporation grants all of its shareholders antidilution rights, the corporation's existing shareholders will be able to block completely the issuance of new shares by exercising those rights, since the total issued shares of a corporation cannot exceed 100 percent.

Because of the dilution problem, you need to be careful when you promise a prospective investor that they will receive 10 percent of the company. It is better to offer prospective investors "X shares of the corporation's common stock, which today constitutes X percent of the corporation's issued shares."

It is very tempting for a newly formed corporation to issue lots of shares to everyone who helps the company get off the ground. That's because the stock is cheap at that point, and because the company founders sincerely want to reward those who contribute their blood, sweat, and tears to the venture. Once someone has become your stockholder, however, there is only one legal way to get rid of him—you must repurchase his shares, often at a significantly higher price. The only people who should receive stock in a new formed corporation are founders, key employees who can be expected to perform for the long term (and who will lose their shares by contract if they don't), and investors who are providing your seed capital. Anyone else should be rewarded with the right to receive shares in the future—options or warrants—but only if they're still making a contribution.

shipping Getting your finished goods from your door to your customer's store. (*See also* freight forwarder.)

s/S

signing bonus A payment given to a new employee to recognize their value and the time and effort required for them to quit their job and join your firm. (*See also* hiring.)

In a tight labor market, companies are pressured to pay signing bonuses to new employees as a final incentive to take the job. Of course, if you don't have to pay a signing bonus, don't. Everything is negotiable and you may be able to get away with a smaller cash outlay by offering to pay for a move, school tuition, or a company car. If you do offer a signing bonus, be sure to stagger the payments. Recruiters suggest paying a portion of the bonus after ninety days, with the balance due after a year on the job. You want to make sure the person is working out and doesn't quit with a bunch of cash in hand. Some employment contracts require the bonus to be returned if the person doesn't stick around, but think of how tough it will be to get the money back after the check is cashed.

SIMPLE 401(k) *See* pension plan.

SIMPLE IRA *See* pension plan.

slash and burn The process of cutting overhead to save your business from ruin.

Sometimes you have to take drastic measures to save your business. It's tough, but the alternatives are filing for bankruptcy protection or just walking away and leaving behind a pile of bills and a pack of unhappy creditors. When your bills exceed your available or expected cash, it's time to slash and burn. Make a detailed list of your monthly expenses to determine what you absolutely need to operate. Anything not on the list of essentials has to go—right now.

When we hit a rough patch and had to cut our expenses, we let go every employee except one—and we reduced his schedule from five to three days a week. We kept the freelance bookkeeper, but reduced her visits from weekly to every other week. We closed two offices and moved into one. We cut off the satellite service, but kept the DSL. We cut off four phone lines, but kept

S/s

the toll-free number. We splurged on bottled water, but put away the credit cards and stopped entertaining clients. We stopped using Federal Express and started using the U.S. Postal Service's Express or Priority Mail.

When we finished cutting operating expenses, we felt more in control and a bit lighter. It was amazing how much money you can save when you look closely at every dollar you spend.

We were careful not to cut out anything that affected the work we did for clients. In fact, Scott Wylie, our chief technology officer, upgraded our video editing system with help from another client he works with. And, we set up Scott's editing suite in our neighbor's office across the hall, trading DSL and tech support services for rent.

Not spending money is not as much fun as spending money, but when the life of your business depends on it, you do what you have to do.

small business Any endeavor in which the principal players feel that their own assets are at risk, and that their own decisions will bring failure or success.

Technically, the federal Small Business Administration calls an enterprise with fewer than 500 employees a small business. That definition varies slightly for government contracts. In 2001 the IRS counted 17,000 businesses with more than 500 employees, and 22.4 million small businesses.

Small Business Administration (SBA) The federal government's resource for businesses of fewer than 500 employees.

The SBA has useful programs and free advice on starting and financing a business, and is a particularly good place to start for companies wishing to sell products and services to the federal government. It also can guarantee loans for start-ups and maintains an online program just for women-owned businesses. The SBA has offices throughout the country. Its website is www.sba.gov.

s/S

Small Business Development Center (SBDC) A network of private and publicly sponsored centers that provide counseling, seminars, and resources to entrepreneurs. (*See also* Small Business Administration, Service Corps of Retired Executives.)

If you are in the start-up phase, run don't walk to the nearest SBDC. These thousand-plus centers come in all shapes and sizes and can be found on college campuses, in SBA offices, and in storefronts in most big and small cities. These private-public partnerships offer a plethora of free and low-cost resources and services for entrepreneurs. You can meet with a SCORE counselor to buff up your business plan or a financial counselor to prepare an application for a government-backed loan. You can borrow books and pamphlets and do online research.

Some SBDCs are modest affairs; one of the most deluxe centers, based in a former bank building in downtown San Jose, California, was funded by twenty corporations and spearheaded by Cisco Systems. It features video conferencing, laptop computers, and office space for a bevy of local lenders and consultants. The best way to find the SBDC nearest your office is to visit **www.sba.gov** and search the list of SBDCs located around the country.

Social Security withholding *See* employment taxes.

software The incredibly complex and expensive programs that drive you crazy when you rely on them to run your business operations.

Most business PCs have enough complex software in them to run a small hospital, but that doesn't mean they will make your life easier. Quite the contrary. Many popular programs are riddled with bugs, quirks, and limitations that will drive you insane. There's nothing you can do about it.

Every small business owner needs programs to do the bookkeeping, accounting, word processing, database management, and e-mail. You'll need a browser for Internet access, and I recommend downloading a free version of Adobe Acrobat to read PDF files. Many programs are pre-installed when you buy a desktop or laptop computer, but you can often customize your system to fit your needs.

S/s

Many industries are lucky (or unlucky) enough to have had proprietary software packages created for them. For instance, your local vet, dentist, or florist can buy a special vertical software package designed to run their particular business from appointment setting to invoicing. Most businesses are held hostage by Microsoft products, especially the latest version of Microsoft Office, which bundles together a suite of products including the most popular business applications: Word, PowerPoint, Excel, Outlook, Microsoft Internet Explorer, and Windows Media Player (for playing audio and video files). You can buy other kinds of business software (Lotus, for example) but then your electronic files won't be compatible with 99 percent of the business world.

No matter what you do for a living, before you buy software, especially an expensive industry-specific program, ask colleagues for their recommendations, and if they're game, a quick demonstration of their system. Spring for the paid tech support offered by the software vendor, especially if you are a novice and will need some hand-holding. Better yet, contract with a smart tech guru who can install, maintain, and troubleshoot your PC software.

sole proprietorship An individual engaged in a trade or business, without any protection against legal liability. (*See also* corporation; partnerships and limited partnerships.)

Unless you have partners in your business, and unless you have formed a legal entity to conduct your business, you are considered a sole proprietorship for legal purposes when you start and own a small business.

A sole proprietorship is a solitary human engaged in a trade or business. You don't need a lawyer to set up a sole proprietorship; all you need is a birth certificate and a pulse. The only piece of legal paperwork you will need is a trade name certificate, and this only if you are doing business using a name other than the name that appears on your birth certificate. For example, John S. Doe, Attorney at Law, is not a trade name, but John Doe & Associates is a trade name. You file this document in the clerk's office of the city, town, or county in which you maintain your business address.

A sole proprietor reports his or her income from the business

s/S

by filling out Schedule C (Income or Loss from a Trade or Business) on his or her Form 1040 each year. If you operate several different sole proprietorships, each one should have its own Schedule C and business checking account to make bookkeeping and accounting easier.

While you can use your Social Security number on Schedule C, it is recommended that you obtain a federal tax identification number from the IRS for the sole proprietorship you operate. You can do this by downloading Form SS-4 from the IRS website at **www.irs.gov** and faxing the completed form to your regional IRS office (the address and fax number will appear on the instructions to the form). You should also obtain a state tax identification number from your state's tax authority for the sole proprietorship you operate.

While sole proprietorships are easy to operate, they do have some negatives:

■ You have unlimited personal liability for every business mistake you make. If you breach a contract, you lose your house; if you get into a traffic accident that's not covered by insurance, you lose your house; if you bake cookies that get people sick, you lose your house. And your stamp collection. And your personally autographed photo of Elvis. When you operate a sole proprietorship, there is no separation between your personal and business assets, so everything is at risk if something goes wrong in your business and you are sued.

■ You pay taxes on your business income at your personal income tax rate, which may be higher than the rate you would pay if you formed a corporation or other legal entity for your business.

Despite the risks of doing business as a sole proprietor, the overwhelming majority of all small businesses in the United States are sole proprietorships. You can limit your risks in a sole proprietorship by buying commercial liability insurance, but this coverage can be expensive depending on the nature of your business.

S/s

spin The process of turning a negative story around. (*See also* crisis PR.)

We've all heard the term *spin doctor* in connection with political figures who need to be bailed out of one mess or another. But often your company will have to disseminate bad news that requires careful handling to avert a media disaster. This is when you need to hire a professional to put a happy face on an unhappy situation. Never handle the release of seriously bad news on your own. An accidental death, worker-related illness, poisoning, bridge collapse, bombing, rape, or murder handled poorly can literally ruin your business. Seek professional help if anything terrible is happening at your business. Hire a good spin doctor and follow his or her treatment plan.

sponsorship, advertising Proven revenue model that gives continual presence to a paid message. (*See also* brand building.)

Every year, corporations around the world spend billions of dollars sponsoring all sorts of events, websites, and organizations. John Hancock Insurance, for example, spent $15 million to be a sponsor of the 2002 Salt Lake City Winter Olympic games. Nike spends millions of dollars to get star athletes in a variety of sports to wear its swoosh logo on ball caps, shirts, uniforms, and shoes.

Landing a sponsorship contract isn't easy. The key is to become the perfect or near perfect bridge between a sponsor and its target audience. Big companies, promoting major brands such as Coke, Pepsi, and Gatorade prefer to sponsor mass-market events like football games and golf tournaments. Sports teams often sell sponsorships for the "Play of the Day" or the play of the minute. Logos are everywhere—on players' hats, shoes, cars, and equipment and all over the stands, scoreboards, and stadiums. Blimps fly overhead, and the stadiums themselves are named after their corporate benefactors, such as the Staples Center, PNC Bank Arena, and Continental Airlines Arena.

Since sponsorship deals require use of the corporate brand, you have to negotiate with a high-level decision maker to put together a lucrative sponsorship deal. Finding the right people can be a

s/S

challenge. Sometimes they are in the marketing department; sometimes they are in the advertising department. Often the outside advertising agency makes recommendations to the corporate client about sponsorship opportunities. We've always been rejected by the agency, but have been successful when selling a sponsorship deal directly to the corporate client.

Big companies seeking to connect with small business owners have sponsored all my national speaking and book promotion tours, and my radio and television segments. In tight economic times, sponsorship dollars shrink, so it's tougher to sign a big contract. You don't need a million-dollar deal. Start small to establish a deep relationship. Join forces with a regional beverage bottler to sponsor a charity race or celebrity tennis match. Do something good for the local community to catch the eye of a national sponsor. Be creative and cook up something unusual that will attract publicity.

THE MID-CAREER MOVE

An obvious way to increase your chances of success is to parlay the skills you learn on the job into a profitable venture. But be careful to adjust your expectations; you're not in the corporate world anymore.

"Before starting my business, I worked in brand management for Quaker Oats," says Sally Kroha, a former brand manager who promoted Rice-a-Roni, Chewy Granola Bars, and Quaker Oatmeal. She founded DazzleDerm Inc., a Chicago-based company that makes Buffing Soap Bags, which turn a bar of soap into a skin exfoliator.

Kroha crafted the first bag on a sewing machine in her basement. "I wanted an easier way to exfoliate my skin," says Kroha, who made sample bags from over 200 materials before she decided on the right type of nylon netting. Users place a bar of soap inside the bag, pull the drawstring, and put their hand inside the back of the bag to scrub their skin. The water hitting the soap inside the netting creates the lather.

S/s

starting a business The process of creating the perfect job for yourself. (*See also* Military Spouse Entrepreneurial Readiness Program; self-employment.)

You need nerves of steel to start a business. But, if you have done your market research and believe there are people who want to buy what you plan to sell, go for it. But don't quit your job until you can collect a salary from your own venture.

Start small, working at home at night and over the weekend. Set up a simple website to act as your twenty-four-hour storefront in cyberspace. Speak with a few veterans who have run successful businesses similar to yours. Listen to their war stories and take good notes.

Visit a franchise expo to get an idea of all the different business opportunities out there. There are very few totally original business concepts, so before you mortgage your house to start a business, make sure there is nothing quite like it.

I recommend working part-time for a business similar to the

She approached the marketing of her invention just the way she ran lines of business for Quaker Oats. "In my former job, I was accountable for the financial results of the product line, developing a business plan and a marketing strategy," says Kroha. "I had a full team of people reporting to me. Now, the steps are the same but I am the cross-functional team."

Kroha works with a team of freelancers and subcontractors who moonlight on her projects. Although she has the talent in place, things don't happen quite as fast as they did at Quaker Oats, she says. "It's harder to get people to jump when it's just you and your little business," says Kroha, who works with a trademark attorney, a patent attorney, and a freelance public relations expert. Her bags are made overseas by a vendor and she sells bags directly to local shops.

s/S

one you want to start. Learn what it really takes on someone else's dime. I once spent a weekend working at a busy Virginia bed and breakfast to write an article about the experience. When I got home, my friends told me they were about to buy a B&B in New Mexico. I told them to work in one before they plunked down the money. They didn't listen to my advice and were totally miserable running the B&B—almost divorcing over the business. They managed to sell it after two years and got back to what they were good at—engineering and public relations.

One of the best books for someone thinking about starting a business is *Kick Start Your Dream Business* by Romanus Wolter (Ten Speed Press, 2001). It is very easy to read, filled with anecdotes and practical information. Wolter works with business owners at several small business centers and incubators in the San Francisco Bay area.

Another good primer is *Small Business for Dummies* by Eric Tyson and Jim Schell (Hungry Minds Inc., 1998).

start-ups Upstart companies bent on proving they have direction. (*See also* incubator; self-employment; starting a business.)

step lease A popular financing vehicle in which rent payments increase during the lease term.

A traditional lease has a fixed rental payment throughout its term. In a step lease, the monthly payments start low and then step up to a payment that is more in line with the current fair rental value of the leased property. This would also allow a company to acquire property (while occasionally used in real estate leases, the step lease is a popular equipment leasing vehicle) and integrate it into its operations without a significant impact on cash flow.

stock A portion of ownership in a corporation that has been divided into shares. (*See also* shareholders.)

S/s

stock options The opportunity to purchase company stock at a pre-set price.

Stock options were once the icing on the cake of incredible job offers made to twenty-somethings working for dot-coms. Millions of dollars in future stock were dangled in front of employees who jumped from company to company with lightning speed. Most of the options ended up being worth nothing, or even worse, went underwater, creating tax nightmares when people had to pay capital gains tax on worthless stock. Stock options are complex legal and financial instruments that require the help of a skilled securities lawyer to negotiate and cash in.

If your company has stock and you expect to expand the company, consider issuing options to employees. You can set up stringent requirements for issuing and redeeming stock. Used wisely, stock options can help keep loyal employees around long enough to taste the fruits of their labors. Speak to other business owners about what worked and what didn't work for them when they issued options.

We've spent a lot of money on legal and accounting fees to issue options to employees in anticipation of selling our company to an outside investor. The options are really worth very little if you are not acquired or invested in, so think twice about going down that road.

strategy A map of unexplored territory intended to help plan and achieve financial and personal goals. (*See also* advisory board.)

You wouldn't drive across country without a map or a visit to the AAA, so why would you try to manage your company without a strategy? Too many business owners are too busy to think about what they are doing. This is a fatal mistake. You should be really thinking about what you are doing at least once a week—and not just at the staff meetings. You, the owner or manager, must be the visionary leader who crafts a plan and a strategy for achieving your financial and personal goals.

Your strategy can change frequently, but base it on a clear map that will take you from point A to point B to point C. If you need help, create a strong board of advisers. This way you can turn to people who know more than you and whose opinions you respect.

s/S

stress The debilitating result of too much to do combined with not enough money or time. (*See also* burnout.)

Entrepreneurs thrive on stress, but too much can do you in.

You must develop a stress-busting strategy or you'll end up in bed with mononucleosis, like I did in the summer of 2001. Entrepreneurs think we are invincible. True, you can go a long way on little sleep and a large supply of Snickers bars. But eventually, poor diet and exhaustion will knock the stuffing out of you.

You don't have to check into a fancy spa to relax. Just do something every day that gives you a break from your business. Read a steamy novel, talk to a friend, smack a ball (golf, tennis, squash), clean the house—anything that helps you let off steam and clear your head. A walk around the block at lunchtime works. So does a swim at the end of the day or a yoga class. Find whatever works for you and stick to it—or regret it.

Subchapter S corporation A corporation that elects to be taxed as if it were a partnership. (*See also* corporation; gross-up clause.)

Many small business owners choose to incorporate their business in order to limit their personal liability for the business's debts, obligations, and liabilities. As a taxable entity, however, a corporation is required to pay federal and state taxes on its net income. If the corporation distributes any of its net income to its shareholders as a dividend, the dividend is taxable to the owners at their personal income tax rates, leading to the double taxation of corporate income.

Some corporations seek to avoid the double taxation problem by electing to be taxed as a partnership under Subchapter S of the federal Internal Revenue Code. The shareholders of a Subchapter S corporation enjoy the same limitation of their personal liability as those of a regular corporation; the Subchapter S election affects only the manner in which the corporation is taxed. A corporation makes a Subchapter S election by filing IRS Form 2553, available with instructions as a free download at the IRS website at **www.irs.gov**, but it may make this election only at certain times of the year. A Subchapter S corporation may elect to convert back into a regular corporation, but if it does so it will

S/s

be barred for three years from re-electing Subchapter S status.

A Subchapter S corporation is not a taxable entity and does not pay federal or, in most states, state income taxes. A Subchapter S corporation's profits and losses pass through to the individual shareholders, who must report their share of the profits and losses on their personal tax returns each year.

What, however, if the Subchapter S corporation decides to keep the $100 in its checking account and not pay the money out to its shareholders? Under current tax law, each shareholder of a Subchapter S corporation must report his or her share of the corporation's net income on his or her personal tax return—this is referred to as the "phantom income" problem and effectively prevents Subchapter S corporations from retaining earnings from one year to the next.

To avoid unhappy shareholders who will have to pay taxes on income they never actually received, Subchapter S corporations

PROS AND CONS OF SUBCHAPTER S

Pros:

■ Shareholders enjoy the same limited liability protection as the shareholders of regular corporations.

■ The corporation does not pay federal income taxes; profits and losses flow through to the owners as they do in a partnership.

Cons:

■ Shareholders have to pay taxes on their percentage share of corporate net income even if the corporation doesn't distribute its income to the shareholders.

■ The corporation may have to pay some state income taxes.

■ All corporations are expensive to form and operate, and require a lot of legal paperwork.

s/S

are usually forced to pay all net income to the shareholders at the end of the business year, or indemnify their shareholders for any phantom tax liability they may incur as a result of undistributed net income (this indemnification is called a gross-up agreement).

A Subchapter S corporation reports its annual income on IRS Form 1120-S (available with instructions as a free download from the IRS website at **www.irs.gov**), but is not required to pay taxes as a legal entity. A Subchapter S corporation must use the calendar year as its fiscal year; using a different fiscal year end will require IRS approval.

The Subchapter S corporation is also subject to a number of rules which are designed to ensure that only small business corporations can make a Subchapter S election. The most important rules are:

- A Subchapter S corporation cannot have more than seventy-five shareholders.
- The shareholders must be natural persons (i.e., human beings), and must be either U.S. citizens or permanent resident aliens (green-card holders).
- A Subchapter S corporation cannot issue preferred stock, which effectively bars it from seeking venture capital.
- A Subchapter S corporation is limited in its ability to deduct losses from passive activities, such as real estate ownership or patent royalties.

A Subchapter S corporation that violates one of these rules reverts to being a regular corporation. In such a case the shareholders would continue to enjoy limited liability, but the corporation might have to pay corporation income taxes and refile its federal and state income tax returns for prior years. Often it is not discovered until much later that one of the Subchapter S rules has been broken.

subcontractor An independent worker or company hired to perform specific tasks. (*See also* independent contractor; outsourcing.)

These self-employed folks set their own hours, use their own tools and equipment, and work for other people besides you. The

S/s

IRS has a twenty-point checklist that separates the subcontractors from the employees, which you can check out at **www.irs.gov**. Subcontractors can't work under your direct supervision, although they can fulfill your company's needs. If you hire a subcontractor, be sure to specify deadlines, the scope of work, the requirements, and all the financial details in writing.

success A form of satisfaction that you have set out to achieve and know how to repeat.

My definition of success includes repetition. There is no such thing as one-time success. Why? Because however complicated it may appear, success is really made up of repeated activities—repeated, sometimes, until you're quite sick of them. So when you've finally achieved what most people call success, the real satisfaction lies in knowing what it took to get there and knowing that you can do it again.

succession planning The unforeseen burden of success. (*See also* estate planning; exit strategy; family business.)

Entrepreneurs like to think they are immortal, but they're not. If you have a business and haven't thought about what would happen to it and your employees if something happened to you, get real and make plans now.

Here's a true story: When a forty-seven-year-old Utah man who owned three small businesses died in a plane crash with his wife, his family was devastated, and so were his employees and customers. He had no succession plan, and his sister, who inherited all his businesses, faced serious financial problems.

"In this case, the situation was especially difficult because the CEO and his wife, who was the bookkeeper, died together," said Michael Gould, a partner with the accounting firm of Mintz Rosenfeld & Co., based in Fairfield, New Jersey. "Like most small business owners, he kept many of the details of the business in his head. Key business decisions needed to be made after his death, and there was a dearth of information."

Gould, who is an accountant and business consultant, worked with the sister to sort out the financial problems. It wasn't easy since

s/S

SURVIVAL PLAN

The following are some tips to help insure a smooth succession:

■ Write down your intentions regarding the future direction of your business. If you planned to expand, promote a key manager, or merge with another company, spell it out in the plan.

■ Keep clear and up-to-date books and records. Make sure your accountant has copies of all current information.

■ Maintain good personnel records. Update files frequently.

■ Share your plan with key employees and advisers so there will be no surprises.

■ Make sure all your agreements are in writing. Handshakes are not legal or binding.

she was emotionally devastated and dreading the responsibility.

"Small business people are traditionally bad record keepers and tend to live day to day," said Gould. "They also don't think about the 'what if' question. Should calamity strike, and they fail to plan, the business often dies with them."

suppliers The people who control the components that you rely on to make your products and deliver them in a timely manner. (*See also* vendors.)

If, like many business owners, you rely on one source for your key ingredients or components, you are a prime candidate for a major disaster. Think about what would happen if your sole supplier went bankrupt, experienced a shortage, or decided your competitor's willingness to pay a few dollars more for the stuff you need was enough to cut you off. Even a broken down delivery truck on a remote highway can mean the difference between profit and loss.

S/s

Lining up multiple suppliers for key elements can be critical to your success. The best time to do this is when everything is going well. If supplies are steady and prices are holding, you have time to go online and research other sources of raw materials. Order catalogs and price lists, call company reps, and comparison shop. You might be surprised if the sales rep offers you a substantial discount on things you buy every week to land your business.

One definite benefit of finding alternative suppliers is that you might be able to negotiate better prices from your current suppliers if you threaten to take your business elsewhere.

Whether or not you decide to change suppliers, establish a relationship with the new supplier by placing a small order. Set up an account and order something from time to time. This second or third source of supplies is better than money in the bank. You'll sleep better with one less thing to worry about.

sweat equity Value added by unpaid labor.

"Don't sweat the small stuff " sounds cool, but if you are in business, nothing is small, especially if you have invested your time and money in building a dream.

During the dot-com mania, sweat equity was nowhere to be seen. Clueless, venture-funded people with little or no experience paid themselves enormous salaries to mismanage thousands of untested business models. When you're spending other people's money, where's the motivation to conserve it? Authentic entrepreneurs who pay themselves virtually nothing know how much effort it takes to get a business off the ground.

While it's tough to quantify the value of sweat equity, you'll need to put a price on your time and effort when it's time to bring in other investors or to sell the business. Be sure to compute not only the dollars you invested in office space and equipment, but also a fair value on your time based on what you would have earned if you were working for a similar company sixty hours a week.

When things are going poorly, it's tough to convince yourself that you made the right decision in starting your own business. If you are working harder than you ever worked in your life and

s/S

earning less than the shipping clerk, it's difficult to justify what you're doing. But, if you build equity through the sweat of your labors as you batten down the hatches and trim the sails, you can often ride out a storm.

The bright side of the days when we were teetering on failure was that so many bigger competitors went out of business that we were getting calls from strategic partners who wouldn't return our calls before. When the dust settled and Onvia.com, Office.com, Work.com, and Smalloffice.com were gone, we received contracts from Apple Computer and Merrill Lynch and MasterCard renewed their advertising contracts.

We wiped the sweat out of our eyes and got back to work.

sweep account A checking account that earns interest overnight.

Picture a broom sweeping your money from your operating account to another that earns interest overnight. Although no brooms are involved, sweep accounts are financial instruments that allow business owners (and consumers) to squeeze a little more interest out of their money. Big brokerage houses like Merrill Lynch that offer such arrangements tend to pay the highest interest on their money market or cash management accounts, as they are called, but your money is not insured by the Federal Deposit Insurance Corp. They are protected by securities industry insurance. A sweep account can be easily linked to your regular business checking account to maximize interest paid.

S/s

target market The aim of all marketing. (*See also* marketing.)

THE GREATEST ASSET that most entrepreneurs bring to the table is their desire to solve a problem they have perceived in the marketplace. In a sense, your initial target is to provide a solution to a problem. Solve the problem, the customers will come. As the business matures, you collect as much information as you can about your customers, then set about to widen that base by aiming at market segments: your customers as subdivided by age, sex, social status, education, location, even the time of day they are most likely to buy. All marketing is targeted. But before you have customers, you target the problem you are solving for them.

taxes Tribute to revenue. (*See also* accountants; audit; enrolled agent; employment taxes.)

There are millions of words written about taxes. I'll add just a few: pay them on time and in full. Take it from me, a former federal court reporter who covered many a tax scofflaw. You don't want to feel the wrath of Uncle Sam—it's not worth saving a few bucks if you risk going to federal prison.

Rely on your tax adviser to make sure you are in full compliance with state, local, and federal tax regulations, especially

THE PERFECT TAXPAYER

This year promise yourself that you won't dump a shoe-box filled with receipts on your accountant or tax adviser's doorstep on March 14 (corporate tax returns are due March 15, personal returns are due on April 15). Here are some tips to help you keep your records in order for your adviser:

■ Prepare an updated annual financial statement, including a profit and loss report. Balance your checking account, at least through December 31.

■ Organize your business checks into categories that match up with the categories you use for your book-keeping system.

■ Separate meal and entertainment expenses, since you can only deduct 50 percent of these costs.

■ Set aside receipts for office equipment and major purchases, because you can deduct the full cost of certain things up to $24,000, rather than depreciating the costs over time.

■ Review credit card statements and circle any big charges that need special attention.

■ Collect receipts obtained for charitable donations, professional society memberships, and other annual fees that may be tax deductible.

■ Do a rough estimate of your income and expenses to get a ballpark figure.

■ Call your accountant or tax adviser *now* to set up an appointment if you haven't already discussed tax strategies.

the ones concerning payroll taxes. Not paying your required payroll taxes is a very serious crime. If you are caught paying people in cash, or under-the-table, without withholding the required taxes, you can end up in jail and losing everything.

T/t

Why jeopardize everything you've worked for?

Not paying your income tax, especially those pesky quarterly estimated tax payments, is a big mistake. When you cash a check from a client or customer, set aside at least 30 percent for the taxes right then. Deposit it in a savings or money-market account and don't touch it until the tax bill is due. It's a simple way to avoid losing sleep and losing your shirt.

As soon as you get into business, hire a seasoned tax adviser. Find someone who is familiar with your particular industry and focuses on the regulations affecting your particular business. Your tax adviser has a challenge: she knows you want to minimize your tax bills, but that if you are planning to attract outside investors or to go public down the road, you will need to show a profit and to pay tax on that profit. You should work with someone who has a view about risk similar to your own. An aggressive adviser who urges you to take questionable deductions is not the right person to prepare your return if you are conservative and don't want to raise any eyebrows at the IRS.

A good tax professional works hard to balance your short- and long-term financial goals based on an in-depth discussion with you and your management team.

In 2001, Congress made 401 changes to the tax code. Although there weren't any big dramatic changes, many of them affect business owners, especially family-owned businesses wanting to pass along the company to the next generation. Although you don't have to be a tax expert, you should keep up with the changes and be prepared with a list of questions for your tax professional.

technology The minimum set of electronic appliances required for efficiency or profit. (*See also* broadband connection; software.)

Technology is a huge boon to small companies. For a few thousand dollars, you and your cat can appear to be a much bigger business. A color laser printer and an Internet-accessible cell phone go a long way to amplify your image. But the wrong technology—or just too much of it—saps your financial resources and drives you crazy. The best advice is simple: make

t/T

sure your specific business activities drive your technology purchases and not vice versa.

Just because all your friends have a groovy, two-pound titanium laptop, doesn't mean you need one, too. Ask yourself what you need the hardware or software to do, then speak to an expert to determine exactly what to buy. It sounds so simple, but millions of dollars are misspent on equipment and software programs every year.

Even if you're smart and your thirteen-year-old knows a lot about computers, I still recommend hiring professional help. Work with somebody who really knows what he or she is doing. There are many independent consultants who specialize in helping small companies figure out what to buy. Be sure to set an adequate but reasonable budget during this exploratory process. You may not need the biggest, fastest computer, but you may need a high-end printer for marketing materials. You don't have to become an expert on technology; you just have to be an informed consumer.

The following is a list of the technology sectors that most small businesses should focus on and keep up to date:

- Computer hardware and software (generic or industry specific)
- Telecommunications equipment, both in the office and mobile (cell phones, pagers, and hybrid devices)
- E-mail programs
- Connections to the Internet (dial-up, DSL, fiber optic lines, cable modem, satellite, and wireless)
- Inter-office networks for sharing files, printers, and other devices
- Portable computers (such as Palm Pilot or Handspring Visor)
- Database management
- Storage for business records (back up systems and optical scanners)

T/t

telemarketing Efficient means of enticing or annoying potential customers.

Telemarketing has its good and its bad aspects. A well-trained and personable internal telemarketing team is an asset when its members are smiling and dialing for dollars all day long. With proper direction and training, they can focus their sales efforts on your current customer base, which makes up most of a company's future revenues. They can answer incoming calls, field customer inquiries, take orders, and be responsible for the handling and resolution of complaints.

Outside telemarketers are the ones often accused of being annoying, aggressive, and of interrupting dinners across America. If you run a mail order or infomercial business, you'll need outside telemarketers. There are good ones and not so good ones. I was surprised at the range of style and experience among the telemarketers I had to hire for a project we did for American Express. I actually interviewed the people before they were assigned to our account by doing fake calls and trying to get a sense of whether they could relate to small business owners or not.

Skilled telemarketers are professionals with pleasant voices and manners. If they are on the receiving end of the calls taking orders, they are more likely to be relaxed and pleasant. If they are making cold calls, they tend to be grumpier and more abrupt.

There are massive telemarketing centers throughout Utah and Nebraska. These areas are ripe with educated, talented people, including many Mormons who have learned a plethora of foreign languages while traveling around the world on spiritual missions.

Compare prices and payment plans. Companies vary in how they want to be compensated and what they pay their workers. Just be careful and employ the telephone as a tool—not a weapon.

telephone The premier business tool for work or interruption. (*See also* customer service.)

The first item on a new business owner's shopping list is usually a telephone. With a telephone and a dedicated fax or Internet line, you are truly in business. No matter how small your company is, don't scrimp on an adequate number of telephone lines, including

t/T

a separate line for your fax machine and/or Internet access. E-mail is great, but a fax is still an important piece of equipment for most companies. Some of the newer fax machines can also make copies and scan documents.

Your phone is your most powerful business tool and your ear to the world. In one day, you can rely on your phone to help you solicit business, make deals, take orders, answer customer questions, and even call home once a while. Good telephone skills are essential. The people answering your phone provide the first impression of your business. If they mumble your company name or answer in a dull tone, you are in big trouble. Give new employees a script to follow and a mirror to make sure they are smiling when they answer the phone. It sounds corny, but a smile, even a forced one, will perk up someone's voice.

Invest in a good phone system, but don't go crazy. Buy a system that accommodates modest growth. Do buy good quality office and cell phones, though. They take a beating and an inexpensive phone makes your business sound cheap.

temp agency A supplier of casual labor. (*See also* employee; leasing employees.)

Savvy entrepreneurs take advantage of the availability of highly skilled talent for rent on a temporary basis. Professional, managerial, and technical workers account for approximately 25 percent of all temporary workers. About 3 million temporary workers are on the job every day, according to the National Association of Temporary and Staffing Services in Alexandria, Virginia. In 1999, industry-wide revenue reached about $14 billion and payroll hit $10 billion.

Unlike freelancers or independent contractors, temps are employed by the agency. They receive their payroll checks and sometimes benefits from the agency. The client writes one check to the agency for the temp's services and doesn't have to worry about anything else.

"With temporary help, you get the skills you need when you need them, for as long as you need them, but you don't have the ongoing costs of a full-time staff," says Jean Ban, cofounder and executive vice president of Paladin, a national temporary staffing service that specializes in placing marketing, advertising, graphic design, and communications professionals.

Dave Lambertson, vice-president and creative director of BHI Design, a Chicago-based graphic design company specializing in corporate communications and trade show graphics, became a Paladin client after a futile search for a traditional, full-time employee. "I must have interviewed hundreds of people, but the quality just wasn't out there," he says. "When you go through the agency, you know your criteria has been met."

Lambertson says free-agent staffing has helped his twenty-six-year-old, $3 million company to be flexible and save money. "You don't have to carry people through slow periods," he says. "You can upsize or downsize quickly without affecting people's lives."

Although many talented workers prefer to take assignments through an agency, many other professionals are hiring themselves out on a temporary basis with great results. Ana Witherow, a San Francisco CPA, was working full time as the manager of professional services for a start-up company. Tired of a two-hour commute, she decided to go into business for herself as a temporary controller. In the late 1990s, she founded Capital Performance. She now works for two early start-ups at a time, each on a half-time basis. She stays with each business for about six months or until it needs a full-time controller. "I love working with different companies, meeting different people and really making an impact," says Witherow.

The best way to find a temp agency is to ask colleagues for recommendations. Most big agencies like Snelling Personnel or Manpower are reputable and can send someone over within a day or so. It's very important to be specific about the skills you require and the exact nature of the job. If the person will be answering the phone, ask for someone with polished phone skills. I get very specific; if I don't want a talkative person, I tell the agency to send me someone quiet.

The best thing about hiring temps is that if they don't work out, you can send them back any time and ask for a replacement.

t/T

trade associations Ready-made personal networks.

No matter what you do, join a trade association. There are thousands of industry groups, from the mundane to the esoteric. Butchers, bakers, candlestick makers—they all have active, busy associations. Use a search engine to find one that fits your needs. And, don't forget to attend the annual meeting or tradeshow. It's a good investment of time and money. You'll meet friends, check out competitors, and enjoy a few free cocktails along the way.

And you don't have to just join an association; you can become an active participant. Start volunteering at the meeting registration desk and work your way up to a committee or board position. Your most valuable business contacts may be made at your trade association.

trademarks and service marks The symbols or signs you use to identify your products and services in an effort to create a recognized brand. (*See also* invention; patent.)

Sometimes the most valuable property a small business has is the name or logo used to identify its products or services. A trademark (used for goods) or service mark (used for services) is the identifying symbol that you put on your goods and services to distinguish them from other people's stuff.

A trademark can consist of words, graphic symbols, or a combination of both. If your trademark consists exclusively of words, the words should be used in a distinctive way; if the words merely describe what the product or service does, it probably will not qualify as a legally protected trademark. Colors may be trademarked if they are sufficiently distinctive and are associated in the public mind with a particular product or service.

You may file to register a trademark that you are not yet using, but sooner or later your trademark actually must be used in commerce and must not conflict with or infringe another trademark for a similar product or service. Your trademark infringes another mark if it would create confusion in the public mind. An antique store that uses the same trademark as a funeral parlor is likely not to infringe the funeral parlor's mark. A brand of paint that uses the same trademark as a brand of

T/t

wallpaper may, however, pose an infringement problem.

The first step in adopting a trademark or service mark is to search the database at the U.S. Patent and Trademark Office to determine that your mark will not infringe someone else's mark. This can be done on the PTO's website at **www.uspto.gov**, but it isn't easy. Determining whether two or more marks are confusingly similar in the public mind is as much an art as it is a science, and you are more likely to avoid infringement problems down the road if you have the search performed by a competent attorney who specializes in trademark law. The cost can run from $500 to $1,500, or even more, depending on the length of the search, the number of hits that may pose infringement problems, and the generally prevailing rates for legal services in your area.

Contrary to popular opinion, you do not have to register your trademarks and service marks with the federal government in order to use them on your packaging, labels, and stationery. Merely placing the letters TM (for goods) or SM (for services) next to your mark tells the world, "I'm using this as a trademark or service mark, so don't even think about using it on your stuff." Of course, if you discover someone is using the same or a similar mark, you will have the burden of proving that you were using it first, that the other guy's use of the mark will create confusion in the public mind, and so forth.

By registering your mark with the U.S. Patent and Trademark Office, you get a legal monopoly on the use of that mark, and any-one else using a confusingly similar mark will have the burden of proving in court that they had it first. You can also register trade-marks and service marks in most states, but your registration will protect you only in that state, while a federal registration covers the entire country. Registering your mark with the Patent and Trademark Office also entitles you to use the registered trademark symbol ®. It is a federal crime to use this symbol if you have *not* officially registered the mark.

The term of a federal trademark registration is ten years, with ten-year renewal terms, but between years five and six you must file an affidavit containing certain information to keep the trade-mark alive. You can also lose a trademark or service mark if you fail

t/T

to use it actively in commerce, if you license it to someone else without adequate quality control or supervision, or if your mark becomes a generic term in the English language. Aspirin, cellophane, and Kleenex were all once originally trademarks that leaked into common usage.

While the Patent and Trademark Office allows you to register marks on its website, you should never attempt to register a mark without the help of a lawyer who specializes in trademarks and other intellectual property or a specialized for-profit service such as **www.trademark.com**. The rules for registration are highly complicated, and it is easy to make a mistake, especially when defining the classifications into which your product or service falls under the trademark laws.

While costs vary in different parts of the country, the average cost of searching and registering a trademark or service mark is between $1,000 and $3,000, and it's money well spent.

trade name A fictitious name or DBA; any business name you use other than the one on your birth certificate. (*See also* DBA; starting a business; trademarks and service marks.)

In virtually every state you are legally permitted to use your name to identify a business. If you are an attorney named John Doe and you wish to call your business John Doe, Attorney at Law, no one can legally stop you, even if there are fifty other John Does practicing law in your town.

If, however, you decide to give yourself a glitzier name, such as John Doe & Associates, you are now using a trade name (known in some places as a fictitious name or a DBA, for "doing business as"). Simply put, any name you use for your business that does not appear on your birth certificate or Social Security card, even if it incorporates a part of your name (such as John's Antiques), is a trade name.

In most states, if you are doing business using a trade name, you must register the name by filing a trade name certificate with the office of the clerk in each town, city, or county (some states require filing by county, others require filing by city or town) within your state in which you will maintain a business address. If your business is statewide, but you have only one mailing address,

T/t

you will need to file a trade name certificate only in the town, city, or county in which you maintain your mailing address.

You can obtain the necessary form from the clerk's office and will have to pay a filing fee, usually an amount between $5 and $15. The form is a simple one—basically all it should say is "I, John Doe, am doing business at thus-and-such an address using the name 'John's Antiques'"—and you will not need the assistance of an attorney in completing the form.

That's the good news. The bad news is that filing a trade name certificate gives you no exclusive legal right whatsoever to use the name in commerce—the filing clerk usually does not check to see if anybody else in town is using the same or a similar name. The certificate is merely notice to the world that if anyone is run over by a truck with John's Antiques stenciled on the side, you're the person who should be sued.

In order to have the exclusive right to use a name in commerce, you must apply to have the name registered as a federal or state trademark.

So why file a trade name certificate in the first place, if it doesn't give you any legal protection? The short answer is the law requires it. The longer answer is that if (heaven forbid) anyone is run over by one of your trucks with John's Antiques stenciled on the side, and you haven't filed a trade name certificate, your failure may lead the local authorities to conclude that you are running a fly-by-night business by hiding behind a fictitious name. Then, what starts out as a simple negligence case for money damages grows into a criminal investigation in which you are fighting to stay out of jail. For a few bucks in fees and a few minutes of your time filing a trade name certificate is cheap insurance against a lot of potential legal nastiness.

trade show An exhibition where every age-old trick of the marketplace is on display.

The Internet may be the fastest way for a company to pitch its products or services to customers worldwide, but sometimes your customers need to feel, touch, watch, or taste your product before they actually cut that check.

t/T

A BEAUTIFUL BOOTH

Here are some trade show tips from Dick Wheeler, owner of Professional Exhibits and Graphics, an exhibit company based in Sunnyvale, California:

- Your graphics should communicate in three seconds or less who you are, what you do, and how the customer can benefit. You must create an impact quickly on a busy trade show floor.
- Make it easy for people to get in and out of your exhibit space.
- Feed your guests. Candy is a magnet for traffic.

And tips for your staff manning the booth:

- Pin name badges on the right side of the body so people shaking hands can read your name.
- No eating, smoking, or sitting down. Your staff should be standing and looking approachable, not conversing with each other.
- Come up with an open-ended question to qualify the leads. Find out if the visitor is a decision-maker, or someone dropping in to just kick the tires and waste your time.
- Learn to politely dismiss a poor prospect.
- Rent a scanner to read the bar codes on badges. It's worth the money to automate the process of following up leads.

Last note: If your business is too localized for a trade show, consider using your vehicle as a rolling billboard. You can buy magnetic signs for your cars or trucks for a few hundred dollars. You can also buy custom designed vinyl wrapping for vans and trucks for about $2,500.

T/t

In today's high-tech world, trade shows are still the second most popular form of marketing (after word-of-mouth), according to the Tradeshow Week's *Databook* research report. According to the trade association's publication, business-to-business trade shows now account for 49 percent of the exhibition industry's $100 billion annual spending.

"People want high-tech, high-touch service, and exhibiting at tradeshows is the best way to provide that," says Dick Wheeler, owner of Professional Exhibits and Graphics, an exhibit company based in Sunnyvale, California (**www.proexhibits.com**). A lively trade show exhibit can quickly build a buzz around a new product. It can also make your small company look bigger and like it's doing a lot more business.

In addition to generating publicity and networking opportunities, trade shows give business people a place to do deals and sign contracts face-to-face. "Very often people will rent a suite just for negotiating," says Wheeler, who recommends doing deals in private—not on the show floor.

Wheeler learned the exhibit business by working for a rival company five years prior to buying Professional Exhibits and Graphics in 1992. Wheeler and his wife, Jody Tatro, the company's CEO, set up their three California offices like a mock trade show, with $600,000 worth of product on their showroom floor.

Although you can buy exhibit booths online from companies, many customers like to visit the booths before they invest. "As you go through the process, you tell them what your budget is and then they give you all of the options," says Stacey Tomlinson, marketing specialist for a software company based in Palo Alto, California. Tomlinson says her company spent about $22,000 on an exhibit for their first trade show. The price included the design work, the booth itself, accents to the booth shape, additional parts, storage crates, a carpet with padding, a carpet bag, and instruction on how to set it up and take it down.

When the show's over, don't stick the booth in a storeroom, set it up in your office. "We're getting more use out of this exhibit because we set it up in-house," says Kevin Toft, creative director of Homeseekers.com, an online listing service for homebuyers, based in Brea, California. "When we put the booth up at the office, it shows stability and strength to our visiting VIPs," says Toft. "It also makes the office look more professional and dynamic."

The cost of a trade show booth depends on how big it is and how elaborate its design and detail. Prices range from $5,000 to $15,000 for a 10 x 10 foot display, $10,000 to $30,000 for 10 x 15, and $20,000 to $60,000 for 20 x 20.

training An essential investment in the future of your company. (*See also* online training.)

Unable to compete with the fat salaries and perks offered by larger firms, small-business owners often face serious challenges when it comes to attracting and keeping good workers. That's when training becomes a powerful way to reward key employees.

Training and education are terrific perks because they benefit both you and your employee. No matter what kind of class, course, or seminar employees attend, it adds to their knowledge base and ultimately boosts morale. Getting out of the office yourself to learn a new skill also expands your network of contacts and gives you a fresh perspective.

Don't be reluctant to let people learn on company time, especially if they are brushing up on their English or learning a new software program.

triple-net lease A lease in which the tenant pays rent to the landlord, as well as all taxes, insurance, and maintenance expenses that arise from the use of the property. (*See also* lease.)

turnaround expert A white knight who saves businesses, but not without causing pain and charging a steep fee. (*See also* accounts receivable financing; bankruptcy; debt restructuring; Service Corps of Retired Executives.)

Turnaround experts have a tough time getting their clients to talk about them. When they are attempting to save a troubled business, the owner is usually too upset to discuss what is going on. After the crisis, when the business is back on track, the business owner just wants to forget that he or she lost almost everything.

T/t

CLASSY MOVES

Here are some tips for offering training as a benefit:

■ Establish a budget. Big companies invest millions of dollars a year in training, but even a few hundred dollars a year can buy valuable skills.

■ Draft a policy outlining who qualifies for training and how long employees must be on the payroll before they can sign up.

■ Require that employees share what they learn with their colleagues in some way, either in writing or by making a brief, informal presentation.

■ Assign one person to collect community college catalogs, seminar brochures, and class schedules from private groups like the Learning Annex or Learning Tree. Post the information where employees can review it.

■ If someone needs specific skills, such as learning a software program, consider teaming up with other small businesses in the area to share the costs of a professional trainer.

■ Encourage people to sign up for non-business classes, such as exercise classes, yoga, or meditation. Anything that reduces stress ultimately benefits everyone.

■ Check with your accountant on the deductibility of training expenses.

"It's one thing to run a company when things are going well," says Joel Getzler, president of Getzler & Co., a Manhattan-based turnaround company. "It takes a totally different mind-set when things aren't going well." At times when things are things aren't going well for thousands of small companies around the country, and many traditional businesses, especially in the apparel and textile industry, are failing, the smart owners reach out for professional help. Getzler says an entrepreneur's unsinkable optimism

t/T

HOMEMAKER TO THE RESCUE

Here's a real success story: Most customers walking into one of the lively and bright Sappington Farmer's Markets in St. Louis, Missouri, have no idea that a former homemaker rescued the business from bankruptcy.

Tessa Greenspan was thrust into entrepreneurship when an investment she'd made in the grocery store as a silent partner in 1981 turned sour. By 1986, the store was $413,000 in debt, including a $40,000 tax bill and a $200,000 bank loan. The two active partners declared personal bankruptcy and handed the keys to Greenspan.

"My entire world changed," she recalls. Though a college graduate, her only work experience was helping out part time in a neighborhood grocery store she and her husband had owned previously. The first thing she did was to hire a good business attorney. Then they developed a plan to save the store:

■ She liquidated her personal investments and took a second mortgage on her home to pay the back taxes.

■ She wrote to every vendor, promising to pay them in full if they would continue to work with her new management team. A majority of vendors agreed to continue selling to the market,

actually hurts his or her chances for saving a troubled business. "They say, 'It will get better tomorrow ... the big order is coming tomorrow,'" says Getzler. "The exact thing [optimism] that got them to where they are starts hurting the business when there is a problem."

A reputable turnaround consultant will do everything from negotiating payment plans with your creditors and suppliers to firing employees. They charge hundreds of dollars an hour and require payment up front. If you hire a professional turnaround consultant, be prepared to take their advice and do exactly what they recommend. Choose someone you trust and feel comfortable communicating with. The turnaround process

T/t

and partial payments on overdue balances were made with each new delivery.

■ The attorney negotiated a favorable payment arrangement with the landlord just as he was about to evict her.

■ She negotiated a deal with her bank whereby she was required to pay interest on only one-third of the loan amount, for which she was personally liable. "The rest, I could pay back without any interest. Even my attorney couldn't believe I was able to work that out," Greenspan says.

■ To increase sales, she transformed the store into an old-fashioned, family-friendly market. A mannequin dressed as a farmer greets customers from a bench with his dog Rusty by his side. Rustic bins brim with fresh produce. A toy train circles above, advertising the day's best bargains.

■ She paid workers out of her own pocket and pitched in to sweep floors and stock shelves.

In 1995, she opened a second store twice the size of the original. She now employs eighty-five people, and the stores generate more than $10 million in annual revenue.

can be long and painful, especially if you've spent years building a successful business.

"The toughest part of my job is to get the company to go along with what we recommend," says Getzler. "Most of the time, we come to some sort of agreement on what should be done. But, sometimes we'll resign if the owner has no interest in fixing things."

Firing people is usually the quickest way to cut overhead costs. Although business owners hate to lose valuable employees, Getzler says finding new talent is manageable if you can save the business. "I'd rather have the problem of finding new people [to hire] than running out of cash and dying," he says.

t/T

FIRST AID DRILL

Here is a must-do list from Getzler & Company, a New York-based turnaround firm:

- **Prepare a cash projection for the next sixty days.** This is the first and most critical step. You will hone your priorities and identify where to cut expenses.
- **Prioritize payments.** Determine which vendors are supplying goods that you absolutely must have to continue operating. If you owe vendors who are not currently supplying your company, hold off on those payments, or at least reduce the amount you pay each month.
- **Review payroll.** Look at every name and ask yourself if this person really contributes to your business. When Getzler & Co. was called in to help a company in trouble, they identified seventy-two of the firm's ninety clerical workers who could be dismissed without slowing down all company operations.

If you are suffering a cash flow crunch, consider some alternatives to prayer. One way to increase your cash flow is to work with an accounts receivable lender. Unlike banks, which base a loan on your collateral and credit history, an accounts receivable lender advances you the cash based on the invoices you have outstanding. This kind of lender pays you a portion of what's owed you, charging a fee based on the total amount financed. (The fee ranges from 3 to 5 percent in most cases.)

If things are going south fast, you may need the services of a liquidator. Jonathan Reich, a bankruptcy attorney, works for Michael Fox International, a Baltimore-based liquidation firm with offices in New York. "Our business has two aspects: appraisals, and the liquidation and auctioning of assets, typically machinery, equipment, real estate, and inventory," says Reich. He says many business owners don't know how to maximize the

T/t

sale of their assets when their business is in trouble. Often the bank insists on an appraisal of assets long before the business owner will call Reich's firm for help, he says, adding that a professional appraisal can cost $5,000 to $20,000 or more depending on the size of the company. "The appraisal report is used extensively as testimony, [in a bankruptcy hearing]," says Reich. "The debtor tries to show the bank is over-secured; the bank takes an opposite view."

He says that if your business is having financial problems, you have to persuade the bank why they shouldn't pull the plug on your loan. "I can often help the owner buy more time with the bank," says Reich. "But, if they owe the bank $10 million and they are worth $2 million, they should sell right away. We can often help find them a merger partner and sell the company as a going concern."

There are myriad resources available to assist troubled business owners. For example, the SBA's Service Corps of Retired Executives (SCORE) provides free counseling services to nearly 300,000 entrepreneurs annually. Visit **www.score.org** for online counseling. The Small Business Development Center Program, which is funded by the SBA and other sources, provides one-stop assistance to small businesses through more than 1,000 branch locations. For more information visit **www.sba.gov**.

t/T

unemployment insurance State-mandated benefits paid to employees who are laid off, usually for the six months after they lose their jobs.

IF YOU PAY YOUR WORKERS IN CASH, skip this section and get ready to go to jail. With every payroll issued, legitimate, ethical employers contribute to a state-sponsored insurance fund that provides money to laid-off workers. Most states provide unemployment insurance benefits for up to six months. The premiums are based on the number of employees you have and, historically, how many employees have collected benefits. While collecting unemployment benefits may sound very cool and romantic, the money is a fraction of the person's salary and will barely cover rent and food.

If you have terminated workers collecting benefits on your policy, monitor their progress and read all state notices carefully. I've had two former employees try to exploit the system by applying to extend their coverage. When notified of their attempts, I filed a written protest in both cases and their benefits ended. Both were healthy and able to find new jobs (even if they were incompetent), so I didn't feel sorry for making them toe the line.

unemployment taxes Mandatory payments to federal and state unemployment insurance funds. (*See also* employment taxes.)

As an employer, you are required by the Federal Unemployment Transfer Act (FUTA) to pay federal unemployment tax if either:

■ in any calendar quarter, you pay wages of $1,500 or more to employees, or

■ in each of twenty different calendar weeks, you had an employee for at least part of a day. The twenty weeks don't have to be consecutive, and the employee doesn't have to be the same person each week. The tax does not apply to certain types of employment (for example, wage payments to co-op education students), and not all payments you make to employees are considered wages subject to tax (for example, payments of worker's compensation insurance premiums can be deducted from wages otherwise subject to tax).

The amount of federal unemployment tax you will have to pay equals a tax base (your annual taxable wages) times a tax rate (published in IRS schedules). For example, if your tax base is $100,000 and your tax rate is 6.2 percent, you will have to pay $6,200 in federal unemployment taxes each year.

In addition, in just about every state you will be required to make periodic payments to a state unemployment insurance fund. You are given a federal tax credit of up to 5.4 percent for payments to your state's unemployment insurance fund. The amount of your state unemployment tax contribution depends on your experience rating. If few of your former employees draw unemployment benefits, your experience rating is good. Accordingly, your tax rate will be toward the low end of the range shown in your state's unemployment tax table.

The federal unemployment tax is reported on IRS Form 940, Employer's Annual Federal Unemployment Tax Return, on an annual basis. The form covers one calendar year, and it is due on January 31 of the following year (you must file Form 940 on a calendar year basis, even if you use a fiscal year). You must, however, calculate the tax due on a quarterly basis—if at the end of any calendar quarter you owe more than $100 in federal unemployment tax, you must make a deposit before the end of the next month (for example, by April 30 for the calendar quarter ending March 31), using IRS Form 8109, Federal Tax Deposit Coupons.

The best source of information about federal unemployment taxes is IRS Publication 15, Circular E—Employer's Tax Guide, which is available as a free download at www.irs.gov. You can learn more about your state's unemployment compensation system by locating the website of your state's Department of Labor. A fifty-state summary of unemployment compensation laws can be found at adp.com/taxfin/toolbox/payroll/uccr.html, but may not be up-to-the-minute. To make sure that federal and state unemployment compensation taxes are paid on time, most small businesses use a payroll service that automatically makes the calculations and deposits on a regular basis. The best-known payroll services are Automatic Data Processing (ADP) at www.adp.com and PayChex at www.paychex.com.

Uniform Franchise Offering Circular (UFOC) A disclosure document that includes a copy of a franchise agreement and states the fees, litigation procedures, and other particulars that the buyer should consider before closing. (*See also* franchise.)

Uniform Partnership Act (UPO) Boilerplate adopted by most states to govern business partnerships. (*See also* partnerships and limited partnerships.)

uniform resource locator (URL) Digital address that leads an Internet user to a specific place on the Web.

The term is so esoteric it's rarely used anymore. People don't ask, "What's your URL?" They ask for your e-mail or Web address. We know that most commercial site addresses start with "www", which stands for World Wide Web, but you don't need to type in the www on most browsers anymore. The main name you choose for your domain is often called a second-level domain and is usually some form of the company name or the service it sells. That name or phrase is followed by a suffix, such

U/u

as .COM, and is officially called the top-level domain (TLD).

The most popular TLD remains COM, short for commercial. Other popular ones are NET for network and ORG for organization. Others gaining popularity are TV for media companies and BIZ for businesses. In 2001, new TLDs were added, increasing your chances of getting just the name you want. PRO is supposed to be limited to professionals; NAME is meant for individuals; INFO is for informational sites; COOP is for cooperatives; MUSEUM for museums; and AERO for airlines, travel agencies, and aerospace firms. Other domain extensions available: SHOP, FAMILY, TECH, LAW, MED, and GOLF. Check the availability of a name at **register.com** or several other registration sites.

union An organized group of workers who pay dues to a central office that represents them in labor and workplace disputes.

Although unions lost members and clout in the late 1980s and 1990s, there are still millions of workers represented by a variety of unions, including the Teamsters. If you are in an industry that depends on union workers, it pays to establish an open, positive relationship with the union leadership as soon as possible.

I learned a lot about unions from two members of my family who were at opposite ends of the spectrum. My paternal grandmother, Estelle Weisman, was a shop steward in the International Ladies Garment Workers Union. She became active in the union that gained power after the Triangle Shirt-Waist Factory blaze killed more than 150 young women on March 25, 1911. They were unable to escape a fire in the Asch building in Washington Square because their employer locked the doors of the sweatshop from the outside. Dozens of girls perished in the elevator shafts where they were taught to hide from city inspectors during raids.

My grandmother was very proud of her union activities as she worked in a variety of garment manufacturing jobs. She rose to the level of inspector in a sweater factory in Los Angeles before retiring.

My maternal grandfather, George Coan, was a vice president of personnel for Howard Clothes, a now defunct chain of men's clothing stores in the Northeast. His charge was dealing with the

u/U

union leaders, resolving complaints, and negotiating contracts. He prided himself in having good relationships with the union executives and workers and always told me how well he treated people no matter what race or color they were.

As challenging as union rules and regulations may be, you must pay attention to them and do what you can to maintain frequent and open communication. If your workers decide to organize and bring in a union, don't panic. Find out everything you can about the union and how its membership has affected operations at similar businesses. Hire an experienced labor attorney to walk you through what to expect. Don't interfere with the organizing efforts or the election—you don't want to get in trouble with the National Labor Relations Board.

URL *See* uniform resource locator.

use tax *See* sales and use taxes.

vacation A treasured few days off during which many Americans wish they were French.

ENTREPRENEURS ARE TERRIBLE VACATION-TAKERS. If you can't force yourself to take time off, and you don't operate a retail store or restaurant, consider closing down the entire company for a week in August and for the week between Christmas and New Year's Day. The French, and most other Europeans, get four to six weeks of vacation a year. (August is the best time to visit Paris if you don't want to see Parisians.) In the United States, employers are not required to grant any paid vacation to employees, but nearly all do (and just try hiring someone without it).

At the beginning of each year, collect requests and create a vacation schedule. Be sure to clarify your vacation-granting policies in writing and distribute the document. Many firms grant requests based on seniority, but be sure to honor vacation requests made when a new employee is hired. If there are too many conflicts, draw straws for prime vacation days. Keep track of every request in writing and post and distribute the schedule to the staff. Make sure you set a company-wide holiday schedule and let people know which federal and state holidays you plan to observe.

In 2001 we closed down SBTV during the second week in

August, giving everyone an extra week of paid vacation. It was a great morale-booster in the middle of a very stressful and tumultuous year. We told all of our clients that we were going to close the office and worked hard to finish all projects before our holiday week. Two staffers were on call for emergencies involving contracts or website operations. We set up an auto-response message on everyone's e-mail, letting people know we weren't checking messages for five days, but provided the emergency phone numbers.

The week between Christmas and New Year's Eve is also a great one to celebrate with a company-wide closure. Everyone is so tired and stressed out by holiday obligations, so why add work to the mix? Many people are out of town or on vacation anyway. It's nearly impossible to move projects along, so don't fight it; close down and make merry.

A final thought: a survey conducted by American Express a few years ago found that time off with pay was the benefit most appreciated by employees. An extra day off here and there to recognize a job well done or a tough deadline met, is far better than a pat on the back or even cash. Be generous with vacation time. It really pays off; especially if you can't give raises or offer other perks.

valuation The total perceived worth of a company's stock or assets, if privately held. (*See also* selling a business.)

During the Internet mania, company valuations were through the roof, as investors liked to say. At one point in the fall of 2000, a big potential investor valued SBTV Corp. at about $6 million by offering about $1.5 million to acquire 25 percent of the stock. Pretty heady stuff for a start-up streaming media company with a short track record and no profits. (The deal fell through when the market started to crash in November 2000, but looking back, we believe that not getting the money probably saved us from extinction. We would have been pushed into spending a few million dollars creating streaming content for a market that wasn't there yet).

When the dot-com market crashed in the spring of 2001, companies valued at millions or hundreds of millions of dollars were basically worthless. WebVan, Kozmo.com, and Pets.com were among the highest fliers and the worst casualties.

Determining the value of your company is not a do-it-yourself project. You must hire an outside professional to examine your assets and liabilities and then crunch the numbers. Find someone familiar with your industry, a person respected by your bankers or other lenders. The size and scope of your business (do you have two branches or twenty?) determines the appraisal fee. A detailed appraisal can take a team of professionals days or weeks to complete and may cost several thousand dollars, according to an executive with an appraisal company. But, you'll need the report if you are trying to renegotiate terms of a loan, about to engage in a merger or acquisition, or planning to go public.

values The rules you live by even when they hurt.

A business without values is morally bankrupt and usually headed toward financial ruin, too. As the founder or manager, you are fully responsible for setting the moral tone around your office. If you lie and cheat, you can expect your employees to follow suit. If you abuse or confuse clients, your staff will, too.

I admit I am not perfect when it comes to values. I work hard to be very upstanding, but when no one else is around to answer the phone, I have pretended to be the receptionist. I even adopt a different tone of voice and throw in a slight British or Southern accent. I answer the phone, put callers on hold, and take only the calls I want to take. (I can't fool my family or friends, though.)

Apart from that kind of minor transgression, we are straight arrows. We don't lie, cheat, or steal from our clients. We do good work and show appreciation in every way possible. We thank them constantly for their support. We are in the service business, and that colors all our decisions. Our values are simple: We are like the Red Cross for small business owners and people looking to start a business. If we make enough money to feed ourselves, that's great. Profit has never been my first and only motivation for being in business. In fact, my highest profile but least profitable venture was a program called Back on Track America, a national coalition I formed to revive the entrepreneurial spirit in the fall of 2001.

I was on the road giving presentations about surviving the recession when terrorists attacked the United States on September 11. When my speaking tour was postponed, I was upset and angry. I felt that if all business conferences and deals and meetings were cancelled then the bad guys won. So, I got on the phone for three weeks straight and called everyone I knew. I assembled a group of major corporations, led by America Online, Merrill Lynch, Wyndham Hotels, MasterCard, ClubCorp, and business associations including SCORE, the Women Presidents' Organization, and the Los Angeles Area Chamber of Commerce, to produce a ten-city tour featuring free conferences.

The price of admission was two business cards. A volunteer faculty of leading business experts and authors traveled around with free tickets provided by Amtrak, teaching seminars and lecturing on getting your business back on track. We reached thousands of business owners between November 15 and January 18, 2002. I was proud of the enormity of the effort and loved hearing from business owners who said our event was the first thing they felt good about attending after September 11.

vendors The people who sell you what you need to make your products or provide your services.

Vendors can make or break your business. Without a steady stream of materials arriving on time at your loading dock or front steps, you can't make your products or serve your clients. In good times, you have your choice of vendors and can play one against the other to get the best price and service. In tough times, supplies dry up and you'll be competing with your competitors for the best supplies.

Successful entrepreneurs always treat their vendors with tender loving care. You are in business with them and should *never* take an adversarial position against them. If you value the relationship, people will go more than the extra mile to help you meet a deadline or fill an unexpectedly big order.

If you are just starting your business, meet personally with several vendors and suppliers. Introduce yourself and explain exactly what you need from them. The first meeting should be informational. Listen to their pitch. You need to learn as much as you can about the industry you're now in, and these folks can help bring you up to speed quickly. They also know your competitors and can be a great source of industry gossip.

After the meetings, review your notes and make some decisions about which company you prefer to deal with. Before signing any long term deals or placing a big order, place a small order with several vendors to compare service and price. Then, you can make an informed decision as the quantities increase.

Keep in touch with your vendors to make sure they keep you informed of seasonal discounts and special promotions. These deals are often used to attract new customers, but if you are a good customer, they should offer you the same incentives if you ask.

venture capital Money invested in your business by professional investors who want to earn ten times their money when they sell out in a few years. Also pejoratively known as *vulture capital*. (*See also* angels.)

Ah, venture capitalists. They were once the most revered and honored guys and gals in America. During the dot-com mania VCs were worshipped by entrepreneurs. They were chased into elevators, e-mailed to death, and mobbed at conventions by hungry business owners desperate for a piece of the staggering $263 billion of venture capital poured into new businesses between 1990 and 2001, according to a survey by PricewaterhouseCooper, Venture Economics, and the National Venture Capital Association. Near half of the total was invested in the bubble years, 1999 and 2000.

Venture capitalists don't want to be your friends. They want to use you to make them rich. They are high-stakes gamblers who raise money from rich people. They buy equity in small companies with scalable ideas. They want your company to take off like a rocket and make oodles of money. They want to see their investment multiply quickly, cash out, and move on to the next deal. They may take a seat on your board and badger you about earnings, and will give you major heart palpitations if things aren't going well.

GETTING TO YES

If you ever wished you could sit down with real venture capitalists and ask them what it takes to get them to open their checkbook, read on. "We look at the opportunity first, then the business, then the management team," says Roger Novak, general partner at Novak Biddle Venture Partners in Reston, Virginia. He and other veteran VCs at a funding conference in New York City shared these insights:

■ The best way to present your company to a venture capitalist is to convince someone whose company has already been funded by the firm to make a personal introduction. This type of referral is much more effective that asking your accountant or attorney to make an overture to a firm he or she doesn't know.

■ Never e-mail business plans or executive summaries to VCs who ask to see them. Send over a hard copy so they don't have to print out your document.

■ Always include contact information in the body of your plan as well as in the executive summary. Cover letters often get separated from the other documents. Carefully edit and proofread the pages to eliminate typos and mistakes. Keep the summary under three pages, if possible.

■ VCs look for industry leaders that can quickly scale up to meet increased sales. If you don't want to get big fast, don't seek venture money.

■ The founding chief executive is often asked to step aside, so be prepared to take the money and leave the management to others.

VCs invest in aggressive managers with a track record. Until women business owners started squawking and forming their own venture networks and conferences, 98 percent of the money went to male-owned businesses. An old boy's network still dominates the venture world. The one serious deal we had cooking in the heyday was made on a golf course. Big VC deals are made on squash courts, in steam rooms, and in sports bars—typically not women-friendly places.

Ironically, many of the biggest, sexiest dot-com deals went south faster than the ones that didn't make it into the now-defunct Industry Standard. For example, Kozmo.com, the New York-based consumer delivery service that expanded to about seven cities, brought in hundreds of millions of dollars and recruited a slew of top retail executives before going bust in 2001. Founder and former CEO, Joseph Park, a former broker for Goldman Sachs, tapped into his network of investors with a simple concept: send a fleet of bike messengers into major cities to deliver goods of all kinds to people within hours or minutes.

I remember asking a friend who lived in the SOHO neighborhood of Manhattan how the service could possibly survive if they didn't charge enough to cover the cost of the guy riding a bike to your house with just a Snickers bar. "I don't know, but it's great," he said. "We call Kozmo all the time."

A source for more detail about the VC game is the National Venture Capital Association, **www.nvca.com**. In February 2002 it reported a small increase in venture funding in the fourth quarter of 2001, suggesting an end to the free-fall that accompanied the dot-com bust. About $37 billion was invested in 2001, compared to $102 billion in 2000. An increasing share of the scarce money in 2001 went to biotech companies.

E-commerce and businesses that rely almost solely on content, like Web-based magazines, were the least likely to get funded in early 2002, according to Jason Calacanis, editor of the *Venture Reporter* magazine. Life sciences, security, software, and nano-technology (ultra-small manufacturing) were the most likely areas for funding, he said.

vesting The process of acquiring ownership in company stock or in a retirement plan.

Vesting is one of the usual means of keeping good employees. Under a gradual vesting plan, employees acquire a percentage of stock or other benefit with each year's service, typically, 25 percent a year for four years. Under a "cliff vesting" plan, the employee acquires all of the benefit at once, say, 100 percent after four years. You may want to dangle a performance-based plan in front of key employees, who would claim stock options or others benefits only if annual earnings per share exceed a target by a specified date. Beware of firing or laying off employees just before the end of a vesting period. Instead have your lawyer write severance agreements that say you will terminate employees on their vesting dates, in exchange for their agreement not to sue.

virtual office A place to work that is leased, borrowed, or rented by the day or hour.

A virtual office provides a flexible and affordable way to bridge the gap between working at home and moving into permanent space. Part-time real estate arrangements, coupled with high technology, create a seamless feeling of having an outside office even on the days when you're working from home, according to Loriann Hoff Oberlin, author of *Working at Home While the Kids Are There Too* (Career Press, 1997).

Tony Todaro was the perfect candidate for a virtual office. He had twenty subcontractors and an impressive roster of high-tech and financial services industry clients, but he was still working out of his home in Redondo Beach, California, a suburb of Los Angeles. At one time, he moved his marketing communications firm, Todaro Communications, Inc. into the eighteenth floor of a Los Angeles high rise. But when the 1994 Northridge earthquake struck, damage to the building sent him back to the home-based world. By 2000, he was looking around again for a real office.

"I needed a place to make formal presentations to clients," said Todaro. He also felt an office would improve his image because, he says, "big companies like to have a feeling of doing

LOOK BIGGER THAN YOU ARE

When is it time to move out of the house? When you have the cash flow to support an office, when you absolutely have to have more space, or when you need to improve your image to attract or retain clients. "If you go through feast or famine periods, it might not be such a great idea to rent a permanent office," advises Loriann Hoff Oberlin, author of *Working at Home While the Kids Are There Too*. "The rent is due each month no matter what. You have to have the kind of business where cash flows in steadily."

Oberlin has these suggestions for looking more professional:

- Join professional organizations and list your membership on your business card. It shows that you belong to a national community of peers.
- Form strategic alliances with other individuals, even if it's informal.
- Add a set of initials after your own on business correspondence, so people think you have a staff.
- If you're operating out of an apartment, list it as a suite on your stationery and cards.
- Always have a professional sounding voice mailbox with an updated outgoing message.
- Limit cell phone calls. They can convey a fly-by-night image if you are making or taking business calls in a noisy Starbucks.
- If and when you choose to move to an outside office, "Start with something modest," Oberlin urges. "You can always move up."

business with a company of their peers."

This time he found a great alternative to a full-time office— classy offices and conference rooms he can use as needed at e-Virtual Suites, in a sleek office building near the Los Angeles International Airport. E-Virtual Suites rents offices and conference rooms as well as providing full-time receptionists.

The company also offers clients a permanent address, a building directory listing, and phone, fax, and voice-mail service. When using the space, Todaro can take advantage of clerical services from word processing, faxing, and copying to mailing, printing, and notarizing. When he's not there, receptionists answer his calls. A pop-up screen on their computer terminals provides information specific to his business. They can also patch calls through to him anywhere in the world. By not having full-time space, and not hiring a receptionist or clerical support, Todaro keeps his overhead low and can pass those savings on to his clients.

E-Virtual charges clients about $165 for a basic package to $339 per month for a deluxe deal. There is a three-month commitment required. Todaro says the price feels just right: "It's high enough to keep the flakes out, but low enough to be affordable."

voice mail Where half of all communication problems are solved. A valuable business tool for saving time, leaving detailed messages, and relaying bad news after normal business hours. (*See also* customer service.)

I love voice mail. Used properly, it can be your best personal assistant. Changing your outgoing message frequently is important and keeps your clients informed about your schedule. Checking your voice mail at certain times throughout the day is the best way to manage incoming information. You should not be checking it every five minutes; if you are working hard, have all your calls sent straight to voice mail and don't check for messages until you take a break.

I leave very detailed messages and love it when people do the same. Tell me why you are calling and exactly what you wanted to tell me. Give me your phone number, repeat it, and tell me when you will be in your office and available. It's hard to believe, but I've completed major projects with people across the country, relying solely on voice mail.

Still, I am still amazed at how many people leave silly "Call me back" voice mail messages. You can be sure I call them back last, if at all, especially if they don't leave me their phone numbers. Of course, I can click around my Microsoft Outlook contact database or dig through my Handspring Visor or card file to find their numbers, but it's a lot easier if they just leave them on the voice mail.

I also leave detailed voice mail messages after hours, although this doesn't work when your target is at the phone later that expected. If I have something quick to say, but have a lot to do and can't get involved in a lengthy chat, I call after hours or on the weekend. Lots of people do check their voice mail over the weekend, so by leaving a message, you are more likely to be called back first thing Monday morning.

If you do change your outgoing message for a special reason, be sure to change it back or update it. You sound careless if you don't.

warranty A promise you make about your goods and services and how they will perform in the future.

WHEN YOU SELL GOODS AND SERVICES, you will often make representations and warranties about them. A representation is a statement of fact as it is today, such as "there is no litigation pending or threatened against our company as of today's date." In contrast, a warranty is an assurance or guarantee that certain facts will be true in the future, such as "this equipment will work underwater." Often, representations and warranties will be combined, such as "these tires are in great shape [representation] and will last for at least 50,000 miles [warranty]."

Most, but not all, warranties in commercial transactions have to do with the condition or performance of the goods being sold. A standard warranty will have four parts: a promise ("these tires will last"), a duration ("for at least 50,000 miles"), a limitation or disclaimer that describes circumstances in which the warranty will not apply ("unless you intentionally puncture them with a sharp metal object"), and a statement saying what you and the customer will do if the warranty is not realized ("if these tires fail before 50,000 miles, you must notify us within thirty days and we will either refund your money or replace your defective tires with tires having the same or similar value, at our option").

Warranties may be either express or implied. Express warranties are those set forth in writing or verbally. Implied warranties are those implied by law, specifically Article 2 of the Uniform Commercial Code of your state, which governs commercial warranties in sales transactions, and local consumer protection statutes. For example, the Uniform Commercial Code provides that in every commercial transaction, even if no express warranties of any kind are made, two implied warranties are deemed to be made: a warranty of merchantability that the product or service is something that can be sold commercially (for example, someone selling chickens they know to be infected with salmonella is selling an unmerchantable product that shouldn't be sold in commerce, regardless of the price that he or she is offering); and a warranty that the product or service is fit for the particular purpose the customer has communicated to the seller.

Special care must be taken when making warranties to consumers. The Magnuson-Moss Warranty Act was enacted by Congress in 1975 to require manufacturers and sellers of consumer products to provide consumers with detailed information about warranty coverage. The act, which is administered by the Federal Trade Commission, applies only to sales of new consumer goods in which a written warranty is given to the consumer. Sales of used merchandise, services (other than workmanship in connection with replacement parts), and commercial goods, and sales in which no written warranty is given to the consumer are not covered by the act. Despite these exceptions, the act has considerable teeth. It requires that anyone making a consumer warranty:

■ Designate or title the written warranty as either full or limited

■ State certain specified information about the coverage of the warranty in a single, clear, and easy-to-read document

■ Ensure that warranties are available where the warranted consumer products are sold so consumers can read them before buying

In addition, the act prohibits manufacturers and sellers of consumer products from:

■ Disclaiming or modifying implied warranties if they use a written warranty. This means that no matter how broad or narrow your written warranty is, your customers always will receive the basic protection of the implied warranty of merchantability. However, if you offer a limited written warranty, the law allows you to include a provision that restricts the duration of implied warranties to the duration of your written warranty—for example, if you offer a two-year limited warranty, you can limit implied warranties to two years.

■ Issuing warranties that contain deceptive or misleading terms. For example, a warranty covering only moving parts on an electronic product that has no moving parts would be deceptive and unlawful.

Consumer warranty disputes are almost always resolved in favor of the consumer, especially if the consumer has been injured as the result of using the product in the manner contemplated by the manufacturer. Accordingly, prior to use all warranty provisions in any contract of sale should be reviewed by an attorney.

website A unique presence on the Internet. (*See also* search engine.)

If you are in business today, you need a website. Period. There were about 50 million websites in 2002 and more are launched every day. You don't need to spend a zillion dollars on some complex, fancy display of Web design. Just register your company name, your name or product name and post basic price and contact information online.

It's so easy to search for and register names. I registered three sites in one weekend and it took less than five minutes. Register.com, Network Solutions (acquired by VeriSign), and lots of other companies are happy to help you out twenty-four hours a day. You just fill in the blank with the name you want, pick the extension (.COM, .ORG, .NET, or others), and within seconds you'll know if it's available. Many registration sites also provide lists of similar names available right there on the page if the one you want is taken. You can also look up who has the name you want and make an offer to buy it.

It costs about $20 to protect a name for a year. It's best to hold a name for at least two years, just in case you need more time to build your site or sell the name. Names were very hot at one point, fetching millions of dollars, but nowadays, names can be had cheap.

I own several domain names, including **janeapplegate.com**, **sbtv.com**, and **sbtv.org**. I regret giving up **applegateway.com** because days after I let the registration lapse, some computer company bought it and now sells computers to people, some of whom think I endorse the company's products.

Although you can design and maintain your own website, I don't recommend it. There are plenty of people who know what they are doing and would be thrilled to help you. We have relied on contract Web designers for years. Don't forget to register your domain name on all appropriate search engines and put it on absolutely everything you print for your business: cards, brochures, letterhead, and mailing labels.

woman-owned business A business certifiably owned or controlled by a woman or women. (*See also* certification.)

In 2002, 6 million U.S. companies were owned by women, and the Small Business Administration estimates more than half of all small businesses will be women-owned in 2003. Business ownership is an attractive option for women at all points along the economic and political spectra. Women start businesses while in high school and college. Women leave the corporate world to make a difference on their own.

As a group, women tend to be more risk-adverse than men when they start a business, conserving their cash. They tend to do more research and ask for help more readily. It's kind of like the jokes about being lost on a road trip; the man will drive for miles, unwilling to admit he's lost. The woman has no time or gas to waste; she is more apt to pull over and asks for directions. For information on applying for certification, visit **www.wbenc.org**.

Women Presidents' Organization (WPO) A New York–based organization with thirty national chapters, targeted at women who run well-established companies. (*See also* Young Entrepreneurs Organization.)

The average WPO member company has been in business for fifteen years and has average annual revenues of $10 million, says WPO founder and president Marsha Firestone. WPO publishes a national directory of members and a newsletter, and also acts as a public relations clearing house by referring the press to members. "We get a lot of calls from the media and refer them to different members," Firestone said. The major benefit of joining the organization is the monthly local meetings, which are limited to no more than twenty-five people. "It's a way for women to use their peers as an informal board of directors," Firestone said.

Unlike the Young Entrepreneurs Organization (YEO), the WPO has no age limit for membership. At the Women Presidents' Organization, female entrepreneurs have the opportunity to get even more specific support for the unique challenges women face in running businesses. The New York-based organization has thirty national chapters and two in Canada, and is targeted at women who run well-established companies. Minimum annual revenue for membership is $1 million.

For more information about the Women President's Organization, call: 212-688-4114 or visit **www.womenpresidentsorg.com**.

word of mouth Still the most powerful form of marketing for small companies. (*See also* brand building; marketing.)

You have to turn your customers into blabbermouths. They need to be encouraged to tell everyone they know about your products and services. You have to ask them to keep talking and give them an incentive to do so. Customer referral rewards are very popular and simple to implement. Just offer me a discount on my next purchase or a free month of something if I send in a new customer or client.

Putting your customer's photo on the wall is a great way to build loyalty and foot traffic. People love to feel special. Think of all those vets and baby doctors with bulletin boards full of happy patients smiling down from the waiting room walls.

Generate buzz about your business in any way you can. Send your products to a celebrity (news anchors and weather reporters are good targets). Send your stuff to a drive-time radio anchor in hopes he or she will mention it on the radio.

RECOMMENDED READING

■ *Full-Frontal PR: Getting People Talking About You, Your Business, or Your Product*, by Richard Laermer with Michael Prichinello (Bloomberg Press, 2003)

workers' compensation (formerly workmen's compensation) A state program designed to provide benefits to employees who are injured from employment-related accidents and certain occupational diseases.

Virtually every state has a workers' compensation statute designed to provide benefits to employees who are injured or become ill as a result of their employment. The goal of these statutes is to provide financial and medical benefits to victims of work-related injuries expediently, and to shift the economic burden for such injuries from the employee to the employer. As a practical matter, the cost is shifted to insurance pools and, ultimately, to the public.

Some states exclude employers who have less than three or four employees, and most states exclude farm labor, domestic servants, and casual workers from coverage if they earn less than a specified amount.

Workers' compensation statutes cover accidental injuries arising out of employment. The term "arising out of" is a term for determining compensation. An injury arises in the course of employment when it occurs during a period of employment at a location where an employee may be performing job duties or an activity at least tangentially related to job duties. To ascertain whether or not accidental injury has arisen out of employment, one must determine when the employment relationship began and ended, whether the employment relationship was uninterrupted, whether the employee went outside the scope of his duties, and if so, how far.

Workers' compensation statutes cover certain occupational diseases. Some statutes define occupational disease generally as disease resulting from the nature of the employment (such as black lung disease for a coal miner), while other statutes include occupational disease under the definition of personal injury, while other statutes list specific occupational diseases which are covered. In recent years, state workers' compensation boards have been grappling with the issue of whether repetitive stress injuries for office workers who spend lots of time at a computer keyboard should be brought within the scope of coverage.

The majority view is that psychological illnesses stemming from emotional stress in the workplace can be eligible for compensation under workers' compensation statutes, even if there is not precipitating physical trauma. However, workers' compensation boards generally proceed with caution when dealing with mental injuries because of the great danger of malingering.

There are several defenses an employer can raise when faced with a workers' compensation claim, including employee misconduct, intoxication, self-inflicted injuries, horseplay, company-sponsored athletic and social events (in some states), assault, or injury sustained during commuting to and from work. The availability of these defenses, and the likelihood of their success, varies widely from state to state.

work made for hire If you did it on company time or used company property to do it, your employer owns it. (*See also* employee; freelancer; independent contractor.)

If you are employed by a small business and you invent or discover something during the course of your employment that relates to your employer's business in any way, you generally do not have any legal rights to that something: It belongs to your employer, lock, stock, and barrel. This legal doctrine is known as work made for hire, and it can create lots of headaches for employees who want to quit and set up their own businesses.

Generally, an employer owns any work product developed, created, or invented by its employees during the course of employment. No legal agreement or other document is required to transfer title to the employer when the inventor or creator is truly an employee. So when exactly is something discovered during the course of employment? The general rule is that anything an employee discovers, invents, or creates while on her employer's time or using the employer's property, is deemed work made for hire unless the employee has a compelling argument to the contrary. The employee must also be willing to fight the employer in a court of law to prove a legal right to the discovery, invention, or creation.

Some courts go further and say that even something created, developed, or invented by the employee on his or her own time is work made for hire if it relates, directly or indirectly, to the employer's business. In such cases, the courts will ask: "If the employee were to take this invention, discovery, or creation and go off on his or her own to make money off of it, would it directly or indirectly compete with any of the employer's lines of business?" If the answer is yes, you will have to hand it over.

The work made for hire rule applies only to inventions, discoveries, and creations by an employee. If an invention, discovery, or creation is made by an independent contractor during the course of performing services for a client or customer, the independent contractor owns the invention, discovery, or creation. That is, unless there is an express, written agreement requiring the independent to treat all such inventions, discoveries, and creations as work made for hire for the client or customer. Such an agreement will require the independent contractor to notify the client immediately of any discoveries, inventions, or creations made while performing services for the client, and that the independent contractor promptly assign all of his or her rights to the discovery, invention, or creation to the client.

Because the law is vigilant in protecting independent contractors, especially in creative lines of work, work made for hire agreements with independent contractors must be drafted very carefully, with comprehensive language covering any possible invention, discovery, or creation that a client or customer might want to claim as proprietary.

wrongful termination Dismissing an employee for the wrong reasons. (*See also* affirmative action; employee; firing employees; performance review.)

Generally, if an employee does not have a written agreement with an employer and has been employed for a relatively short period of time (say, five years or less), he or she is considered an employee at will under the law. This means the employee can be fired for any reason, even an unfair one, with or without notice.

Over the years, however, the law has recognized a number of significant exceptions to the doctrine of employment at will. If you terminate an employee at will for one of the following reasons, you may be exposing your company, and perhaps yourself, to a claim of wrongful termination:

■ You directed a worker to violate any law, ordinance, regulation, or statute, the employee refused, and you fired that employee in retaliation for refusing your directive.

■ Your employee complained, or has threatened to complain, about your company's violation of a law, ordinance, regulation or statute, and you fire that employee in retaliation.

■ Your true reason for firing the employee is based, even in part, on that employee's race, age, gender, religion, disability, or national origin (or, in a growing number of states, on the employee's sexual orientation, pregnancy, or legal immigrant status).

If your employee has a written employment agreement that prevents him or her from being fired without cause, and you dismiss the employee anyway because of a reduction in staff or a business downturn, you will generally not be liable for wrongful termination, although the employee may sue you for breach of the employment agreement. Note that even if the employee does not have a written agreement, oral promises and/or written promises such as those found in an employee handbook or manual may create legal rights, the frustration of which may lead to a breach of contract suit.

What if, instead of firing a difficult person, you make the employee's life so difficult that he quits of his own accord? The employee in such a case may or may not be able to sue you for constructive discharge, which is a legal way of saying, "You made my life so miserable I had no alternative but to quit." Say, for example, that you have an argument with an employee over a business matter, and two days later you ask the employee to make a difficult business trip to a faraway plant. If the employee quits under these circumstances, he or she would have a hard time arguing constructive discharge—especially if business travel was a normal, routine part of his job. On the other hand, say an employee refuses your improper sexual advances, and two days later you move her office to an unheated basement, double her workload, and make rude comments in public about her job performance. If the employee quits under these circumstances, she may well have a claim for constructive discharge as well as a rather solid case of sexual harassment under federal, and possibly state, law.

Joseph Varon, an attorney in Fairfield, Connecticut, who specializes in wrongful termination and employment discrimination cases, says, "You wouldn't believe how many wrongful termination cases stem from the employer's failure to document performance problems. An employer cannot terminate an employee on the grounds of poor performance when the employee has never received any performance evaluations or has been given positive critiques right up to the day of the dismissal. Failing to give frequent, and progressively more discouraging, performance evaluations will invite employees to claim that their termination for poor performance was merely a pretext for some illegal or wrongful motive."

Young Entrepreneurs Organization (YEO) An international organization for business owners under the age of forty. (*See also* Women Presidents' Organization.)

YEO IS MORE THAN a way to exchange business cards. Membership is by invitation only and highly selective: You must be the founder, current owner, or controlling shareholder of a company earning $1 million or more in gross annual revenues.

Founded in 1987 and based in Alexandria, Virginia, YEO has 2,500 members in local chapters across twenty-two nations. A similar group, the Young Presidents' Organization (YPO), is based in Irving, Texas, and accepts men up to forty and women up to forty-four years of age. The Women Presidents' Organization, based in New York, has no age restriction.

Some YEO members say the most important benefit is a program called Forum, in which members meet for candid discussions about personal and professional issues. The sessions are guided by a trained moderator and follow strict rules of confidentiality.

"It's nice to talk about issues with someone who is not in your company," said Harold Solomon, whose Telekey Inc., based in Atlanta, Georgia, sells prepaid long-distance calling cards. "People listen and respond, and give practical advice or offer resources. There is complete secrecy. It never goes outside the room."

Another YEO program is the Inventory of Skills (IOS), in which members submit a particular problem and are immediately put in contact with an expert in YEO's network. When Solomon experienced problems processing credit card orders, he turned to the IOS. "The next day, I got a call from the president of the largest credit card processor in the United States," Solomon recalled. "He called me, with my eight employees."

YEO can be reached at 703-519-6700 or through their website **www.yeo.org**.

zero tolerance Taking a firm position by prohibiting any and all unprofessional or offensive behavior among employees. (*See also* Equal Employment Opportunity Commission; firing employees; sexual harassment.)

WHEN IT COMES TO sexual harassment, racial discrimination, and locker room behavior, a zero tolerance position is the best way to go. Make it clear to all employees, in writing when they are hired, and in your company policy manual, that you will not tolerate any illegal or offensive behavior around the office. Period.

Be prepared to carefully document infractions in writing. Counsel the employee and be firm in your contention that you will fire them if they don't control their actions or language. If the problem is not resolved or worsens, talk with a labor attorney and begin taking steps to terminate the offending worker. There are plenty of talented people out there looking for jobs and you can't afford to defend yourself against a lawsuit or EEOC complaint. Remember: Life is too short to work with anyone who gives you a headache or a stomachache.

Conclusion

IF YOU HAVE READ this book cover to cover, I thank you. You are definitely more knowledgeable for having perused the alphabetical roster of key business terms. We've worked hard to provide clear, concise answers to most, if not all, of your tough questions—plus a few laughs and a sprinkle of inspiration.

This book was born out of thousands of hours of research and interviews. We think it was worth the effort and hope you do, too. In the introduction, I reminded you that you'll never work harder than when you work for yourself, and by now, I am sure you agree with me. Running an entrepreneurial venture requires enormous dedication, persistence, and stamina. Only the strong survive to tell their stories.

If you are still working for yourself, consider this: You've descended from a long line of hearty American entrepreneurs. The pursuit of the American dream has been around longer than America itself. Just think of the folks who fled persecution in England and Continental Europe to start anew in the colonies. They fed their families by becoming merchants, blacksmiths, or purveyors of silk, tea, and coffee. They managed trading posts, general stores, taverns, and hostels. They all started and ran small businesses.

It's amazing to think that these early entrepreneurs faced the very same problems you face today: how to manage unproductive employees, how to negotiate with vendors, and how to survive tough times. They ran their small businesses with less technology than we have today: no electricity, indoor plumbing, cars, trucks, trains, airplanes, computers, Internet access, or cell phones. Chances are, they grew their businesses through word of mouth and by providing excellent customer service and high quality goods. They filled orders promptly and asked their customers how they could serve them better.

If you think about it, nothing much has changed today—the basics of small business success are still the same: sticking to the basics works. I hope this book has helped you—and will continue helping you—by providing a foundation of solutions to help guide you as you build upon those basics.

★★★

BEFORE YOU GET BACK TO WORK, consider my personal motto: Life is too short to work with anyone who gives you a headache or a stomachache. Think about it. If you dread walking into your office, it's time to make some changes.

Resources

BOOKS

Advertising, Marketing, and Public Relations

Advertising Without an Agency, by Kathy J. Kobliski (Oasis Press, 1998)

Full-Frontal PR: Getting People Talking About You, Your Business, or Your Product, by Richard Laermer with Michael Prichinello (Bloomberg Press, 2003)

Guerrilla Publicity, by Rick Frishman (Adams Media, 2002)

Loyalty-Based Selling, by Tim Smith (AMACOM, 2001)

The PR Crisis Bible, by Robin Cohn (St. Martin's Press, 2000)

The Wizard of Ads, by Roy Hollister Williams (Bard Press, 1999)

Business Planning

Business Continuity Planning: A Step-By-Step Guide, by Kenneth L. Fulmer (Rothstein, 2000)

Business Plans for Dummies, by Paul Tiffany and Steven Peterson (Hungry Minds, 1997)

Manager's Guide to Contingency Planning for Disasters, by Kenneth N. Myers (John Wiley & Sons, 1999)

The Board Book: Making Your Corporate Board a Strategic Force in Your Company's Success, by Susan Shultz (AMACOM, 2000)

The Complete Book of Business Plans: Simple Steps to Writing a Powerful Business Plan, by Joseph Covello (Sourcebooks, 1994)

The Successful Business Plan: Secrets and Strategies, by Rhonda Abrams (Running Media, 2000)

Family Businesses

Family Business Ownership, by John L. Ward, Ph.D. and Craig E. Aronoff, Ph.D. Family Enterprise Publishers, 2001)

Keeping the Family Business Healthy, by John L. Ward (Business Owner Resources, 1987)

The Family Business Succession Handbook, edited by Mark Fischetti (Family Business, 1997)

Finances

422 Tax Deductions for Your Small Business, by Bernard Kamoroff, CPA (Bell Springs, 2001)

A Commonsense Guide to Your 401(k), by Mary Rowland (Bloomberg Press, 1997)

CCH Business Owner's Toolkit Tax Guide 2002, edited by Paul Gada (CCH Inc., 2002)

How to Sell Your Business—and Get What You Want!, by Colin Gabriel (Gwent Press, 1998)

J.K. Lasser's Your Winning Retirement Plan, by Henry K. Hebeler (John Wiley & Sons, 2001)

Keep or Sell Your Business ... How to Make the Decision Every Private Company Faces, by Mike Cohn with Jayne Pearl (Dearborn Trade, 2000)

Stand Up to the IRS, by Frederick W. Daily (Nolo Press, 1998)

Tax Savvy for Small Business, by Frederick W. Daily (Nolo Press, 2001)

The Complete Idiot's Guide to 401(k) Plans, by Wayne G. Bogosian, et al. (Prentice Hall, 2001)

The Wall Street Journal Guide to Planning Your Financial Future, by Alan M. Siegel (Fireside, 1998)

Where Did the Money Go?, by Ellen Rohr (Max Rohr Publishing Inc., 1999)

You've Earned It, Don't Lose It, by Suze Orman and Linda Mead (Newmarket Press, 1997)

Starting and Growing Your Business

Asia for Women on Business, by Tracey Wilen and Patricia Wilen (Stone Bridge Press, 1995)

Casual Power: How to Power Up Your Nonverbal Communication and Dress Down for Success, by Sherry Maysonave (Bright Books Inc., 1999)

Europe for Women in Business, by Tracey Wilen (Wilen Publishing, 1998)

How to Create a Buy-Sell Agreement & Control the Destiny of Your Small Business (includes PC disk), by Anthony Mancuso and Bethany K. Laurence (Nolo Press, 1999)

Kick Start Your Dream Business, by Romanus Wolter (Ten Speed Press, 2001)

Small Business for Dummies, by Eric Tyson and Jim Schell (Hungry Minds Inc., 1998)

Start and Run a Profitable Exporting Business, by Laurel Delaney (Self-Counsel Press, 1998)

Taming the Paper Tiger at Home, by Barbara Hemphill (Kiplinger, 1998)

Taming the Paper Tiger at Work, by Barbara Hemphill (Kiplinger, 1998)

The Copyright Handbook, by Stephen Fishman (Nolo Press, 2000)

Working at Home While the Kids Are There Too, Loriann Hoff Oberlin (Career Press, 1997)

Working Solo, by Terri Lonier (John Wiley & Sons, 1998)

CERTIFICATION

National Minority Supplier Diversity Council
www.nmsdcus.org/index.html
1040 Avenue of the Americas, 2nd Floor
New York, NY 10018
212-944-2430

Women's Business Development Center in Chicago
www.wbdc.org
8 South Michigan Ave., Suite 400
Chicago, IL
312-853-3477

Women's Business Enterprise National Council
www.wbenc.org
1120 Connecticut Ave., NW, Suite 950
Washington, DC 20036
202-872-5515

EXPORT TRAINING

Small Business Association (SBA)
www.sba.gov
409 3rd Street SW
Washington, DC 20416
800-827-5722
The SBA offers free seven-week export training classes at Export Assistance Centers around the United States.

Stat-USA/Internet, a service of the U.S. Department of Commerce
www.stat-usa.gov
HCBC Room 4885
U.S. Department of Commerce
Washington, DC 20230
800-STAT-USA

TamTam
www.tamtam.com
3609 S. Wadsworth Blvd., Suite 550
Denver, CO 80235
303-986-8202

TradeCompass
www.tradecompass.com
1510 H Street, NW
Washington, DC 20005
800-598-3220

Worldskip
www.worldskip.com
530 Water Street, Suite 740
Oakland, CA 94607
877-818-SKIP

GOVERNMENT OFFICES

Immigration and Naturalization Service (INS)
www.ins.usdoj.gov

Manufacturing Extension Partnership (MEP)
www.mep.nist.gov
800-637-4634

MEP is a national network of about 400 nonprofit centers organized in 1986
by the National Institute for Standards and Technology.

Occupational Safety and Health Administration (OSHA)
www.osha.gov
200 Constitution Avenue
Washington, DC 20210
800-321-OSHA

U.S. Copyright Office
www.loc.gov/copyright/forms
101 Independence Ave. SE
Washington, DC 20559-6000
202-707-3000

You can register a work by sending a properly completed application form
free from the site.

U.S. Department of Commerce
www.commerce.gov
1401 Constitution Ave. NW
Washington, DC 20230
800-USA-TRADE

U.S. Equal Employment Opportunity Commission
www.eeoc.gov
1801 L Street NW
Washington, DC 20507
800-669-4000

U.S. National Relations Labor Board
www.nlrb.gov
1099 14th Street
Washington, DC 20570-0001
202-273-1700

U.S. Patent and Trademark Office
www.uspto.gov
General Information Services Division
Crystal Plaza 3, Room 2C02
Washington, DC 20231
800-786-9199

While you can register a company or product name in your state, it's best to have federal trademark protection.

LEGAL CONCERNS

ADP Payroll & Tax Monitor
www.adp.com/taxfin/toolbox/payroll/uccr.html

This handy site provides a fifty-state summary of unemployment compensation laws.

Americans with Disabilities Act
www.eeoc.gov
800-669-3362

Contact them for a copy of the ADA Enforcement Guide.

FindLaw
www.findlaw.com
1235 Pear Avenue
Mountain View, CA 94043
650-210-1900

This site can help you search for lawyers by both specialty and zip code.

ONLINE TRAINING

Freeskills
www.freeskills.com

OnLine Training Institute
www.oltraining.com
561-357-0841

ORGANIZATIONS AND NETWORKS

American Express small business network
www.americanexpress.com

Better Business Bureau
www.bbb.org
Council of Better Business Bureaus
4200 Wilson Blvd., Suite 800
Arlington, VA 22203-1838
703-276-0100

Council of Smaller Enterprises (COSE)
www.cose.org
Tower City Center
50 Public Square, Suite 200
Cleveland, OH 44113-2291
888-304-GROW

The Franchise Connection, a nationwide franchise network
www.frannet.com
888-322-FRAN

Institute for the Accreditation of Professional Employer Organizations
www.iapeo.org
Three Financial Centre, Suite 401
900 S. Shackleford Road
Little Rock, AR 72211
501-219-2045

National Business Incubation Association
www.nbia.org
20 E. Circle Drive, Suite 190
Athens, OH 45701-3571
740-593-4331

National Federation of Independent Business
www.nfib.org
800-NFIB-NOW

National Small Business United
www.nsbu.org
1156 15th Street NW, Suite 1100
Washington, DC 20005
202-293-8830

National Venture Capital Association
www.nvca.com
1655 North Fort Meyer Drive, Suite 850
Arlington, VA 22200
703-524-2549

Service Corps of Retired Executives (SCORE)
www.score.org
409 3rd Street, SW, 6th Floor
Washington, DC 20024
800-634-0245

Small Business Association (SBA)
www.sba.gov
409 3rd Street SW
Washington, DC 20416
800-827-5722

Small Business Development Center (SBDC)
www.sba.gov/sbdc

Women's Business Enterprise National Council
www.wbenc.org
1120 Connecticut Ave., NW, Suite 950
Washington, DC 20036
202-872-5515

Information on getting certified as a business owned or controlled by a woman or women.

Women President's Organization
www.womenpresidentsorg.com
155 East 55th Street, Suite 303
New York, NY 10022
212-688-4114

World Intellectual Property Organization (WIPO)
www.wipo.org
P.O. Box 18
CH-1211 Geneva 20 Switzerland
41-22-733-54-28

Inventors can submit a world-wide patent application for the seventy-nine nations that currently subscribe to the Patent Cooperation Treaty of 1978, while paying the fees imposed by only ten of those nations.

Writer's Guild of America
www.wga.org
7000 West Third Street
Los Angeles, CA 90048
800-548-4532

Young Entrepreneurs Organization (YEO)
www.yeo.org
1199 N. Fairfax Street
Alexandria, VA 22314-1437
703-519-6700

PAYROLL SERVICES

Automatic Data Processing, Inc. (ADP)
www.adp.com
1 ADP Boulevard
Roseland, NJ 07068
800-CALL-ADP

PayChex, Inc.
www.paychex.com
911 Panorama Trail South
Rochester, NY 14625-0397
800-322-7292

PayMaxx, Inc.
www.paymaxx.com
302 South Royal Oaks Blvd.
Franklin, TN 37064
877-PAYMAXX

TECHNOLOGY AND SOFTWARE

Anonymizer, Inc.
www.anonymizer.com
5694 Mission Center Road #426
San Diego, CA 92108-4380
888-270-0141
Offers services to protect your identity while visiting websites.

Broadband Reports

www.broadbandreports.com

41-51 East 11th Street

New York, NY 10003

A website dedicated to DSL questions and service options.

D&B

www.dnb.com

One Diamond Hill Road

Murray Hill, NJ 07374-1218

908-665-5000

Palo Alto Software

www.paloalto.com

144 E. 14th Avenue

Eugene, OR 97401

541-683-6162

Their Business Plan Pro software is one of the most popular and easy-to-use programs.

QuickBooks

www.quickbooks.com

2535 Garcia Avenue

Mountain View, CA 94043

650-944-6000

Intuit's QuickBooks Pro includes a module to keep track of inventory information based on the invoice.

Register.com

www.register.com

575 Eighth Avenue, 11th Floor

New York, NY 10018

800-899-9723

Allows you to register domain names.

VeriSign

www.verisign.com

487 East Middlefield Road

Mountain View, CA 94043

650-961-7500

Allows you to register domain names.

index

About Bloomberg

BLOOMBERG L.P., founded in 1981, is a global information services, news, and media company. Headquartered in New York, the company has nine sales offices, two data centers, and 87 news bureaus worldwide.

Bloomberg, serving customers in 126 countries around the world, holds a unique position within the financial services industry by providing an unparalleled range of features in a single package, the BLOOMBERG PROFESSIONAL® service. By addressing the demand for investment performance and efficiency through an exceptional combination of information, analytic, electronic trading, and Straight Through Processing tools, Bloomberg has built a worldwide customer base of corporations, issuers, financial intermediaries, and institutional investors.

BLOOMBERG NEWS®, founded in 1990, provides stories and columns on business, general news, politics, and sports to leading newspapers and magazines throughout the world. BLOOMBERG TELEVISION®, a 24-hour business and financial news network, is produced and distributed globally in seven different languages. BLOOMBERG RADIO℠ is an international radio network anchored by flagship station BLOOMBERG® WBBR 1130 in New York.

In addition to the BLOOMBERG PRESS® line of books, Bloomberg publishes *BLOOMBERG MARKETS*™, *BLOOMBERG PERSONAL FINANCE*®, and *BLOOMBERG WEALTH MANAGER*®. To learn more about Bloomberg, call a sales representative at:

Frankfurt:	49-69-92041-280	São Paulo:	5511-3048-4506
Hong Kong:	852-2977-6900	Singapore:	65-6212-1100
London:	44-20-7330-7500	Sydney:	612-9777-8686
New York:	1-212-318-2200	Tokyo:	813-3201-8910
San Francisco:	1-415-912-2970		

FOR IN-DEPTH MARKET INFORMATION AND NEWS, visit the Bloomberg website at **www.bloomberg.com**, which draws from the news and power of the BLOOMBERG PROFESSIONAL® service and Bloomberg's host of media products to provide high-quality news and information in multiple languages on stocks, bonds, currencies, and commodities.

About the Author

JANE APPLEGATE is America's leading small business expert and executive producer and CEO of SBTV (Small Business TV), the first online network exclusively devoted to covering small business. The author of four books, including *201 Great Ideas for Your Small Business,* Applegate was also a writer and commentator for CNNfn, Bloomberg, CNBC, and ABC in San Francisco. Her syndicated "Succeeding in Small Business" column appeared in print and online until she stopped writing it in 2002.

In 1994, Applegate was named National Media Advocate of the Year by the U.S. Small Business Administration. In 2000, Applegate was awarded the Artemis Award by the Euro-American Women's Council as one of the top ten leading international businesswomen. Applegate has keynoted hundreds of small business conferences throughout the U.S. and abroad and has represented the United States at international business conferences held in Moscow, Paris, Athens, and London. She serves on the advisory board of the Women Presidents' Organization.

Applegate lives in Pelham, New York. She and her husband, Joe, an editor at *Newsweek,* have two children.

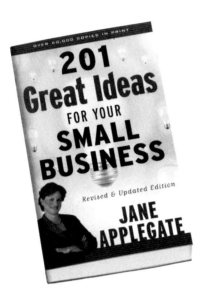

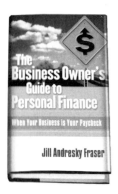